THE HEART SET FREE

THE HEART SET FREE

SIN AND REDEMPTION IN THE GOSPELS,
AUGUSTINE, DANTE, AND FLANNERY O'CONNOR

KIM PAFFENROTH

continuum

NEW YORK • LONDON

The Continuum International Publishing Group
15 East 26th Street, New York, NY 10010

The Continuum International Publishing Group Ltd
The Tower Building, 11 York Road, London SE1 7NX

Cover illustration by William C. Lebeda
Cover design: Lee Singer and William C. Lebeda designs

Library of Congress Cataloging-in-Publication Data

Paffenroth, Kim, 1966–
  The heart set free : sin and redemption in the Gospels, Augustine, Dante, and Flannery O'Connor / Kim Paffenroth.
    p. cm.
  Includes bibliographical references and index.
  ISBN 0-8264-1613-6 (pbk.)
  1. Sin. 2. Christian life—Catholic authors. 3. Jesus Christ—Teachings. 4. Augustine, Saint, Bishop of Hippo. Confessiones. 5. Dante Alighieri, 1265-1321. Divina commedia. 6. O'Connor, Flannery—Religion. I. Title.
  BV4625.P34 2005
  230'.092'2—dc22

                                                              2004027517

"For this my son was dead, and is alive again;
he was lost, and is found."
And they began to make merry.

Luke 15:24 (RSV)

Drifting on a sea of doubt
And no one ever heard me shout
That I was lost and couldn't find my way.

I was lost and found.
I had run aground.
I was lost but now I'm found.

"Lost and Found," lyrics by Glenn Tipton/
Judas Priest, from the album *Demolition*

CONTENTS

PREFACE

This work examines four of the greatest theological and literary minds of the Christian tradition—Jesus, Augustine, Dante, and Flannery O'Connor—in a way that makes their prophetic and poetic challenge to our sinfulness accessible and relevant to the modern Christian. These thinkers offer timeless criticisms of four of the greatest and most flawed societies of all time—Israel, Rome, medieval Europe, and America—and they do so in a way that raises their critiques out of the particular historical context and renders them relevant today. To show this current relevance, for each of these figures, I give the readers a twofold analysis. First, I focus on two sins that he or she thinks pervade and degrade society and the individuals in it, and then the two actions that he or she offers as the shocking, redemptive alternatives. Then the second half of each chapter guides readers through serious study, reflection, and prayer on three specific texts. The section on study is intended to guide readers more carefully and with more detail through a relevant passage that might be obscure due to its literary and historical context. The section for reflection should be more straightforward in its meaning, but more difficult in its application, and therefore asks for meditation and association more than study. And the section on prayer should relate both intellectual and ethical considerations to form a personal and affective experience of the ideas raised in these texts, the challenges they pose, and the beauty they offer. All of this should help show how these sins are still a part of our lives today, and how their alternatives can become a part of our lives through analysis, introspection, and prayer. Each chapter also includes an annotated bibliography of accessible works suggested for further reading and reflection.

In the first chapter, I look at some of Jesus' sayings as they relate to the people's need for retribution and their feeling of arrogance. Jesus' society—Jewish, Roman, and Greek are indistinguishable on this point—cannot respond to him positively because of these sins. Jews and Greeks, together with modern Christians, are heavily invested in their own honor, and cannot really conceive of turning the other cheek or of accepting everyone as equals, and they cannot accept a Messiah who overturns these values and distinctions. In the section on study, I look at part of the Sermon on the Mount, since some of the examples Jesus uses are somewhat obscure to modern Christians due to their historical context of Roman occupation of Palestine. Recovering this life situation helps us appreciate how radical and difficult it is to follow Jesus' command. In the section for reflection, I look at Jesus' equally difficult saying to the disciples on being servants: here what Jesus is saying may seem clear enough; but while we would like to follow it better than the disciples do, our reaction to it is probably no better than theirs. Finally, for prayer I offer Luke's unique saying at Jesus' rejection in Nazareth, asking how might we proclaim the acceptable year of the Lord in a way that transforms our sinful lives.

In chapter 2, I consider Augustine's critique of the pride and ambition he sees in the culture of the late Roman Empire, attributes he finally acknowledges are ruining his own life. Since these two qualities are so much more positive than those in the first chapter, they are that much more insidious: seldom do we consider the negative possibilities of pride or ambition—we even encourage our children to display these qualities in abundance. In the section on study, I look at a passage from *Confessions*, book 5, that could be quite obscure without some idea of Manichaean theology, but which does not rely on the truth of that theology for its relevance. We all excuse ourselves all the time, without necessarily having any idea that God is a big, shining substance. For reflection, I consider the events of Augustine's retirement to Cassiciacum, as he flees a world of earthly ambitions that is startlingly similar to the one in which we live, one we usually feel poses no threat to our faith.

The community of love and study into which he immerses himself could strike one at first as quite odd, but its beauty and simplicity are definitely worthy of our consideration and emulation. And for prayer, I think nothing is more beautiful and helpful than the opening paragraph of the *Confessions*, as Augustine lays out how distracted and fractured our lives have become without God.

In chapter 3, Dante shows us how our lives will always be lived out of love, but some loves are destructive and some are life-giving. It is hard to imagine a counsel more relevant today than his, for so many people today subscribe partially or completely to the idea that he attacks—the idea that all love is necessarily good (*Purg.* 18.36). The strength of Dante is that he so beautifully disassembles that idea, while showing us what real love is. For study, I examine Paolo and Francesca in *Inferno*, both because their story is obscure to us and, of more importance, because readers are often distracted by their sympathy for the lovers, so that they think there is something noble in their love, when Dante is really using them as a prime example of what is wrong with lust and how it differs from real love. For real love, I ask readers to reflect on Dante's discussion of it in the middle of *Purgatory*, and see how such a minute dissection of it might help us to understand and experience it better in our own lives. Finally, for a prayerful experience of Dante's idea of love, I recite his graphic description of it in *Paradise*, for it is here that earthly and heavenly loves combine, the one leading to the other at the same time as it is completed by it.

Finally, I consider the God-centered writing of Flannery O'Connor, for whom the human sins of self-deception and self-righteousness can be cured only by divine intervention in revelation and grace. While the three previous chapters focus on our preparation to receive grace, she focuses on the rather scary moment when grace finally comes: the experience is so shattering and unexpected that it is most often fatal to her characters. For the study of self-deception, I examine the last part of the exchange between the grandmother and the Misfit in "A Good Man Is Hard to Find." Here the difficulty with understanding is entirely literary: O'Connor subverts our expectations of how we are to react to a grandmother or a criminal, to show us how faulty our perceptions really are and to jolt us into questioning our values. For reflection, I consider the final gracious moment granted to Mr. Head in "The Artificial Nigger." O'Connor's writing is as beautiful and clear as anyone's at this point, but it is hard to see Mr. Head's obvious need for grace as similar to our own, for he is so self-righteous and distasteful. But without this application, O'Connor's brilliant and humane point would be lost. For prayer, I turn to that of the little girl in "A Temple of the Holy Ghost": with or without its grotesque aspects, this prayer captures much of O'Connor's anguish at human creatureliness, but directs it beautifully toward praise of its awesome Creator.

All of these thinkers connect social and political ills with much deeper theological and anthropological analysis, so that their conclusions cannot be discounted as "signs of the times," or the way people thought "back then" about a particular problem—e.g., war, racism, corruption, etc.—that is now supposedly past: if their descriptions of the sickness in human nature were ever accurate, then they are always accurate and demand our attention as the profound calls for personal and societal introspection and change that they really are. These calls for personal devotion and change remain relevant and should be taken up by the modern Christian, so that intellectually as well as spiritually, the redemptive truth of these writings can begin to set us free. As intellectually challenging as these works are, I am confident that everyone can experience and be inspired by their beauty and truth.

ACKNOWLEDGMENTS

First, I would like to thank all my students over the years. It is their challenging questions and perceptive insights—filtered through my more mature but mediocre mind—that should be heard on every page of this book. The independent study that I did of O'Connor with Christine Casino at Iona College was especially helpful in focusing my analysis of her stories. Also, a former student from my first semester of teaching eleven years ago, Jenny Shank, has enhanced my interpretations by sharing with me her subtle analyses, always expressed with an elegance and grace that I have seldom seen elsewhere, attributes I myself never achieve.

I express my thanks to my colleagues in the Religious Studies Department at Iona College—Brian Brown, Kathleen Deignan, Robert Durning, Elena Procario-Foley, and Barbara Srozenski—for furthering my work with their encouragement and support. Their experience of teaching and scholarship as a calling and not a task has been inspiring to me. Further, the dean of Arts and Sciences, Alex Eodice, granted me a teaching reduction in the academic year 2003–4 that allowed me valuable time to finish this project. The staff at Ryan library has been enormously helpful, especially those who obtained so many books and articles for me on interlibrary loan—Susan Robinson, Jacyln Marchionni, Mallory Genovesi, and Koren Collura. Jenna Freedman did the Iona community a huge service by building up the library's holdings in literature and theology, before Barnard College had the good fortune of taking her from us. While working in the Hesburgh Library at the University of Notre Dame, I was helped by Marilyn Bierwagen, Theodore J. Cachey, Jr., Rita Erskine, and Sara Weber. Finally, two student assistants—Angela Harris and Lauren Maimone— were very patient and efficient in helping me in my research, and Angela's questions and challenges have greatly improved the analysis.

I am very grateful to my network of friends and colleagues all over the continent, who constantly provide me with feedback that enriches my writing. I would especially note the inquiries and acumen of Debra Romanick Baldwin, Tom Bertonneau, Rick Bolles, Phillip Cary, Marylu Hill, Kevin Hughes, Robert Kennedy, Dan Morehead, Dave Schindler Jr., and Brian Weimer. My former boss, Jack Doody, has decidedly influ- enced my analysis of these works, especially Dante: we still reminisce about the class on *Paradiso* that he sat in on seven years ago, an enjoy- able memory of when we began to realize how many goals and beliefs we shared. Although not himself a scholar, Bob Jarrell's humor and good sense have also shaped my life and work for the last twenty years. And for more than twenty years, my friends Berry Credle, Scott Field, Kerry Forbes, Bill Lebeda, Alex Parker, Kim Prack, Daphne Schleft, and Shahin Sharifi have in their various ways influenced me, proving that old friends are the best friends. Bill also generously gave his time to design the beautiful cover for this book. Besides my old friends, I also continue to love the music I did twenty-five years ago: the sinister yet pleasant tunes of Judas Priest have often been playing as I typed, and they were kind enough to let their lyrics grace the beginning of this book.

Financial support for this project was generously provided by the Louisville Institute, the Earhart Foundation, and the Devers Program in Dante Studies at the University of Notre Dame.

Thanks go to my editor at Continuum International Publishing, Henry Carrigan. Without his enthusiasm for my idea, I would not have been able to make my analysis of these thinkers available to a wider cir- cle of Christian readers.

As always, I offer my thanks to my wife, Marlis, and our children, Charles and Sophia, for putting up with my idiosyncrasies, especially my ongoing fascination with the darker side of human life and nature. I think there are a few paragraphs in these pages that show that I do sometimes see the light that will dispel the darkness, as their love has brightened my life. And may God's grace shine eternally on my father, George G. Paffenroth, who was taken from us during the final proof-reading of this manuscript.

Finally, this book is dedicated to three teachers with whom I first studied most of these works. Brother Sixtus Robert Smith, FSC, has quietly and humbly inspired generations of students—as he inspired me— to love and pursue ideas, wherever they may lead. Dr. Harriet Crabtree was the teaching assistant in a class on religion and literature that I attended at Harvard Divinity School; she is one of the most intelligent, dedicated, and charming people I have known, and her keen wit pushed me to analyze literature more deeply than I had before. Finally, the late Rev. Richard Bumpass patiently spent many hours helping me read the New Testament for the first time, as he generously helped every student who came to him with any intellectual or spiritual question. His untimely death in 1993 took from the Annapolis student community the kindest and most tireless servant it has ever had. I could never be the teacher or minister that any of them have been: I can only be thankful that their graciousness has made me a better student.

Kim Paffenroth
Cornwall on Hudson, NY

1

JESUS
Life in the Kingdom of God

Introduction

The events, sayings, and meaning of Jesus' life are, of course, recounted in the four canonical Gospels, as well as in numerous apocryphal ones. In this chapter I am interested in Jesus' ethical teachings, however, so I will focus on the three canonical Gospels—Matthew, Mark, and Luke—where his ethical teachings are mostly found. These Gospels are known as the Synoptic ("seen together") Gospels, because their accounts of Jesus' life are so closely parallel to one another. They were probably written a generation or two after Jesus' life, between 70 and 90 C.E., though they are based on recollections of his deeds and words that had been handed down orally by believers. Of these records, Mark was probably written first, with Matthew and Luke written ten or twenty years later.[1]

Since these are literary works not composed by Jesus himself, I will often distinguish between the evangelist and Jesus: for example, given the nature of our sources, it is more accurate to say that "Luke emphasizes Jesus' teaching and practice of forgiveness," than to jump directly to "Jesus emphasized forgiveness." This does not, I think, diminish or dilute the truthfulness or applicability of these Gospel teachings. Rather, it simply distinguishes between the raw data—what Jesus said—

and a later interpretation of that data—what the evangelist wrote. And for a believer, both levels of the tradition are true: indeed, the evangelist's interpretation may make more clear and explicit what Jesus stated in a briefer, more obscure form. Furthermore, I have chosen two ethical injunctions—forgiveness and service to others—that are at the heart of Jesus' ministry and are repeated throughout all the Gospels. Therefore, the difference between Jesus' own voice and what the evangelists have chosen to emphasize is minimal. Indeed, many have taken just these two ideas as the essence of Jesus' teaching.[2] If I wanted to claim that these are "authentic" teachings of Jesus, probably no one would disagree with me. But I find such a claim unnecessarily belittling to the evangelists' own work as faithful interpreters and transmitters of Jesus' message, as well as dismissive of other teachings that might be labeled "inauthentic" simply because they are not attested as frequently or dispersed as widely.

Religiously, Jesus was raised in the Judaism of his time, to practice Jewish law (torah) and live in covenant with the God of Israel. Politically, socially, and economically, he lived in the Roman Empire, benefiting from the commerce and culture it brought to Palestine, and suffering from its economic exploitation and harsh political and military oppression. From either of these perspectives, Roman or Jewish, Jesus' teaching on forgiveness and service to others was a radical, extreme demand, and it remains a challenge to us today. In the first century or the twenty-first, the human tendency is to retaliate for wrongs done to oneself and to look out for oneself, not to serve others selflessly.

Retribution and Forgiveness

Measured retribution is the basis of all earthly justice: when someone does harm to another, then the perpetrator should himself be penalized, lest people get the idea that they can get away with harming others. Anything less increases the risk of further injury and injustice. At the other extreme, however, the retributive harm should be measured and commensurate with the first injury, for anything more would be revenge, which might also lead to further violence, if the overly punished person seeks to even the score. The Bible, like many other law codes, therefore develops a system of retributive, fair, equal justice to protect society: "Show no pity: life for life, eye for eye, tooth for tooth, hand for hand, foot for foot" (Deut 19:21; cf. Exod 21:24–25; Lev 24:20).

But while equal retribution has the enormous advantage of stopping the spiral downward into further violence and injustice, Jesus bases his message on forgiveness, which offers the riskier but higher goal of "a spiral of forgiveness,"[3] a spiral upward into further mercy, compassion, love, and closer communion with God. Forgiveness is essential to Jesus' teaching in the Gospels. Even more than being a central teaching of his, it is the foundation on which Christian life and community are to be founded: "The ability to forgive is clearly not just one of several items in a repertoire of qualities desirable in a follower of Jesus drawn up by the New Testament! It is rather an absolutely necessary dimension of Christian existence."[4] Some of Jesus' most radical teachings on retribution and forgiveness are in the passage from the Sermon on the Mount that we will examine later (Matt 5:38–48), but there are numerous references throughout all the Gospels to Jesus' teaching and practice of forgiveness. There are also numerous examples of how his audience frequently finds such teaching unacceptable, preferring the more normal approach of paying others back for their supposed misdeeds.

The Synoptic Gospels open with the preaching of forgiveness: "John the baptizer appeared in the wilderness, proclaiming a baptism of repentance for the forgiveness of sins" (Mark 1:4; cf. Luke 3:3).[5] The same idea, with forgiveness only implied, is expressed more dramatically in Matthew by John the Baptist proclaiming directly, "Repent, for the kingdom of heaven has come near" (Matt 3:2), a call repeated by Jesus himself as his first reported preaching (4:17; cf. Mark 1:15). John the Baptist and Jesus have come to announce that the kingdom of heaven is breaking into the sinful world of the Roman Empire, and it will bring with it healing, forgiveness, and redemption. And since the kingdom has begun, Jesus heals and forgives, for that is what life will be like in the kingdom, free of death, disease, and sin. The combining of these is seen in the healing of the paralytic:

> When he [Jesus] returned to Capernaum after some days, it was reported that he was at home. So many gathered around that there was no longer room for them, not even in front of the door; and he was speaking the word to them. Then some people came, bringing to him a paralyzed man, carried by four of them. And when they could not bring him to Jesus because of the crowd, they removed the roof above him; and after having

dug through it, they let down the mat on which the paralytic lay. When Jesus saw their faith, he said to the paralytic, "Son, your sins are forgiven." Now some of the scribes were sitting there, questioning in their hearts, "Why does this fellow speak in this way? It is blasphemy! Who can forgive sins but God alone?" At once Jesus perceived in his spirit that they were discussing these questions among themselves; and he said to them, "Why do you raise such questions in your hearts? Which is easier, to say to the paralytic, 'Your sins are forgiven,' or to say, 'Stand up and take your mat and walk'? But so that you may know that the Son of Man has authority on earth to forgive sins"—he said to the paralytic—"I say to you, stand up, take your mat and go to your home." And he stood up, and immediately took the mat and went out before all of them; so that they were all amazed and glorified God, saying, "We have never seen anything like this!" (Mark 2:1–12; cf. Matt 9:1–8; Luke 5:17–26)

Those present at this scene of healing and forgiveness attack Jesus, believing that sin can be forgiven only by God, but sin and disease are both symptoms that Jesus as God's agent has come to eradicate as part of the beginning of the kingdom.[6]

Luke crafts an even more beautiful scene of forgiveness and restoration, as a sinful woman anoints Jesus' feet:

One of the Pharisees asked Jesus to eat with him, and he went into the Pharisee's house and took his place at the table. And a woman in the city, who was a sinner, having learned that he was eating at the Pharisee's house, brought an alabaster jar of ointment. She stood behind him at his feet, weeping, and began to bathe his feet with her tears and to dry them with her hair. Then she continued kissing his feet and anointing them with the ointment. Now when the Pharisee who had invited him saw it, he said to himself, "If this man were a prophet, he would have known who and what kind of woman this is who is touching him—that she is a sinner." Jesus spoke up and said to him, "Simon, I have something to say to you." "Teacher," he replied, "Speak." "A certain creditor had two debtors; one owed five hundred denarii, and the other fifty. When they could not pay, he canceled the debts for both of them. Now which of them will love him more?" Simon answered, "I suppose the one for whom he canceled the greater debt." And Jesus said to him, "You have judged rightly." Then turning toward the woman, he said to Simon, "Do you see this woman? I entered your house; you gave me no water for my feet, but she has bathed my feet with her tears and dried them with her hair. You gave me no kiss, but from the time I came in she has not stopped kissing my feet. You did not anoint my head with oil, but she has anointed my feet with ointment. Therefore, I tell you, her sins, which were many, have been forgiven; hence she has shown great love. But the one to whom little is forgiven, loves little." Then he said to her, "Your sins are forgiven." But those who were at the table with him began to say among themselves, "Who is this who even forgives sins?" And he said to the woman, "Your faith has saved you; go in peace." (Luke 7:36–50)[7]

While Jesus' host thinks only of the woman's sinfulness and inwardly condemns Jesus for associating with her, Jesus is totally focused on her goodness, just as he had recognized the faith of those who broke open the roof to help their friend be healed. Jesus recognizes the change that forgiveness makes in people's lives: "It is her experience of being forgiven them [her sins], that empowers her to love. Forgiveness changes her."[8] While some are again incredulous or condemn Jesus' act of forgiving, others trust in, long for, and accept Jesus' forgiveness, and thereby begin their restoration to right physical, moral, and social health. "In these episodes, cultic and ethical barriers are overcome, and the person previously excluded finds herself or himself reincorporated into the community, and by extension reincorporated into the covenant relationship with God."[9] Believing in Jesus' forgiveness makes it possible, while disbelieving or mocking it shows how one is incapable of receiving it, for it shows that one "loves little."

Jesus' mission of forgiveness culminates in his death for the forgiveness of sins. Luke underscores forgiveness at the crucifixion, "Then Jesus said, 'Father, forgive them; for they do not know what they are doing'" (Luke 23:34).[10] Matthew shows how Jesus' forgiveness and his fellowship with sinners is commemorated in the Lord's Supper: "Then he took a cup, and after giving thanks he gave it to them, saying, 'Drink from it, all of you; for this is my blood of the covenant, which is poured out for many for the forgiveness of sins'" (Matt 26:27–28).[11] And at the end of Luke, Jesus commissions the disciples to continue this ministry of forgiveness until he returns and the kingdom is fully realized: "[Jesus] said to them, 'Thus it is written, that the Messiah is to suffer and to rise from the dead on the third day, and that repentance and forgiveness of sins is to be proclaimed in his name to all nations'" (Luke 24:46–47). The Gospels begin and end with a proclamation of God's forgiveness to all, and the miraculous new kingdom that this ushers in.

But between these teachings of God's forgiveness, the Gospels include exhortations for people to forgive one another. In essence, Jesus demands that his followers be as forgiving as he is, and as forgiving as the God they worship, a message repeated elsewhere in the New Testament: "Just as the Lord has forgiven you, so you also must forgive" (Col 3:13).[12] Since there is no limit to divine forgiveness, there should be no limit to human forgiveness: "The willingness to forgive must be boundless."[13] Matthew and Luke express this boundlessness with different numbers, but the intent is the same:

> Then Peter came and said to him, "Lord, if another member of the church sins against me, how often should I forgive? As many as seven times?" Jesus said to him, "Not seven times, but, I tell you, seventy times seven." (Matt 18:21–22)
>
> [Jesus said,] "If another disciple sins, you must rebuke the offender, and if there is repentance, you must forgive. And if the same person sins against you seven times a day, and turns back to you seven times and says, 'I repent,' you must forgive." (Luke 17:3–4)

No matter how much we or the disciples may want an exact rule—a point beyond which we could say that we have forgiven "enough" and then we can stop—Jesus insists that this is the wrong way to look at it. Forgiving is not something one does "enough" of, a duty to fulfill that then ends. Instead, it is the kind of duty that one does when one loves someone, and one does it gladly, constantly, and always. This makes it another instance of the Golden Rule: "In everything do to others as you would have them do to you" (Matt 7:12; cf. Luke 6:31). Since we want and need endless forgiveness from other people, we must extend it to them.

But the Gospels go further than just making forgiveness a matter of reciprocity and fairness between people: they make forgiveness between people the basis and prerequisite for receiving forgiveness from God. This is shown dramatically in the parable of the unforgiving servant (Matt 18:23–35):

> "For this reason the kingdom of heaven may be compared to a king who wished to settle accounts with his slaves. When he began the reckoning,

one who owed him ten thousand talents was brought to him; and, as he could not pay, his lord ordered him to be sold, together with his wife and children and all his possessions, and payment to be made. So the slave fell on his knees before him, saying, 'Have patience with me, and I will pay you everything.' And out of pity for him, the lord of that slave released him and forgave him the debt. But that same slave, as he went out, came upon one of his fellow slaves who owed him a hundred denarii [6,000 denarii = 1 talent];[14] and seizing him by the throat, he said, 'Pay what you owe.' Then his fellow slave fell down and pleaded with him, 'Have patience with me, and I will pay you.' But he refused; then he went and threw him into prison until he would pay the debt. When his fellow slaves saw what had happened, they were greatly distressed, and they went and reported to their lord all that had taken place. Then his lord summoned him and said to him, 'You wicked slave! I forgave you all that debt because you pleaded with me. Should you not have had mercy on your fellow slave, as I had mercy on you?' And in anger his lord handed him over to be tortured until he would pay his entire debt. So my heavenly Father will also do to every one of you, if you do not forgive your brother or sister from your heart." (Matt 18:23–35)

Exactly opposite to the sinful woman, who is forgiven much and loves much, the unforgiving servant is forgiven much, but loves little, or not at all. God's gratuitous and enormous forgiveness initiates the action, but we are expected to learn from and follow his example. If we do not, then we revert to a situation of the retributive kind of justice, and we are repaid in kind, equal to how unforgiving we have been to others: "Being willing to receive forgiveness for one's own debts, but not to forgive others in turn, is in effect to deny the new economy of mercy in favor of the old one in which the bonds and obligations leading to indebtedness still hold sway."[15] Receiving God's mercy obligates us to share it with others.

Similarly, Matthew and Mark make forgivingness the prerequisite for effective prayer: "Whenever you stand praying, forgive, if you have anything against anyone; so that your Father in heaven may also forgive you your trespasses" (Mark 11:25; cf. Matt 5:23–24). And Matthew and Luke put our forgiving others at the center of the Lord's Prayer,[16] the paradigm of Christian prayer, and a central element of Christian worship in most denominations: "And forgive us our debts, as we also have forgiven our debtors" (Matt 6:12); "And forgive us our sins, for we ourselves forgive everyone indebted to us" (Luke 11:4). Asking for God's forgiveness can only be done effectively so long as we have forgiven others: "Should we refuse to forgive our neighbor, we shall no longer experience the forgiveness of God—not because God ever ceases to love or forgive (he cannot because he is forgiving love), but because our failure to respond to his forgiveness by forgiving our neighbor closes us up to his forgiveness and love."[17] God keeps on giving, but we refuse the gift whenever we refuse to pass the gift of God's forgiveness on to other people.

We can, and often do, pay others back for the wrongs they have done to us or to others. If we do so in a fair and balanced way, our lives may even be called just or honorable for doing this, but they could not be called saved, or even "savable," unless we practice forgiving. Forgiving others opens us up to and prepares us for God's forgiveness, while not forgiving others hardens us, insulates us from God, and makes us incapable as well as undeserving of receiving forgiveness from him.

Arrogance and Service

Closely related to the sins of pride and self-righteousness (discussed in later chapters), there is arrogance, the almost instinctual human habit of thinking that we are better than other people. Religiously, this can be expressed in an inflated opinion of our own goodness, in which case it is closer to self-righteousness and less related to other people. Arrogance can also manifest itself in an overestimation and condemnation of others' supposed sinfulness; this is closer to contempt or bigotry and is what I am most interested in here, since Jesus seems to have encountered it constantly in his ministry.

One of the most famous New Testament parables, the parable of the Good Samaritan, is intended to counteract this feeling of bigotry, even though few modern readers would guess it:

> But wanting to justify himself, he asked Jesus, "And who is my neighbor?" Jesus replied, "A man was going down from Jerusalem to Jericho, and fell into the hands of robbers, who stripped him, beat him, and went away, leaving him half dead. Now by chance a priest was going down that road; and when he saw him, he passed by on the other side. So likewise a Levite, when he came to the place and saw him, passed by on the other side. But a Samaritan while traveling came near him; and when he saw him, he was moved with pity. He went to him and bandaged his wounds, having

poured oil and wine on them. Then he put him on his own animal, brought him to an inn, and took care of him. The next day he took out two denarii, gave them to the innkeeper, and said, 'Take care of him; and when I come back, I will repay you whatever more you spend.' Which of these three, do you think, was a neighbor to the man who fell into the hands of the robbers?" He said, "The one who showed him mercy." Jesus said to him, "Go and do likewise." (Luke 10:29–36)

The parable is a wonderful description of what it is to love and serve, and an exhortation to "Go and do likewise." But behind it is the assumption that the audience expects and lives according to different ideas. What is the point of the third person—the loving, helpful person—being a Samaritan? If the contrast is supposed to be with hypocritical clergy, then the third person should have been a lay Israelite; instead, it is a foreigner. Samaritans continue to live in northern Israel, and since the Assyrian invasion of Israel in 722 B.C.E., they have been cut off from Judaism as it developed in the south, so the two groups regard each other as heretical.[18] By Jesus' time, Jews and Samaritans regarded each other with mutual suspicion and animosity: "Jews do not share things in common with Samaritans" (John 4:9). The disciples had shown how they agreed with this negative evaluation of Samaritans in an earlier episode in Luke's Gospel. When a Samaritan village refuses to receive Jesus, James and John—whose arrogance we will see underscored in a different story below—are eager to retaliate, against Jesus' wishes. "When his disciples James and John saw it, they said, 'Lord, do you want us to command fire to come down from heaven and consume them?' But he turned and rebuked them" (9:54–55; cf. 17:15–18). Jesus shocks his audience and his disciples by praising Samaritans, not judging or destroying them.

The parable's exhortation to love, therefore, is directed not only to emulating the generous, selfless assistance offered to the injured man, but also to emulating the Samaritan's overlooking of ethnic prejudices to offer such assistance. Even more provocatively, the parable is intended to subvert the audience's own prejudices that it is scandalous that a Samaritan should be the one offering such loving aid. The parable follows on Jesus' exhortation to love "your neighbor as yourself" (Luke 10:27). This leads to the question, "Who is my neighbor?" In other words, "Whom am I supposed to love?" The parable then offers a

startling new definition of neighbor when Jesus ends with the conclusion that one is supposed to love a Samaritan, an enemy that one has
been raised to despise and distrust.

Another of Jesus' most famous parables, the parable of the Prodigal
Son,[19] also includes an unexpected exhortation to eschew arrogance and
feelings of superiority and judgment of others. The first part of the
parable (Luke 15:11–24) is more familiar to most Christians:[20] A son
asks his father for his inheritance before the father dies, and the father
hands over the money. The son squanders it foolishly and sinfully to the
point where he is on the brink of death. When he goes back to his father,
his father accepts him gladly and without hesitation. The father even
throws a big party for his son's return, killing the fatted calf.

But the parable doesn't end on this joyful note. It continues on to a
more ambiguous and challenging ending:

> Now his elder son was in the field; and when he came and approached
> the house, he heard music and dancing. He called one of the slaves and
> asked what was going on. He replied, "Your brother has come, and your
> father has killed the fatted calf, because he has got him back safe and
> sound." Then he became angry and refused to go in. His father came out
> and began to plead with him. But he answered his father, "Listen! For all
> these years I have been working like a slave for you, and I have never dis-
> obeyed your command; yet you have never given me even a young goat
> so that I might celebrate with my friends. But when this son of yours
> came back, who has devoured your property with prostitutes, you killed
> the fatted calf for him!" Then the father said to him, "Son, you are always
> with me, and all that is mine is yours. But we had to celebrate and rejoice,
> because this brother of yours was dead and has come to life; he was lost
> and has been found." (15:25–32)

Unlike the good Samaritan, in the case of the elder brother feeling superior to the younger, there's every indication that his prejudice is well-
founded. His brother has been a fool, sinner, and spendthrift, as well as
ungrateful and disrespectful to their father. But there seems a large difference between his complaints and accusations being correct in some
factual sense, and their being appropriate for the occasion. Something
good has happened, something over which he should rejoice, something that trumps the accuracy of his complaints. Whom is he hurting

by sulking rather than rejoicing? Certainly himself mostly, and maybe his father a little, but not his sinful brother against whom he has stored up so much envy and resentment. His brother has been brought back safely from a life-threatening situation, and all the elder brother can do is dwell on how it is his brother's fault for getting into that life-threatening situation in the first place. Like his father, he should feel sudden joy at the future, not sullen, calculating disappointment over the past.

The parable ends with this challenging note to avoid being like the judgmental older brother, precisely because we are more often like him. "Rather, reading the parables as they were meant to be read is to be 'once more astonished' by the gospel—to so *engage with the text* in all of its detail, contingency, and after-life in the tradition, that, like Jacob after his struggle with God at the Jabbok, we come away marked for life."[21] Most of us are not prodigals, sinking into debauchery to the point of being near death. Instead, we are more often just as petty, condemning, and vindictive as the older brother here, keeping careful track of each and every one of our virtuous acts, and even more meticulous records of others' misdeeds. How many of us really rejoice more "over one sinner who repents than over ninety-nine righteous persons who need no repentance" (Luke 15:7)?[22] I certainly prefer that my neighbors and co-workers be "righteous persons," rather than repentant sinners; there's just too much risk of recidivism. But if we think of where this attitude leads us, we may begin to see its uselessness. This is shown most clearly in family situations, such as in this parable. How many of us have held bitter, self-destructive grudges against our own family members for decades? My own mother left this world unreconciled to her siblings: Was her animosity toward them justified? Were they not repentant enough toward her for what she deemed their bad behavior? I really have no idea, but the more appropriate response is "Who cares?" I can't see that her bad feelings helped her in any way. If instead we give up our own feelings of superiority and stop excluding those we deem worse sinners than ourselves, we certainly risk disappointment or betrayal. But it is the only way to share in the love of God, the Father, who reminds us, "You are always with me, and all that is mine is yours."

But this nonjudgmental attitude should extend even to those outside our family, as shown in the parable of the Pharisee and the tax collector:

He also told this parable to some who trusted in themselves that they were righteous and regarded others with contempt: "Two men went up to the temple to pray, one a Pharisee and the other a tax collector. The Pharisee, standing by himself, was praying thus, 'God, I thank you that I am not like other people: thieves, rogues, adulterers, or even like this tax collector. I fast twice a week; I give a tenth of all my income.' But the tax collector, standing far off, would not even look up to heaven, but was beating his breast and saying, 'God, be merciful to me, a sinner!' I tell you, this man went down to his home justified rather than the other; for all who exalt themselves will be humbled, but all who humble themselves will be exalted." (Luke 18:9–14)

With good reason, tax collectors of the time were deemed especially sinful for their collaboration with Roman rule and the resulting extortion and violence that they carried out as part of their service (cf. the story of Zacchaeus the tax collector, Luke 19:1–10).[23] But as above with the prodigal son, the tax collector's sinfulness is not the issue; it is taken for granted. Nor is the Pharisee accused of hypocrisy. As with the prodigal's older brother, there is no reason here to doubt the Pharisee's claims of righteousness. But exactly as in that parable, the problem is with the resulting attitude of arrogance. If one really thought, even with some good reason, that one was morally superior to another person, the right kind of prayer would be to ask God to help that other person to become better, while humbly acknowledging the limitedness and fallibility of one's own evaluation of the situation. It seems impossible to be humble while condemning others, even more impossible to be so while rejoicing at such condemnation, rejoicing that another person is supposedly heading toward punishment or damnation. God will judge such a lack of humility and compassion more harshly than the sinfulness that we arrogantly judge: "Do not judge, so that you may not be judged. For with the judgment you make you will be judged" (Matt 7:1–2; cf. Luke 6:37–38). Our perspective is so narrow and inaccurate that to pass judgment on another is improperly to usurp a role that only God can fulfill: "All judging is here excluded, because only God knows the heart where alone the ethical quality of the action is determined."[24] Judging oneself unfavorably, on the other hand, as the tax collector does, is not just more honest and accurate. It also shows the right attitude of humility and utter dependence on God. Only with such an attitude can one be truly "justified" by God, rather than trying ineffectively to be so by oneself.

People with feelings of superiority surrounded Jesus, even while he, truly superior to everyone around him, made himself the equal and even the servant of all. Paul beautifully describes this character in one of the earliest New Testament writings (ca. 52 C.E.):

Do nothing from selfish ambition or conceit, but in humility regard others as better than yourselves. Let each of you look not to your own interests, but to the interests of others. Let the same mind be in you that was in Christ Jesus,

who, though he was in the form of God,
  did not regard equality with God
  as something to be exploited,
but emptied himself,
  taking the form of a slave,
  being born in human likeness.
And being found in human form,
  he humbled himself
  and became obedient to the point of death—
  even death on a cross. (Phil 2:3–8)

Jesus provided a perfect example and gave his constant exhortation to embrace the opposite extreme from arrogance, to live in equality and service to others. In spite of that, the arrogance of those around him, especially his own disciples, is so intransigent that they show little sign of changing, even by the end of the Gospels, as we will see (below, in the section for reflection).

For Study: On Love of Enemies—Matthew 5:38–48

You have heard that it was said, "An eye for an eye and a tooth for a tooth." But I say to you, Do not resist an evildoer. But if anyone strikes you on the right cheek, turn the other also; and if anyone wants to sue you and take your coat, give your cloak as well; and if anyone forces you to go one mile, go also the second mile. Give to everyone who begs from you, and do not refuse anyone who wants to borrow from you.

You have heard that it was said, "You shall love your neighbor and hate your enemy." But I say to you, Love your enemies and pray for those who persecute you, so that you may be children of your Father in heaven;

for he makes his sun rise on the evil and on the good, and sends rain on the righteous and on the unrighteous. For if you love those who love you, what reward do you have? Do not even the tax collectors do the same? And if you greet only your brothers and sisters, what more are you doing than others? Do not even the Gentiles do the same? Be perfect, therefore, as your heavenly Father is perfect. (Matt 5:38–48)

The Christian ideal of turning the other cheek is so widely known, and yet so little practiced by most of us, that its standing in Christianity is, I think, ambiguous. Are Christians just being hypocritical and ignoring an ethical injunction because it is inconvenient? Or is this teaching meant as an ideal, and not really to be practiced? Or are we just not trying hard enough?

It is important to sort out the examples that Jesus uses here. First, there is turning the other cheek to accept another blow. This does not seem to be any act of violence or pugilism, but one that is meant more to humiliate and degrade, rather than physically injure. It is specified as a slap to the right cheek, which means the blow was either delivered with the left hand, which was deemed unclean and therefore insulting, or with the back of the right hand, which was also deemed a gesture of disrespect, not assault: "We are dealing here with insult, not a fistfight. The intention is clearly not to injure but to humiliate."[25] The second example also involves humiliation, for the two garments being given away here would leave the person naked. The third example is taken from the situation of the Roman's humiliating, oppressive occupation of Palestine: Roman soldiers were allowed to force conquered people to carry the army's supplies for only one mile, not more. So in these examples, the point seems to be less a willingness to suffer physical injury, than a willingness to suffer humiliation. The spiritual benefit for Jesus' followers would be a diminution of the self, a cure to the kind of sinful pride we will see Augustine attack so vehemently: "A host of writers, from Chrysostom [church father, ca. 347–407 C.E.] to the present, stress the spiritual benefits to be gained by voluntarily undergoing humiliation and the mortification of the ego."[26] Christians can turn humiliation that is inflicted on them into humility that they willingly accept. Going even further than forgivingness, love of enemies—of those who do not even ask for forgiveness and who continue to abuse and degrade one— is the ultimate imitation of Jesus and God: "Be perfect, therefore, as your heavenly Father is perfect." But exactly as God can turn even his enemies and their actions to some good purpose, so can love of enemies turn a scene of humiliation into one that gives us a glimpse into the depths of divine love, humble and overpowering.

What is the practical, immediate value of turning the other cheek? Or are its rewards only spiritual, at the expense of physical harm to oneself? For Jesus, the imitation of God—"so that you may be children of your Father in heaven. . . . Be perfect, therefore, as your heavenly Father is perfect"—may be the only motive, since God receives no benefit from the people on whom he makes it rain. So too we will get nothing from this virtuous action, other than the virtue itself.[27] But even in Jesus' society, these acts may have had practical benefits: "Jesus' sayings in vs. 39b–41 envision the rejection of both passivity and violence for a third way which seeks to recover the humanity of both oppressed and oppressor through acts of defiant vulnerability."[28] Both Mohandas K. Gandhi (1869–1948) and Martin Luther King Jr. (1929–68) based their practice of nonviolence partly on Jesus' teaching. Both testified that nonviolent resistance was not only some spiritual exercise, but also the most effective means to accomplish their goals of peace and justice for their people, as well as for their oppressors.[29]

Although these great spiritual leaders have defended their teachings much more eloquently than I could, I would offer this simplified version. As my students know, I tend to boil things down to little two-by-two matrixes, which show the four possible outcomes in a situation with two variables. In this case, let us consider a situation in which someone has violently wronged you. Your choices are to respond with violence, or not; that's the one side of the matrix. The other variable is whether the person wronging you is capable of being shamed into stopping the violence and taking up better behavior, or whether that attacker is so violently inhumane that only violence can stop that party. Unfortunately, this side of the matrix is totally outside of your control, as well as finally unknown to you. You can only inaccurately guess at your assailant's moral development and sensibilities. If one responds violently against a person who might have been persuaded nonviolently, one risks doing harm or even killing that person; one may even turn a potential friend into a dead enemy. Even if the violent response is nonlethal, the enemy remains just an enemy, subdued, but not converted. If one responds violently against a person who will listen only to violence, the outcome is still the same— a subdued or dead enemy. And making people into corpses is no great accomplishment; bacteria and viruses do it every minute of every day.

What Gandhi and King saw in Jesus' teaching was the value of a higher way, a way that would result not just in this animal response of killing or subduing another animal, but of making both human beings more human and closer to God. The worst that could result from your nonviolence would be if the person was intractably violent, and your nonviolence led to your death. Even then, at least you would have committed no wrong yourself: you would have suffered an injustice, not committed one. Besides Gandhi and King, this is basically the argument of the Greek philosopher Socrates (469–399 B.C.E.),[30] as well as part of the Old Testament background to the New Testament teaching.[31] If, however, you used nonviolence against a person with a conscience, you would have made an enemy into a friend, not a corpse. Gandhi and King deemed this best outcome so valuable that it was worth risking the worst outcome of one's own death. In this case you have not merely done something that is just by human standards, such as killing an unjust person. Instead, you have done something beyond and more divine than justice, helping to turn an unjust person into a righteous one.

But what about extreme instances of violence and injustice— terrorists, tyrannical police states, serial killers, rapists? What would turning the other cheek mean in such cases, except the continuation of injustice and the spiral downward into further violence? Such scenarios strain both the applicability of Jesus' teaching and the courage of his followers, and the breadth of interpretations is therefore wide. In a curiously ambivalent essay on Jesus' teaching of nonretaliation, maneuvering between seemingly dismissing it and praising it, Dungan seems both embarrassed and proud to insert a much less ambiguous anecdote into his final footnote. Thereby he shows some of the hope and value of nonretaliation:

> My father used to tell this story about the time when he came the closest to getting shot in all his years as a missionary. It was 1941, and he was still in China although the rest of the family had gone home a year earlier. He was free to roam about since the Japanese had not yet declared war on America. One day he was on his way to deliver a message or some medicines through Japanese lines in Shanghai to another part of the city. The errand was not entirely without danger, since foreigners were being shot without provocation. As he walked along, he happened to glance into a store window and admired the carvings inside. Then he noticed in the glass of the window that a Japanese soldier had started across the street

toward him, and was cocking his rifle. "For a split second, I felt terrified. Then I remembered Jesus' example. I turned around, looked the Japanese soldier straight in the eyes and said in Chinese, "Peace, brother." He faltered and a startled look appeared on his face. "You are Christian?" he asked. "Yes," said my father. "Peace, brother," the Japanese soldier said, and held out his hand in greeting.[32]

An enemy had become, however briefly, a friend. In a more famous, public display, Pope John Paul II publicly forgave the man who had tried to murder him, immediately after the shooting. Later the pope visited him in prison, after which the pope said, "I spoke to him as a brother whom I have pardoned and who has my complete trust."[33] While the former anecdote might be dismissed as a helpless man making a gambit to save his life by appearing friendly to an enemy soldier, the pope's forgiveness was given for no ulterior motive. The only motive it could have had was to reconcile with a man he regarded as a fellow, beloved child of God. And it was given to a man who was a prisoner and therefore in the powerless, vulnerable position.

Here are concrete, practical examples of the "spiral of forgiveness,"[34] in which love, however briefly, disarms violence and hate and starts the halting, haphazard process toward peace and reconciliation, even salvation. They are extreme, in which innocent men are threatened by armed men driven by fanatical, almost insane devotion to some cause, and with whom love or reason would appear all but hopeless. Even in such cases, there is reason to practice Jesus' teaching in a literal way. But let us assume, just for the sake of cynicism, that such extreme actions are, like Jesus' cross, far beyond the courage of most of us, or that they only succeed in such rare cases that we have to discount them as impractical and useless in our regular circumstances. If we are considering regular circumstances, then let's not consider situations where madmen are shooting at us. For almost all of us, our lives are full of many more "regular" opportunities to practice forgivingness, or to practice cruelty and revenge, than when we are exchanging gunfire with someone.[35] I carry many grudges against people who have done me much less harm than shooting at me. I have been violent toward people who were unarmed and whom I could easily have ignored, rather than strike. All of us are eminently capable, but intractably reluctant, to practice Jesus' injunction in ordinary circumstances: "We are not asked to do the impossible. Most of us have only to swallow pride, show ourselves a little more loving than the other, make some gesture God can use to change a human heart."[36] Turning the other cheek is a call to subdue a sinful part of ourselves—"to swallow pride"—and thereby to begin healing our relations with others. Even if the others prove irreconcilable, the sinful part of ourselves should still be curbed, and such self-control brings us all slightly closer to a right relation with God.

For Reflection: On Being a Servant of All—Mark 10:35–45

James and John, the sons of Zebedee, came forward to him and said to him, "Teacher, we want you to do for us whatever we ask of you." And he said to them, "What is it you want me to do for you?" And they said to him, "Grant us to sit, one at your right hand and one at your left, in your glory." But Jesus said to them, "You do not know what you are asking. Are you able to drink the cup that I drink, or be baptized with the baptism that I am baptized with?" They replied, "We are able." Then Jesus said to them, "The cup that I drink you will drink; and with the baptism with which I am baptized, you will be baptized; but to sit at my right hand or at my left is not mine to grant, but it is for those for whom it has been prepared."

And when the ten heard this, they began to be angry with James and John. So Jesus called them and said to them, "You know that among the Gentiles those whom they recognize as their rulers lord it over them, and their great ones are tyrants over them. But it is not so among you; but whoever wishes to become great among you must be your servant, and whoever wishes to be first among you must be slave of all. For the Son of Man came not to be served but to serve, and to give his life a ransom for many." (Mark 10:35–45)

This is one of the many times in the Gospels when Jesus is misunderstood, even by his own disciples. Other instances, when he is misunderstood by strangers or opponents, are easier for readers to accept, for we can surmise that such people are prejudiced against Jesus by their own sinful selfishness and stubbornness. We expect such characters in the Gospel story to reject and misunderstand Jesus. But what are we to make of these repeated scenes in which those closest to him seem so willful in their ignorance of his mission and message?

Such misunderstanding on the part of his disciples is found in all the Gospels, but it is especially stressed in Mark. He structures the central section of his Gospel (8:22–10:52) around repeated scenes of the disciples misunderstanding Jesus, after the phenomenal success of Jesus' teaching and healing in the first half of the Gospel.[37] This central section begins and ends significantly with Jesus healing blind men (8:22–26; 10:46–52), a signal that Jesus has the power to heal any physical blindness present in the world, but leaving the dramatic tension as the story unfolds. Can he heal mental, spiritual blindness, the inability to "see" who he is and what it means to follow him? This more difficult obstacle is shown in his first interaction with the disciples in this section. He asks them, "But who do you say that I am?" Peter, acting as the spokesperson for the group, responds, "You are the Christ [Messiah]" (Mark 8:29). Since the Gospel's narrator begins the whole book with this title for Jesus (1:1), we know that Peter is in some sense correct in his assessment of Jesus. But the story quickly turns to one of incomprehension, frustration, and hostility between Jesus and his followers.

The abrupt shift in the story from acceptance to rejection comes when Jesus goes on to explain a part of his mission that the disciples had never heard of before in the narrative. "Then he began to teach them that the Son of Man must undergo great suffering, and be rejected by the elders, the chief priests, and the scribes, and be killed, and after three days rise again. He said all this quite openly" (8:31–32). Peter rebukes Jesus for such a shocking, unacceptable teaching, and Jesus turns against him with a harsh saying: "Get behind me, Satan! For you are setting your mind not on divine things but on human things" (8:33). He then teaches the disciples the further shocking revelation that they too are expected to participate in suffering and death (8:34–9:1), a lesson that the ghastly murder of John the Baptist earlier in the Gospel also intimates (6:14–29). A simple look at the Gospel's contents up until this turning point will show how dramatic is the shift, and how we are to understand the disciples' reaction. Till this point in Mark, Jesus has performed numerous miracles, especially healings and exorcisms, showing his power over evil and mortality, and authenticating the Gospel's claims that Jesus is the promised Messiah who would defeat Israel's enemies—including all biological, cosmic, political, or military threats. After this buildup, when Peter proclaims Jesus the "Christ," it would seem that what he means by "Christ" is a "powerful, miracle-working Messiah sent to save his people Israel." So when Jesus explains that, instead, his life will be one of humiliation and death, Peter's incomprehension and rejection is completely understandable. It is, indeed, almost inevitable.

Even though the disciples' initial shock at Jesus' true mission is understandable, as readers we could still hope, based on his success in curing physical blindness, that Jesus would also be able to open the eyes of his disciples to this new, difficult teaching. But such is not the case, especially not as Mark has presented it. For this first scene of shock begins a cycle of three similar scenes, each of them presented in the same form: Jesus predicts his suffering, humiliation, and death (8:31; 9:31; 10:32–34), the disciples misunderstand him (8:32–33; 9:32; 10:35–41), and he teaches them further as to the necessity of his and their suffering (8:34–9:1; 9:33–37; 10:42–45). Our passage (above) for reflection is from the third of these cycles, and the disciples' reaction shows that they have absorbed none of Jesus' teaching. After he has repeatedly told them that his ministry—and theirs—is about painful sacrifice, not glory, and about humble service, not commanding authority, they still ignorantly ask for glory and a place of honor. They even bicker about who among them should get these "rewards" that Jesus has refused for himself, and which he has tried unsuccessfully to teach them to refuse as well. Here Jesus tries to teach them one more time. He doesn't even say that they won't get what they want: instead, he tells them they should not even want such a "reward" in the first place. Jesus does not make a sacrifice so that he can then be glorified, the way James and John are thinking of it. His sacrifice is his glory: "For the Son of Man came not to be served but to serve, and to give his life a ransom for many" (Mark 10:45).

Although the image of the disciples' obduracy is brought out so vividly in Mark, Jesus gives a related description of his paradoxical "glory" near the end of Matthew that also addresses the problem with how the disciples are thinking about service. "When the Son of Man comes in his glory, and all the angels with him, then he will sit on the throne of his glory" (25:31). Here is a scene more like what James and John had in mind. But the way that the Son of Man judges all who come before him is still unexpected. He praises and rewards the first group to come before him, listing all the wonderful, kind, and generous things they have done for him, to which these people reply with some confusion:

"Lord, when was it that we saw you hungry and gave you food, or thirsty and gave you something to drink? And when was it that we saw you a stranger and welcomed you, or naked and gave you clothing? And when was it that we saw you sick or in prison and visited you?" And the king will answer them, "Truly I tell you, just as you did it to one of the least of these who are members of my family, you did it to me." (25:37–40)

The Son of Man then turns to those who have not done these things to "the least of these" and punishes them as though they had hurt and neglected him (25:41–45). Jesus does reward the righteous. But what Jesus does, which James and John cannot understand, is to identify completely with everyone who suffers an act of cruelty, or even simple neglect; he also rejoices at every act of kindness done to anyone. The starving, poor, sick, imprisoned, and outcast are not objects of pity for him: they are his family. And one does not ask to be rewarded for helping one's family. One does that out of love, with no thought of reward. This is what the righteous in this story also seem to understand when they act so incredulous at being rewarded by Jesus, whom they didn't even know or worship in their lifetimes, and whom they certainly didn't seek to please with their actions.[38] Ironically, it is these anonymous, non-Israelite "nations [Gentiles]" (25:32) who practice Jesus' message of love better than his closest followers.

Unlike Jesus, few of us identify with the least of our brothers and sisters. At least, seldom if ever do we go so far as feeling the hurts and injustices inflicted on them as though they were inflicted on us. We may try to help them, but in the end, they're on their own. We seldom really love the afflicted for their own sake, but for the benefits that loving them is expected to bring us. We are exactly like James and John in this scene. We expect following Jesus to "pay off." If it means so much hard work and sacrifice now, it should at least offer us honors and benefits later. If we help the poor and sick now, deep down we expect all that effort back, with interest. That's just being prudent and realistic, as the Bible itself teaches in a verse often used to encourage thriftiness and foresight: "Send out your bread upon the waters, for after many days you will get it back" (Eccl 11:1). All the other sacrifices we make—dieting, exercising, student loans, working a second job, studying hard in school—all these are forms of delayed gratification. We do something undesirable now, give up something desirable in the present, to get something more desirable in the future. That's about all the sacrifice we are prepared to handle, and even that is too much for most of us most of the time. Let's admit that we're not even as strong and patient as James and John. They at least are willing to live a life of sacrifice and humiliation now, forgoing all reward for their hard work and drinking the bitter cup, until the kingdom comes. If anything, we're usually much more like the other disciples, the nagging scolds who see James and John asking for exactly what we ourselves lust after. Then we get angry with them, not because we think their request is wrong and misguided in its object, but because we think we deserve the preference and not they.

But Jesus' deflection of their request shows that his reward is not such a delayed gratification. Rather, it is a new and unexpected kind of blessing. Humbly loving and serving others is not a chore to be endured until the real reward of sitting on a throne somewhere, presumably lording over others, is finally realized. Humbly serving and loving others *is* the form of eternal life, and it should be gladly embraced now and forever. At about the same time that Jesus was giving this hard lesson to his disciples, the Hindu scripture *Bhagavad-Gita* was written (ca. 1st century C.E.). It articulates the similar concept of dharma (duty), the performance of all life's duties—familial, social, religious, professional—out of a selfless devotion to God, not out of selfish desire for one's own good or some future reward. All the while one knows that such devotion is the only real fulfillment and satisfaction in life.[39] From completely different theologies, Hindus and Christians have both perceived and tried to follow the difficult truth that devoted service is not just the means to salvation; it is also the end or goal of a saved life.

For Prayer: The Acceptable Year of the Lord—Luke 4:18–19

> The Spirit of the Lord is upon me,
>> because he has anointed me
>>> to bring good news to the poor.
> He has sent me to proclaim release to the captives
>> and recovery of sight to the blind,
>>> to let the oppressed go free,
> to proclaim the year of the Lord's favor. (Luke 4:18–19)

According to Luke, this is how Jesus begins his public ministry, immediately after the devil has tempted him in the wilderness (4:1–13). Although there are similar incidents in Matthew and Mark (Matt 13:53–58; Mark 6:1–6), Luke's placement of Jesus' visit to Nazareth as his ministry begins is clearly meant to accentuate its importance, to present it as an epitome and inauguration of his whole ministry.[40]

Such a programmatic quality is clearly shown in the content of Jesus' reading from Isa 61:1–2 in the synagogue. Jesus' ministry, as well as the discipleship to which he calls us, is one that brings complete and unexpected deliverance and rehabilitation to those who suffer economic, political, or physical degradation. Following Jesus is not only about a personal relationship with God, or even love and kindness to those close to us. It is also about complete commitment to and concern for any and all who need the most practical and physical of help. This is shown throughout Jesus' ministry of healing and exorcisms, and in his preaching of social and economic justice. And he powerfully and selflessly continues to free captives right up until his final breath. In another scene unique to Luke's Gospel, Jesus says to the thief on the cross next to his, "Truly I tell you, today you will be with me in Paradise" (Luke 23:43). The thief's guilt or innocence is not the issue—his guilt in the story is made explicit, while his contrition is quite indirect (23:40–42). Instead, the issue is his status as a child of God, to whom mercy must always be extended, no matter how wicked he has been, or how weak and in need of help Jesus himself is.

But the negative outcome of such compassion is apparent in the Nazareth crowd's reaction to Jesus. Jesus has reiterated the words of the prophet Isaiah and recommitted himself to living out the principles of the Hebrew prophets, who constantly called for the just treatment of others, while constantly questioning the justice of the present social, political, and economic order that has made people poor or outcasts or imprisoned. The people listening to Jesus initially respond quite positively to his message: "All spoke well of him and were amazed at the gracious words that came from his mouth" (Luke 4:22). But exactly like the Hebrew prophets, Jesus turns against his audience. He accuses them first of wanting such miraculous assistance only for themselves (4:23), and then he reminds them that in the Hebrew Bible, such aid had often come from God to the least expected recipients, especially to non-Israelites (4:24–27). "God's grace is for all, without distinction of nationality and race. That was too much for the people of Nazareth."[41] The crowd's reaction then turns to violent rejection, to the point that they try to kill Jesus (4:28–29). Throughout his Gospel, Luke stresses this image of Jesus as a prophet like those of the Hebrew Bible, enthusiastically accepted at first, until people realize the radical, accusatory nature of his prophecy. When they realize that he has come to announce "God's impartial grace,"[42] a grace that will save many people whom they do not think deserve saving, then the people persecute and kill him, as they did to the prophets before him.[43] But lest we react in exactly the same wrong way as the Nazareth crowd does, we should observe that such a tendency to exclude others from our calculation of who is saved is hardly unique to Judaism. "Religious people, in general, find it difficult to allow God to act with a generosity that extends . . . salvation beyond the narrow confines of their tradition."[44] Most of us have heard the assertion that "those people" are damned sinners, falling outside of God's plan for salvation, much more loudly and frequently from Christians than we will ever hear it from Jews, or Muslims, for that matter. Yet, Christians are always quick to point out any statement by people of other faiths as an excuse for their own narrow-minded exclusion or bigotry.

But even if we could overlook Jesus' radical inclusion of outsiders, his message still often makes us stumble. When presented with the general exhortation to help everyone, we and the Nazareth crowd respond enthusiastically. But when it is revealed that such an exhortation demands more of us, and is directed to us almost exclusively as the givers of the aid, rather than its recipients, our enthusiasm wanes. It may even turn to bitter resentment at the seeming unfairness of such a demand: "I'm too busy to help. Why can't the poor just get a job? I have to work for a living. No one ever gave me a handout. Why should prisoners get free training and education in prison? I had to pay for mine!" Unlike the worshippers in the Nazareth synagogue, we add hypocrisy to our sins, claiming to follow Jesus while all the time making excuses, avoiding service, and diluting his message down to irrelevance.

Jesus proclamation of the "year of the Lord's favor" (Luke 4:19) points us to another difficulty in applying his words. Here Luke takes up the idea of the Jubilee year from the Hebrew Bible[45] and applies it to Jesus' ministry and to the coming kingdom of God (see also 1:46–55). The Jubilee was meant to be a return to the way things were, the way things are supposed to be, and not some miraculous overturning or shattering of the world.[46] God's will for the earth and for his people was reestablished by the most mundane of actions: debts were forgiven, prisoners and slaves were freed, land was returned to its original owners. With this image and throughout his Gospel, Luke goes a long way to limiting and redirecting Christian eschatological expectation or apocalyptic fervor. He rightly intuits that too much apocalypticism loses in credibility or healthiness what it gains in enthusiasm and commitment. Luke's description makes the Jubilee and the kingdom eminently practical and related to our everyday lives.[47] To think of the kingdom in terms too apocalyptic—to focus on the details and timetable of the end times and even to seek to plan for or manipulate the specifics of them—threatens to make the kingdom absurd or irrelevant. On the other hand, its description in the Gospels is a highly relevant and earthly description of a God-directed, God-centered community that seeks and longs for God's presence, practices God's justice and mercy, and calmly and steadily prepares for Jesus' return and eternal dominion.[48] Luke captures this more immediate experience of the kingdom in another passage unique to his Gospel: "Once Jesus was asked by the Pharisees when the kingdom of God was coming, and he answered, 'The kingdom of God is not coming with things that can be observed; nor will they say, "Look, here it is!" or "There it is!" For, in fact, the kingdom of God is among you'" (17:20–21). Here is an experience of God's reign in our lives that is present, ongoing, and vital, and not postponed to some future apocalypse or even till our own deaths.

Such an eager but not fanatical or otherworldly expectation of the coming of the kingdom of God gives us a simple rule to live by. Every time we wonder about the ethics or justice of what we are about to do— and I think we should constantly wonder about these qualities, lest we commit sins by mistake or bad habit or the influence of others—we can simply ask, "Will this action build up the kingdom, or not? Is this how things are done in the kingdom, or in our sinful world? Will this action lead to the liberation of those who suffer, or to their further pain and enslavement?" Nearly two thousand years after Jesus lived in Palestine and quoted the Hebrew prophet Isaiah, Gandhi also gave his own version of this way of life in strikingly similar terms:

> I will give you a talisman. Whenever you are in doubt, or when the self becomes too much with you, apply the following test. Recall the face of the poorest and the weakest man whom you may have seen, and ask yourself, if the step you contemplate is going to be of any use to him. Will he gain anything by it? Will it restore him to a control over his own life and destiny? In other words, will it lead to swaraj [freedom, self-rule] for the hungry and spiritually starving millions? Then you will find your doubts and your self melting away.[49]

26

It is a testimony to the truth and universal applicability of Jesus' message, as well as to the innately Christian character of Gandhi and the millions who have sought to follow his message of peace and love, that they are in profound agreement as to the ideals and goals of human life and community.

But as simple and beautiful as the rules of both Jesus and Gandhi are, twenty centuries of Christian history have clearly demonstrated how difficult they are to implement in our fallen, violent world. Both Gandhi and Jesus were killed for their commitment to loving and helping others. Most of us will never undergo such an extreme sacrifice for the gospel, but the kingdom only begins to break into our fallen world and into our sinful lives insofar as we overlook our own hardships and commit ourselves to alleviating the suffering of others. However, the obstacles to such commitment are enormous, so that I do not believe that we can achieve such commitment solely on our own. We must humbly pray for it, the way Jesus did when even he faltered in the face of such an extreme and constant self-sacrifice: "Father, . . . not what I want, but what you want" (Mark 14:36//Matt 26:39//Luke 22:42). We can always pray with confidence, however, for we can always be sure that what God wants is for us to have the strength to help others, for us to be the imperfect instruments of his perfect love.

For Further Reading

Burridge, R. A. *Four Gospels, One Jesus? A Symbolic Reading.* Grand Rapids: Eerdmans, 1995. A lovely presentation of each of the four Gospels, with sensitivity to the distinctive perspective of each, and their relevance for believers today.

Johnson, L. T. *Living Jesus: Learning the Heart of the Gospel.* San Francisco: HarperSanFrancisco, 2000. An elegant, eloquent debunking of historical Jesus research in favor of a study of Jesus that makes his person and ministry a real, living presence in one's life.

Throckmorton, B. H. *Jesus Christ: The Message of the Gospels, the Hope of the Church.* Louisville: Westminster John Knox, 1998. More historical than the other two recommended works, this book gives us a more likely historical reconstruction of Jesus than much scholarship today, focusing on the crucial idea of "dominion (kingdom) of God."

Notes

1. On the dating of New Testament books, see P. Perkins, *Reading the New Testament*, 2d ed. (New York: Paulist Press, 1988), 2–4.

2. E.g., G. Soares-Prabhu, "'As We Forgive': Interhuman Forgiveness in the Teaching of Jesus," in *Forgiveness*, eds. C. Floristan and C. Duquoc (Edinburgh: T & T Clark, 1986), 57–66, esp. 57: "Yet the Indian reader would at once identify active concern and forgiveness as the two poles, positive and negative, of the *dharma* [in Hinduism, duty; in Buddhism, teaching or path] of Jesus—of that complex blend of worldview and values, of beliefs and prescriptions, which 'holds together' the followers of Jesus, and integrates them into a recognisable community. For if these are not exclusively Christian attitudes, the importance given to them in the teaching of Jesus, and the concrete forms they assume in the New Testament, give them a specifically Christian significance."

3. Ibid., 60.

4. Ibid., 59.

5. On the Markan passage, see P. G. Bolt, "'With a View to the Forgiveness of Sins': Jesus and Forgiveness in Mark's Gospel," *The Reformed Theological Review* 57 (1998): 53–69, esp. 53–56.

6. See ibid.: "Here the link between Jesus' healing and his role as the Servant who brings forgiveness to the nation is clear and explicit"; J. A. Fitzmyer, *The Gospel according to Luke*, 2 vols. (New York: Doubleday, 1981–83), 1:580, 584: "The general sense of the . . . story presents Jesus as the Son of Man, a heaven-sent agent, able to do what people normally ascribe to Yahweh alone. . . . In curing the man and forgiving his sins, Jesus fulfills the mission for which he has been sent." All of this healing and forgiving is done outside of the temple and its sacrifices, which Christians interpret Jesus as replacing: see K. O. Sandnes, "The Death of Jesus for Human Sins: The Historical Basis for a Theological Concept," *Theology and Life* 15/16 (1993): 45–52, esp. the conclusion on 52: "He exercised forgiveness of sins outside the sacrificial system, and thus embodied in himself the function of the sacrifices."

7. On the passage, see Fitzmyer, *Luke*, 1:683–94; J. J. Kilgallen, "A Proposal for Interpreting Luke 7, 36–50," *Biblica* 72 (1991): 305–30; idem., "Luke 7:41–42 and Forgiveness of Sins," *Expository Times* 111 (1999): 46–47.

8. Soares-Prabhu, "As We Forgive," 64.

9. S. H. Ringe, *Jesus, Liberation, and the Biblical Jubilee* (Philadelphia: Fortress Press, 1985), 66.

10. The verse is of doubtful authenticity: see Fitzmyer, *Luke*, 2:1503–4. But the similarity to Acts 7:60 actually increases the likelihood this verse is authentic to Luke, since the same author wrote both books and similarities between them are to be expected; the theme of forgiveness is also Lukan, frequent in both his Gospel and Acts (Acts 2:38; 5:31; 10:43; 13:38; 26:18; see Fitzmyer, *Luke*,

1:223–24). For a good argument in favor of its authenticity, see T. M. Bolin, "A Reassessment of the Textual Problem of Luke 23:34a," *Proceedings, Eastern Great Lakes and Midwest Biblical Societies* 12 (1992): 131–44.

11. Cf. H. U. von Balthasar, "Jesus and forgiveness," *Communio* 11 (1984): 322–34, esp. 333: "To be more explicit: he is both, indivisibly, the one sent by the Father to be physician and healer by divine authority and the one who totally identified with sinners in a solidarity demonstrated perfectly by the institution of the Eucharist just prior to the Cross."

12. Quoted by Soares-Prabhu, "As We Forgive," 60.

13. Fitzmyer, *Luke*, 2:1140.

14. From the chart at http://www.ntimages.com/Coin-chart.htm (site visited June 10, 2004).

15. Ringe, *Biblical Jubilee*, 76.

16. See Soares-Prabhu, "As We Forgive," 59: "The promise to forgive those who have injured us stands out strikingly as the sole reference to human activity in the Lord's Prayer. This, evidently, strongly highlights the significance of forgiveness in the *dharma* of Jesus."

17. Ibid., 60.

18. See Fitzmyer, *Luke*, 1:829, with bibliography.

19. Cf. S. C. Barton, "Parables on God's Love and Forgiveness (Luke 15:1–32)," in *The Challenge of Jesus' Parables*, ed. R. N. Longenecker (Grand Rapids: Eerdmans, 2000), 199–216, esp. 201: "The three parables of Luke 15 are among the most famous parables of Jesus and have been transmitted by Luke with consummate literary skill."

20. This is not to endorse the suggestion that the two parts were originally separate: see the thorough discussion in Fitzmyer, *Luke*, 2:1082–94.

21. Barton, "Parables," 200, emphasis in original.

22. Cf. the wonderfully passionate conclusion of Barton, "Parables," 215: "It is, therefore, quite legitimate—indeed essential—to ask: *Do we believe* it to be true that 'there is joy in heaven before the angels of God over one sinner who repents'? Do we believe it to be true that God is like that shepherd, that woman, and that forgiving father? Do we believe it to be true that Jesus embodied such an understanding of God in his practice of eating with 'sinners,' and that to be a follower of Jesus means to engage in practices that are in creative fidelity with his teaching and example? No amount of agreement *in principle* will show in any convincing way that what is affirmed is true. In Bonhoeffer's terms, what is necessary is the step beyond 'agreement in principle.' What is necessary is the step (as he provocatively put it) from being a theologian to being a Christian. In other words, what will show it to be true is whether or not the testimony of the parables to the overflowing grace and forgiveness of God, which leads to repentance, becomes embodied in our own lives and practices."

23. On tax collectors, See Fitzmyer, *Luke*, 1:469–70.

24. Soares-Prabhu, "As We Forgive," 63, who goes on in the next sentence to comment on the modernity of such a nonjudgmental attitude: "In an age which has been alerted to the hidden motives of human behaviour, personal and social, by the great 'masters of suspicion', Nietzsche, Freud and Marx, the logic of Jesus' prohibition becomes obvious, even if its practice remains as difficult as ever."

25. W. Wink, "Neither Passivity nor Violence: Jesus' Third Way (Matt. 5:38–42 par.)," in *The Love of Enemy and Nonretaliation in the New Testament*, ed. W. M. Swartley (Louisville: Westminster John Knox Press, 1992), 102–25, quotation on 105.

26. Ibid., 102.

27. D. Gill, "Socrates and Jesus on Non-Retaliation and Love of Enemies," *Horizons* 18 (1991): 246–62, esp. 257: "Nor does it appear to be a strategy for avoiding trouble or winning over the offending party."

28. Wink, "Neither Passivity nor Violence," 115.

29. Cf. D. L. Dungan, "Jesus and Violence," in *Jesus, the Gospels, and the Church: Essays in Honor of William R. Farmer*, ed. E. P. Sanders (Macon, GA: Mercer University Press, 1987), 135–62, esp. 149: "If it succeeded in awakening the pangs of conscience within the opponent, by accepting voluntary suffering at his hands, it [nonviolent resistance] was in fact the best and quickest way to work toward better relationships in the future."

30. See the clear discussion and comparison of Gill, "Socrates and Jesus."

31. See J. Vijayakumar, "Non-Violence and Peaceful Co-Existence: A Biblical Perspective," in *Bible Speaks Today: Essays in Honour of Gnana Robinson*, ed. D. J. Muthunayagom (Delhi: Indian Society for Promoting Christian Knowledge, 2000), 45–55, esp. 46: "*Hamas*: This is a word used very frequently in the Old Testament to refer to violence. Both the noun and the verb together occur about sixty times in the Old Testament. While most of the time it is translated as violence, it is also translated as wrong, injustice, oppression, wickedness, falsehood, cruelty, unrighteousness, and damage. . . . Seen in the light of its cognate *adikia* which is used by the Septuagint in most cases to render *hamas*, it basically denotes causing injustice."

32. Dungan, "Jesus and Violence," 162.

33. W. J. Burghardt, "A Brother Whom I have Pardoned," *The Living Pulpit* 3 (1994): 10–11, esp. (quotation from) 10.

34. Soares-Prabhu, "As We Forgive," 60.

35. Cf. R. Horsley, "Ethics and Exegesis: 'Love Your Enemies' and the Doctrine of Nonviolence," in *The Love of Enemy and Nonretaliation in the New Testament*, ed. W. M. Swartley (Louisville: Westminster John Knox Press, 1992), 72–99, esp. 85: "As we shall see, the content of nearly all the sayings indicates a context of local interaction with personal enemies, not one of relations with foreign or political foes." Even Dungan, "Jesus and Violence," 145, admits the everyday nature of Jesus' teaching: "Furthermore, I agree with Richard Horsley that the

sociological context of these sayings is not some sort of universal brotherhood, but the everyday, common life of the Galilean villages."

36. Burghardt, "A Brother," 11.

37. Often recognized: see B. Ehrman, *The New Testament: A Historical Introduction to the Early Christian Writings*, 2d ed. (New York: Oxford University Press, 2000), 67–69.

38. This is one of the passages, together with Matt 7:21, often cited in support of the possibility that non-Christians, people who grew up somewhere never having heard the name or teachings of Jesus, would be judged on their intuitive, "natural" practice of Christianity, rather than on their simple lack of belief in someone of whom they'd never heard. We will look at this idea again in the chapter on Dante, because it is a problem with which he too wrestled.

39. Cf. Soares-Prabhu, "As We Forgive," 61: "We are back here at the bedrock of the *dharma* of Jesus, in which relationships with God are normally mediated through relationships with our fellow human beings."

40. See Fitzmyer, *Luke*, 1:529, "The Lucan story, transposed to this point in the Gospel, has a definite programmatic character. . . . The fulfillment-story stresses the success of his teaching under the guidance of the Spirit, but the rejection story symbolizes the opposition that his ministry will evoke among his own"; also P. Hertig, "The Jubilee Mission of Jesus in the Gospel of Luke: Reversals of Fortunes," *Missiology: An International Review* 26 (1998): 167–79, esp. 167: "There may be no better way to get to the heart of Jesus' mission than to study Jesus' inaugural address in his hometown Nazareth sermon. There Jesus proclaimed that he was the anointed one of God and introduced a jubilee era that is programmatic in Luke's Gospel for his holistic mission of grace."

41. J. Pritchard, "Jesus and Jubilee," *Epworth Review* 26 (1999): 52–59, quotation from 55.

42. Hertig, "Jubilee Mission," 169.

43. For a brief but effective treatment of this theme, see Ehrman, *Historical Introduction*, 103–21.

44. M. Prior, *Jesus the Liberator: Nazareth Liberation Theology (Luke 4:16–30)* (Sheffield, UK: Sheffield Academic Press, 1995), 99, as quoted in Hertig, "Jubilee Mission," 170.

45. See Ringe, *Biblical Jubilee*; also J. H. Yoder, *The Politics of Jesus*, 2d ed.(Grand Rapids: Eerdmans, 1994), esp. 60–75.

46. Cf. M. Barker, "The Time Is Fulfilled: Jesus and Jubilee," *Scottish Journal of Theology* 53 (2000): 22–32, esp. 23: "The command to eat only what grows of itself in the field (Lev. 25:12) and the older injunction to share this equally with the poor and the animals (Exod. 23:11), indicate that the Sabbath year was a time when the land and the people returned to their original state."

47. Cf. Pritchard, "Jesus and Jubilee," who relates it to present-day forgiveness of Third-World debts.

48. Cf. Hertig, "Jubilee Mission," 177: "There has been a sad tendency in evangelicalism to reject such prophetic texts through oversimplifications or interpretations irrelevant to real life. Mark Noll has observed that prophecy tends to draw Christians into apocalyptic speculation rather than into prophetic engagement with the world around them. . . . However, the present jubilee era we live in calls for Christians everywhere to embrace the holistic mission of Jesus by engaging in the real world through Jesus' spiritually and socially inclusive mission of mercy and love."

49. Widely quoted as the epitome of Gandhi's teaching. Online: http://www.gandhiinstitute.org/aboutmkg.html (site visited May 20, 2004).

2

ST. AUGUSTINE
Human Glory and God's Glory

Introduction

Augustine was born in 354 C.E. in Thagaste, a town in North Africa in what is present-day Algeria.[1] His mother, Monica, was an especially devout Catholic Christian her whole life, but his father, Patricius, was a Roman pagan until near the end of his life, when he finally converted to his wife's faith. The marriage was stormy in other ways: Patricius was frequently unfaithful and had a violent temper (see *Conf.* 9.9.19), though Augustine insists that Patricius did not beat Monica or even argue with her. Her personality was so irenic and soothing that she calmed him down, despite all his shortcomings, before blows or even words were exchanged. The one thing both parents shared, however, was a steadfast and self-sacrificing determination for the success of their one son—they had other children, although they're barely mentioned by Augustine himself—a determination that Augustine himself inherited from them and practiced throughout his life.[2] But determination in itself is not really a virtue, just a strong personality trait, as we shall see when Augustine discusses its negative expressions, pride and ambition.

During his life, Augustine experimented with many philosophical schools and religious movements. Indeed, it seems to be a part of what makes him fascinating and frustrating to so many readers of his

Confessions. He didn't follow either of the spiritual paths must of us are used to: he didn't grow up in a tradition and always stay with it, nor did he grow up in a tradition and then abandon it completely for another. Instead, he grew up nominally as a Christian, then questioned and doubted Christianity while investigating and even embracing several other philosophical and religious perspectives. Eventually, in early adulthood he fully committed himself to Christianity. Augustine tells us that at the age of nineteen he read a book by the pagan statesman and philosopher Cicero (lived ca. 106–43 B.C.E.), *Hortensius*, and that this book changed his life radically: "This book really changed my temperament, and it changed my prayers to you, O Lord, and gave me different aspirations and desires. Suddenly all my empty hopes were now worthless to me, and with an unbelievable burning in my heart I craved the immortality of wisdom."[3] Christian readers are understandably puzzled and intrigued that a pagan author helps Augustine down the right path, to pray to the one true God and to seek after the truth.[4] Clearly, Augustine is not telling us a simple story of how he dabbled in various wrong ways of looking at the world, and then rejected them when he found the right way, Christianity. Instead, each attempt at truth, even when transcended, is valued for the partial truth it contains, and gratefully accepted for the loving providence it shows from God, who has secretly guided the whole journey, no matter how circuitous or painful. This valuing of truth even when enunciated by non-Christians is especially noticeable in Augustine's continuing commitment to Platonist philosophy, which he deems compatible with Christian belief, just incomplete without the message and especially the humility of Christ. "Conversion and baptism did nothing to crush the pedagogic and humanistic instinct. The Neoplatonic influences set him on the way to seeing the liberal arts . . . as a highly desirable mental training. . . . He expressly denied that holy scripture represented the sole medium of divine revelation."[5] Less compatible were the Manichees, a pseudo-Christian, dualistic sect of which Augustine himself was a member for about ten years of his adult life.[6] We will discuss them further (below). But he comes to look upon even this group with compassion, not anger or regret (see *Conf.* 9.4.8), for they too are mysteriously part of God's plan, a plan that is guided only by love.

Another painful subplot that winds itself through the *Confessions* is Augustine's emotional life. Every reader has been impressed—most positively, but many negatively—by Augustine's passionate personality. Unlike any of the other church fathers—or most any other subsequent Christian theologian, for that matter—Augustine loved passionately in his own life, and left us a uniquely personal, but at the same time universal, analysis of human emotions. "No thinker in the Early Church was so preoccupied with the nature of human relationships."[7] "Among the great theologians, Augustine is pre-eminently the psychologist."[8] "He was 'the first modern man' in the sense that with him the reader feels himself addressed at a level of extraordinary psychological depth."[9] He was passionately devoted to his friends,[10] some of whom stuck with him throughout his life and surrounded him constantly both before he became a Christian and after his conversion and ordination. "Augustine, as we shall see, will hardly ever spend a moment of his life without some friend, even some blood-relative, close by him."[11] Augustine's account of his feelings for a friend who died young is one of the most moving depictions of grief in any literature (*Conf.* 4.4.7–6.11). He was also very close to his pious mother, as different as her personality and spiritual journey were from his.[12] But such passion and loyalty make the relationships he neglected all the more disturbing to his readers. Augustine expresses no affection for his father.[13] He also lived with a woman for thirteen years, who bore him a son, and yet he turned her out when the liaison became an impediment to a socially advantageous marriage for him. The only apology we should make for him is that he admits he was a cad—even though such an arrangement was not really regarded as shameful at the time. He admits that she was a stronger person than he, and admits that he painfully missed her for long after her departure (see *Conf.* 6.15.25).[14]

Simultaneous with these intellectual and spiritual wanderings, and this stormy personal life, Augustine's professional life, on the other hand, was in high gear. He took up the study and subsequently the teaching of rhetoric, first in Carthage, the largest nearby city, and then in Italy. His was a powerful and influential career in his time, for skill at speaking eloquently and persuasively was absolutely necessary in his world for success in politics or law. Augustine describes how he himself was very talented at speaking and writing. He tells us how he won a poetry contest, receiving the prize from the proconsul (the governor of the province) himself (*Conf.* 4.3.5); his abilities were being recognized and rewarded. Soon after, Augustine dedicated his first written work,

On the Beautiful and the Fitting, to a famous orator in Rome (*Conf.* 4.14.21), looking to ingratiate and advance himself more. Augustine's rise seemed steady and assured, so much so that he could realistically dream of a governorship and a marriage to a wealthy heiress (*Conf.* 6.11.19). Augustine was on the fast track of his time for advancement, power, wealth, an advantageous marriage—everything that people would deem as worldly success, then or now.

But just as he came to see his parents' determination for worldly success as a mostly negative thing, so too he slowly grew to believe that worldly success as defined in his society was deeply flawed, negative, even damning. He became so disenchanted with his supposedly successful life that he quit his job teaching rhetoric, and, following what he believed was a sign from God in 386, he finally decided to embrace Christianity wholeheartedly. He and a group of friends and family retreated from the world after Augustine's conversion until his baptism the following Easter, going to a wealthy friend's country estate at Cassiciacum (near Milan, Italy) to read, discuss, meditate, and pray. Augustine's mother died shortly after his baptism, and he returned to North Africa. There he intended to live a quiet life of withdrawal and contemplation with others, similar to what he had enjoyed at Cassiciacum, a religious community similar to what would later be formalized and regulated as monasteries.[15] But the church members and hierarchy quickly noticed and valued Augustine's eloquence and brilliance so much that they wanted him as a spokesperson and defender of the church, not just a contemplative member. So they forced him— more or less against his will—to be first a priest (391) and then a bishop (395).[16] He served as bishop of the city of Hippo, where he was tireless and effective in his aid to his parishioners, in his correspondence and work with other bishops, in his debates with heretics and non-Christians, and in his copious writing. Much of it—unlike most other writings from antiquity—has survived to the present,[17] and most of it is now available in translation. He died during the Vandal siege of Hippo in 430.

These facts of Augustine's life are mostly gleaned from his best-known work, *Confessions*, which he wrote in about 400. The main thrust of the book is not to relate autobiographical details, however. Augustine set out to trace his philosophical and theological problems, probings, dead ends, and finally, resolutions, as these unfolded over thirty-three years of his life.[18] The final four books of *Confessions* show these resolutions in his more abstract contemplation of time, mind, and Scripture. One of the overriding problems for Augustine—in *Confessions* and elsewhere in his works—is the problem of evil in the world and sin in our lives. As my brief sketch of his life demonstrates, a large part of Augustine's analysis of sin is that it often comes from mistakenly choosing lesser goods—such as worldly success, but also including sensual pleasures—over greater goods—especially loving and obeying God. And when the lesser and greater goods are given the wrong relative value by us, then the final, ultimate good—eternal happiness—is lost. What Augustine intuits in his own experience of sin, he powerfully and influentially generalizes to the whole human race. We see this in his later works, where he further develops the idea of original sin, including his other well-known work, *The City of God* (written ca. 413–426), where he applies this critique to all of Roman society—its religion, culture, politics, economics, everything.

Augustine's preoccupation with sin and its terrible effects on our world has often horrified readers and critics over the centuries, and many have dismissed him as a neurotic prude who hates life, sexuality, himself, other people—pretty much everything but God. And since a love of God predicated and based on a hatred of everything else doesn't seem helpful or healthy, many have found little in Augustine that they would wish to emulate or even consider, but just an ugly, if influential, relic from the past. But this is not, I think, the only or best way to read him. As stark and even depressing as his description of sin is, it is not the final word, or even his primary focus. Augustine only describes the disease so vividly and its terminal condition as so dire in the context of joyfully and gratefully praising the only Physician who can cure it—the God of Jesus Christ. He has complete assurance that God will cure it, indeed, that God has already begun to do so. In the next chapter we will see that Dante is not primarily about punishment and damnation—even though that is the most vivid part of his work and the part everyone remembers—but about love and blessedness. So too, Augustine is not finally about the strength and horrors of sin, but about the graciousness, love, and power of the God who can and does heal and redeem us from sin.[19]

I have chosen to analyze here the two related sins of pride and ambition, both because they weigh down Augustine's own life so much, and because they are equally or even more prevalent in our modern world.

Today people do not usually even regard them as sins, thereby making Augustine's own experience and condemnation of them all the more timely to us. Further, Augustine does not believe that we must simply wait for God's grace and redemption to come upon us in our sinfulness. Instead, he gives us practical and beneficial spiritual exercises to curb these sins, eloquently praising and persuasively recommending the counterbalancing virtues of humility and contemplation to us in our distracted, overburdened lives.

Pride and Humility

First, what exactly do we mean by speaking of "pride" as a sin? In our modern usage pride is almost universally praised and encouraged as a good trait, something people need in order to be comfortable with themselves, accomplish their goals, and lead happy, fulfilling lives. We constantly encourage it in our children: "Stand up for yourself, take pride in what you do, make me proud." To understand the implications of a word, it is often helpful to consider what we would think of as its opposite. The opposite of the quality just described as pride would be "shame," the usually unhealthy degradation, humiliation, and debasement of the self. So what we're really talking about in our modern use of the word "pride" is self-worth, self-respect, self-esteem, honor, integrity.[20] In this pairing, pride is spiritually and psychologically healthy; shame is a spiritual and psychological disease, sometimes endured for good reasons to curb or cure a deeper disorder, sometimes carried to neurotic extremes. With these meanings, neither pride nor shame would in itself be a sin.

But when we set "humility" in opposition to "pride," we are clearly talking about a different quality. Humility is the right valuing of oneself, seeing one's own faults and shortcomings as well as one's accomplishments, while being deferent and considerate and not overbearing toward others. The sinful sense of "pride," then, is the opposite of the virtue of humility. Internally or personally, it is the ultimate disorder in one's soul, inaccurately and irrationally valuing oneself above all else, instead of putting oneself in the right relation of humility toward God and other people. Rather than the healthy feeling of self-worth described above, pride is a smug feeling of self-enclosed self-satisfaction. But, ironically, since we cannot really satisfy ourselves but can find rest and enjoyment only in God, such pride is completely self-defeating, leading to ultimate dissatisfaction, "dissipation . . . diminution, which the self-satisfied soul unavoidably suffers, if it seeks to enjoy its own power in perverse imitation of God."[21]

When such a proud, self-satisfied person interacts with other people, the results are equally disastrous. One's complacent self-satisfaction can cause one not to pursue further virtues, but to assume and advertise to others that one already has them. This is hypocrisy, which many of us consider as the most distasteful of sins.[22] More destructively, if one is so satisfied with oneself and one's supposed accomplishments, one inevitably is dissatisfied with others and their supposed failures, and such dissatisfaction is expressed as contempt,[23] arrogance, even abuse and domination. All of these are rendered more insidious by their being rationalized as fitting and proper, when they are in fact the total disintegration and perverting of human relations.[24] And in one's relation with God, pride is even more destructive, for God is the one person before whom the only right relation is complete humility: "For pride means an arrogation on the creature's part of something that properly belongs to God alone. . . . To act as though one has no limits is nothing other than to play at being God."[25]

It is not hard to see why Augustine would so emphasize this negative, sinful aspect of pride, for it was his own besetting sin. "According to his own testimony, pride . . . had ruled his will until the time of his conversion, and still, fourteen years later, was the most difficult temptation to resist."[26] His excelling at his studies, his relentless pursuit of his career, his callous disregard for others' feelings—all were symptoms and punishments of a sinful soul that thought itself better than others and sought to dominate and exploit them. By the time he writes the *Confessions*, Augustine believes that it was nothing other than pride that had painfully kept him from God for so long. He reveals "that from early youth he had been increasingly conscious of an acute moral and intellectual struggle within himself. As he depicts them, the issues or opposing tensions involved in this conflict were his own sinful pride and the love of God, Who resists the proud but gives grace to the humble."[27] But more than just his own worst sin, Augustine came to see pride as the epitome and worst of all sins. Whether Augustine thought all sins stem from pride or are instances of pride is debated,[28] but looking at Augustine's most famous analysis of sin in *Confessions*, book 2, shows how fundamental he thought pride was.

The incident is perhaps the most famous in *Confessions*. Augustine is sixteen, and he and some friends steal pears from a neighbor's tree.[29] What anyone else would discount as a typically adolescent and fairly harmless prank—a friend and I set off a rather large and potentially dangerous explosion in a supermarket dumpster at that age—Augustine spends the next several pages analyzing as the worst of sins. Generations of readers—the German philosopher Nietzsche most famously—have understandably and derisively thought this a rather absurd, melodramatic overreaction.[30] But Augustine's choice of this incident as uniquely revealing of how sin works is in fact careful and insightful. It comes right after his honest appraisal of his sexual exploits at the time (*Conf.* 2.1.1–3.8), sins that are embarrassing and immature for their lack of self-control. These sins are understandable because they pursue some things that humans naturally and legitimately desire—physical pleasure and emotional companionship—yet just do so inordinately, without control or restraint. But in the pear theft, Augustine can find no equivalent goal. Unlike wanton sex to a teenager, the pears are not appealing: "I stole that of which I had plenty, even of much better quality" (*Conf.* 2.4.9). And he and his companions throw them to pigs instead of eating them. That is what confuses him about this sin and causes him to look more deeply into it. And when he does, the final problem and terror of a sin that cannot be explained away or mitigated rise up before Augustine.[31] He did something evil for its own sake, knowing it to be evil, and loving the evil in it: "It was foul, but I loved it. I loved to perish; I loved my own ruin, not that for which I ruined myself, but rather I loved my very ruin itself"(*Conf.* 2.4.9). A few paragraphs later he will draw the further implication that if he could love the sheer nothingness and negation of stealing for no reason, then he could love any conceivable sin: "For what would I not be capable of, if I even loved a crime done for no reason?" (*Conf.* 2.7.15). Augustine had found the inadequacy of all other explanations of evil, and this is exactly why his analysis would come to dominate and define Christian theology. People do not just sin out of ignorance or because of a mistake—the plausible and optimistic analysis of such powerful ethical teachers as Confucius and Socrates. Rather, they sometimes sin just because they want to, with full and accurate knowledge of what they're doing and its consequences, and without even an expectation of some appealing reward, but just for the sake of sinning. To say that we are doing something "for the hell of it" turns out to be much more than an empty phrase. It is quite an accurate assessment of our darkest, inexplicable, motiveless acts of rebellion and destruction.

But Augustine won't let his analysis go at that, even though it's gotten him deeper into understanding sin than almost any other thinker. He keeps probing, because he believes that we must do everything we do for *some* reason: a motiveless, evil act is not like a seizure or a trance; it is still chosen over other options. If he didn't steal to get the pears, or to hurt his neighbor, or to show off in front of his friends—this last motive certainly facilitates his act, but doesn't seem to *cause* it (*Conf.* 2.8.16–9.17)—then why *did* he do it? What he finally decides is that the theft, in its furtiveness and in its transgression of rules just for the sake of disobedience, must have been some kind of attempt to be like God, to be in control and to be free, even though the attempt was so petty and ineffective. Augustine cries out the question of how it could be that he, "a captive, imitated a stunted liberty, by avoiding punishment for doing something forbidden, making a dismal imitation of omnipotence?" (*Conf.* 2.6.14). Augustine had finally found the root of his sin—the desire to be God by oneself and for oneself, which is as proud as it is pathetic. For Augustine, "all formal sin can be ultimately defined in terms of a basic—though perverted—propensity to imitate the Divine through the use of purely human resources and capacities. Such a desire particularly distinguishes the proud, who aim at a lofty grandeur belonging by right to the Deity alone."[32] We are created in God's image (Gen 1:27), but instead of turning to God to worship the true divine image, our pride foolishly turns us away from him to worship our own selves, stunted images of God. Augustine describes this as a catastrophic loss of everything, including ourselves: "Whoever lets God go and loves himself, letting God go in loving himself, remains not even in himself, but goes out of himself too. He is exiled from his own heart through contempt of the inward and love for the outward."[33] It is an image of utter dissolution and dissipation, as our selves let go of the solidity of God for the disappointing, ghostly shadow of our own proud selves.

Augustine drew this description from his own personal experience of pride, which was keeping him from God, and found it in the deuterocanonical book of Sirach (or Ecclesiasticus, or Ben Sira), written about 180 B.C.E.[34] He knew and frequently quoted the passage from a suspect Latin text: "Pride is the beginning of all sin" (Sir 10:13).[35] The immediately preceding verse exactly describes pride as we have been analyzing it in Augustine: "The beginning of pride is human effrontery in withdrawing one's heart from one's Maker" (Sir 10:12).[36] These verses are part of Augustine's analysis of the falls of Satan and of Adam and Eve. He shows how their disobedience was first based on pride, on withdrawing their hearts from their Maker and relying on their own resources, even before their outward disobedience:

> It was in secret that the first human beings began to be evil; and the result was that they slipped into open disobedience. For they would not have arrived at the evil act if an evil will had not preceded it. Now, could anything but pride have been the start of the evil will? For "pride is the start of every kind of sin." And what is pride except a longing for a perverse kind of exaltation? For it is a perverse kind of exaltation to abandon the basis on which the mind should be firmly fixed, and to become, as it were, based on oneself, and so remain. This happens when a man is too pleased with himself: and a man is self-complacent when he deserts that changeless Good in which, rather than in himself, he ought to have found his satisfaction.[37]

The actual disobedient act is, in a way, less momentous than the inner disposition, just as Augustine had described his own sinning with a tree in *Confessions*. It is the inner disposition that alienates one from God, that pulls one from one's true and life-giving origins into a sterile world of false self-sufficiency and self-delusion. And at such proud self-destruction, even God himself can only turn away: "Pride is a denial of God, which leads to abandonment by God."[38]

Augustine also says that he read "certain books of the Platonists" (*Conf.* 7.9.13), and right after this, he comes to another startling conclusion about how evil works. There is no *substance* of evil; it is not some *thing* that exists, or some *thing* that we can choose. Evil is not *what* we choose, but *how* we choose: "In effect, moral evil is best described with an adverb than a noun: it means choosing evilly rather than choosing an evil."[39] It is the choice itself, the turning away from a good to the corruption or diminution of that good, from existence toward disintegration and nonexistence (*Conf.* 7.12.18–7.13.19; see also 3.7.12).[40] As he amalgamated his own experience with the Genesis story of Adam and Eve, he also saw his fall and theirs as very similar to what the Platonists described as the fall of every soul away from its heavenly home of unchanging truth and contemplation, and into the physical world of changeability and falsity. The Platonists—as well as the Manichees—would have attributed more blame to the corrupting influence of matter and flesh on the soul than would Augustine, who always maintained the goodness of creation as described in the first chapter of Genesis. But both the Platonists' and Augustine's interpretation of Genesis described the soul's first turn toward negativity and nonexistence as an act of pride, a disordered love of a lesser good—oneself—instead of a greater good—the One (for Platonists) or God. "That is, it is not a falling away to evil natures; the defection is evil in itself, as a defection from him who supremely exists to something of a lower degree of reality; and this is contrary to the order of nature" (*City of God* 12.8).[41] Rebellion and disobedience are only the outward symptoms of the deeper disease and the cause of sin—pride.[42]

But although Augustine sensed the compatibility between the Platonist and Christian ideas of a fall into negativity, falsehood, and mortality, he also sensed the inadequacy of the Platonists' position. They too were ultimately and devastatingly guilty of pride: "This is the sin of pride, which Augustine finds particularly prominent in Satan, the pagan Platonists, and himself."[43] It stems from the fact that the Greeks would have had a quite different sense of pride, somewhat akin to a rather overgrown, overbearing self-esteem, or a more humane, manageable arrogance: perhaps "condescension" would best identify it. For Plato, such pride is not fundamentally bad. The desire to do things by and for oneself, to look down on others who are clearly beneath oneself, and even to dominate others, insofar as they deserve or even like to be dominated—such pride is simply a matter of rightly evaluating oneself and rightly asserting one's superiority. It could become excessive or violent, like any other normal urge, and thereby become sinful. "To be sure, the Greeks did not conceive of pride in the Biblical sense, that is, the spirit which prompts disobedience to God. For the Greeks *hybris* was an ethical concept, that of excess which oversteps the bounds of decent behavior."[44] But when rightly exercised, it would be part of a virtuous life, and a person who was missing it entirely would be considered base and ignoble. And, as we might concede, no one had more of a right to be proud of themselves than the philosophers. Augustine himself admits that they intuited so many truths about God: "The pride of Platonism is based, [Augustine] admits, on a real measure of spiritual apprehension granted to such rare souls as Plotinus himself."[45] Simply put, for the Greek philosophers pride was not a vice, and Augustine saw this as a deep flaw in their ethical thinking. It thereby became the root of their sinfulness by blinding them to their own sin, as it had blinded Augustine for so long.

But perhaps the more important corollary to this is that for the Greek philosophers, humility is not a virtue, and it certainly should be avoided, not embraced. For them, humility is simply the servile attitude of weak, base people. Greek philosophers, especially the Platonists, knew and taught many truths about God. But the simple truth about human beings—that all must be humble before one another and more especially before their Creator—they could never accept or teach: "Humility was the one lesson that Augustine's philosophical teachers had excluded from their curriculum."[46] "The way of humility cannot be learnt in the books of the philosophers."[47] Indeed, this is made more ironic by the fact that it was their accurate learning about God that made the philosophers incapable and disdainful of the virtue of humility: "By science the soul can recognize God as maker of the world, but unless the soul at the same time acknowledges the superiority of God to the rational seeker, unless the soul religiously disposes itself to worship, its pride will corrupt its own discovery."[48] Knowing things about God had made them prideful and not humble before God.

Christian humility is not the same as the weakness, passivity, or servility that the Greeks rightly condemned. Humility is really the right evaluating of oneself. But totally unlike the Platonists' pride, Christian humility brings God into the relation as the one whom we have sinned against and abandoned. The right evaluation of oneself must necessarily be as one who is extremely insignificant, and, of more importance, as one who is completely undeserving and needy.[49] And since other human beings are brought into consideration as fellow creatures made in the image of God, any feelings of superiority over them are also excluded; the only right feelings toward them are equality and compassion.[50] This kind of humility is based on the painfully recurring experience of one's own limitations and on one's intense, constant need for others; it is simple "submission to the facts of experience."[51] But it paradoxically leads to the right exercise of power, for by humbly serving others, one becomes an instrument of God's will. Rightly and reasonably giving up on the weakness of one's own will and the foolishness of one's own plans, one obeys God's omnipotent will and helps to enact his infinitely wise and benevolent providence.[52]

Augustine believes that the "facts of experience" are so universal and obvious that it should be possible for any reasonably honest, mature person to achieve the kind of humility that acknowledges human limitations, weakness, and complete dependence on God. "[Augustine] claims that Porphyry's own words—'granted to a few'—should have compelled him to acknowledge that this apprehension was a gift and not an achievement."[53] But there is a more paradoxical humility and "gift" that is anything but obvious and goes beyond human comprehension. That is divine humility, based not on weakness, but on omnipotence. The incarnation "demonstrated the divine humility, . . . at once the antithesis to and the remedy for the human self-assertion which divides persons from God and sets them against each other."[54] This "remedy" is a gift utterly unexpected and undeserved, "the remedy that could never be imagined,"[55] for it fully expresses the infinite, incomprehensible love of the Giver. But to accept this unbelievably humble gift is also unbelievably humbling, for this gift is not deserved and can never be repaid: if one accepts it, one must humbly remain in God's debt forever. Even if one refuses the gifts of God's incarnation, love, and sacrifice, one is still in God's debt forever for one's very being. But one can at least choose to ignore this, or even hate and resent God for it, and those reactions often prove less burdensome than this humility. The humility that outrageously embraces the mystery of the incarnation is the more important humility that the Platonists lack (see *Conf.* 7.9.13–14),[56] but it is the humility that defines Christianity and makes eternal life possible. Thus, Augustine preached to what must have been a crowd astonished at his challenge and rhetoric: "You are so overcome with the burden of your own pride . . . that only God's humility can raise you."[57]

Ambition and Contemplation

The ancient world, much like our own, was one that praised and rewarded the life of ambition, action, and accomplishment, of improving oneself and getting ahead of others to command their respect and obedience. For men, this could be accomplished in many ways—the military, politics, the courts, commerce, sports, literature, art, and even philosophy. Here again, Augustine came to see the insufficiency of Greek philosophy to curb human sinful urges, because the philosophers were as guilty of ambition as anyone else, making philosophizing into yet another competition to be won in order to further oneself and gain honor.[58] At best, the philosophers could thereby distract and redirect men who might have pursued more destructive, predatory types of domination in politics or the military, but this is hardly a victory over sin, just a less harmful indulgence in it. And even when they turned inward to practice contemplation, there was an ambitious bent to it. All the time they believed that they themselves would lift themselves up to the Divine, returning unaided to their true spiritual home.[59] They did not humbly beg to be taken back by the Father they had abandoned, as in the image of the prodigal son (Luke 15:11–32), which Augustine invokes so many times in the *Confessions*.[60] The philosophers talked beautifully about the superiority of contemplation to earthly ambitions, but then they degraded it by making it just another kind of ambition.[61]

But ambition, whoever is indulging in it, offers only the most limited and frailest of satisfaction, for it turns away from God to pursue human values that are flawed and fleeting: "Ambition involves seeking glory and honor, but God alone is to be given honor and glory. God's glory is eternal and thus not dependent, as human honor is, upon the opinion of faulty and fickle human beings."[62] Ambition therefore can never bring rest and fulfillment, but only endless toil and restlessness; and the same can be said for a contemplation like the philosophers', which is only another kind of ambitious, futile activity. Augustine vividly describes his own realization of this futility in book 6 of *Confessions* (6.6.9–10) when he sees a drunken beggar, for Augustine suddenly and painfully realizes that the drunk is happier than he is. Augustine sees clearly that all his pretensions and intellect and accomplishments only make him more anxious and apprehensive about the future and ruin his enjoyment of the present. Meanwhile, the drunk is happily oblivious to the future and thoroughly enjoys the present. And if one objects that the drunk is happy over a false object, Augustine candidly and poignantly counters that his ambition is even worse, for it leads him to turn away from God just as surely and even more addictively than wine ever could. The drunk will at least wake up sober, but in the morning, Augustine laments, he himself will still be ambitious and wandering further from God.

What Augustine attempts, therefore, is an improved sense and practice of contemplation, one that will offer Christians the same kind of access to God that the Platonists claim, but without falling into their ambition and false self-sufficiency. "Augustine is using the sophisticated ingenuousness of autobiography to serve a specific apologetic end: disabusing pagan Platonists of their soteriological claims while certifying that the great cognitive benefits of contemplation are accessible to Christians."[63] On the one hand, Augustine tries to be even more Platonic than the Platonists, making contemplation more truly inward and completely unworldly: "Higher truths still, truly abstract notions, can only be attained by introspection . . . still further removed from the physical world which supplies the mind with its bodily images."[64] But on the other hand, Augustine adds a distinctively biblical and anti-Platonic, anti-Manichaean focus for contemplation—the created world, the good and beautiful creation of God, still brimming, even in its fallen state, with signs of God's presence (see *Conf.* 10.6.8–10).[65] Altogether, it is a complicated and beautiful reworking of philosophical contemplation: to make it more inward by making it less concerned with outer honor and glory, but also to make it more outward, by turning its gaze on the goodness of creation.

Both the inward turn of contemplation away from ambition and its outward turn toward God's awesome and beautiful creation begin to heal the soul by filling it with humility and love (*caritas*), without which it would be unable to continue in contemplation. "Therefore we are often unable to perceive, or even tolerate, the unchangeable light of God's presence. Our minds must be gradually healed and renewed to be capable of such unspeakable bliss."[66] Without humility, the joys of contemplation are fleeting, as Augustine himself experiences several times in the *Confessions*. God in effect taunts the overly intelligent and haughty by letting them see him, while keeping them frustrated and longing by not being able to hold on to the vision for more than a moment.[67] And without love of others, contemplation always carries a danger of becoming insular, lonely, sterile, or even sanctimonious. Augustine's ability to use contemplation instead to build up loving relationships is an enormous improvement in its practice.[68] Augustine experiences such humility and love in the climactic scene of contemplation in the *Confessions*. Unlike the earlier scenes of contemplation, experienced alone by Augustine and with frustration over their brevity and difficulty, Augustine and his mother, Monica, finally contemplate God *together*, and for a moment they are ecstatically united with the Wisdom of God (*Conf.* 9.10.23–26). Throughout his life, Augustine had always been dismissive of his pious mother's wishes and disdainful toward her simple, unintellectual faith. She too seems to have indulged in some uncharitable attitudes toward her wayward son. He was intellectually arrogant toward her; she was spiritually arrogant toward him. But in this moment of real contemplation and understanding, they both sur-render their pride and are humble toward one another, thereby uniting themselves to each other and to God in love.

The close connection between contemplation, humility, and love (*caritas*) means that contemplation is the surest foundation and goal for a community, much more so than the busy, competitive lives that usu-ally occupy and divide us from one another, as well as fracturing us within ourselves. Augustine himself experienced this kind of contem-plative community with his friends and family at Cassiciacum, and it did not matter how different were the intellectual abilities or training of the people assembled there. They could help each other in this quest, because their goal was a wisdom that did not induce pride, nor could it be pursued with ambition. Rather, it was a wisdom freely and equally available to all. "For Augustine's 'true philosophy' was also the religion of a universal church. It must therefore be widened to take in all kinds of mind: a sort of universal franchise of wisdom had to be established. . . . The 'highest pitch' of wisdom was available to any moderately educated and serious mind."[69] And just as God has made this wisdom available to all who seek it in humility and love, such humble, loving wisdom makes God available to all who seek him.

Even in his earlier friendships, while still struggling for the truth out-side of Christianity, Augustine gave a vivid description of the unity and love that constantly fills a community dedicated to contemplation:

> There were other things done with them that captivated my mind more: talking together and laughing together, and happily taking turns at giv-ing in to each other's wishes; reading well-phrased books together, joking together, and showing each other respect; disagreeing sometimes, but without anger, as a person disagrees with him- or herself, the infrequency of our disagreements making our many agreements all the more enjoy-able; teaching and learning from one another, sadly longing for those

who were absent, and joyfully welcoming those who joined us. Such signs, coming from hearts that loved and were loved in return, were shown in our faces, voices, eyes, and a thousand pleasant gestures, and were like kindling to inflame our minds and make the many of us into one. (*Conf.* 4.8.13)

Ambition often tears apart a community or even a family with suspicion over each other's motives, and competition over finite resources—often including the tragically mistaken notion that love itself is a finite resource over which one must fight. Contemplation, on the other hand, unites people in a life of complete openness and cooperation, focusing all of them toward a goal that is infinite, and that even increases when shared. Contemplation fulfills and perfects both the individual and the community; it is the activity for which both were originally constituted, and to which both can still return, even in our fallen state.[70]

For Study: Pride Blinds Us to Sin—*Confessions* 5.10.18

For it still seemed to me that it was not really we who sin, but rather some other nature within us that sins. Being above guilt delighted my pride; and when I did something bad, it delighted my pride not to confess that I did it, so that you might heal my soul, that had sinned against you. Instead, I loved to excuse myself, and to accuse something else that was within me, but was not really I. But truly I was a single, whole being, and it was my own impiety that had divided me against myself. And that sin was made more incurable, insofar as I judged myself not to be a sinner. (*Conf.* 5.10.18)

This is how Augustine describes the conception of sin that he held when he was about twenty years old. To understand exactly what he is describing here, though, it is necessary to examine more closely the Manichaean influences on Augustine. At this point in his life his thoughts provide a clear example of how our intellect and our will conspire together to create and perpetuate a sinful outlook and life.

Mani lived in third-century Persia (216–277 C.E.) and founded a religion that combined elements of Zoroastrianism and Christianity.[71] The religion was quite successful and spread throughout the Roman world. It was especially popular in the East, where it spread as far as China and was practiced there until the late Middle Ages. It appears that the Manichees often attracted converts away from Catholicism by worshiping in a much more beautiful, aesthetically pleasing manner, with more elegantly decorated sacred books, as well as more beautiful church buildings and music.[72] From everything we know of him, Augustine would hardly seem to be one to be swayed by such aesthetic considerations. Yet, on one issue—the ugly, banal Latin translation of the Bible that was current in the Catholic church of his time—even he must have been made more skeptical of the Catholic church's claims to truth, since they were expressed in such low, simplistic language.[73] As many of us have felt in our rebellious youth, whatever the tradition in which we were raised, the religion of his mother looked like a common superstition expressed with no artfulness or grace, and propped up only by authority and tradition. Meanwhile, the new mythology of the Manichees appeared exotic, attractive, and perhaps most of all, it promised him reason rather than authority for its beliefs.[74]

And the question on which Augustine sought reason and clarity was one on which the Manichees were especially focused and forceful—the origin and nature of evil. "Above all, the Manichees urged that they had the only satisfactory answer to the problem of evil: it was an ineradicable force inherent in the physicality of the material world."[75] Apparently the Christian believers and clergy that Augustine knew in his youth were not so clear or convincing in their description of evil. Augustine sensed this ambiguity or hesitation and gravitated to the Manichees' strongly held and clearly defined position. And if Augustine had any qualms about embracing a wholly non-Christian worldview, then it was easy enough to state the Manichaean position in more or less Christian terms. There is nothing unorthodox in saying that good and evil are locked in a struggle in our world, and our physical bodies present us with a plethora of opportunities and temptations to sin. The unchristian character of the Manichaean teaching is only apparent when pushed back to the origins of the world and of evil, rather than to evil's presence in the current world. The Manichees believed that evil had always existed, that it was coeternal with and coequal to God, and they believed that it was physical, not spiritual. In technical terms, the Manichees were dualists—believing in two eternal, opposed principles in the universe—and gnostics—believing in the intractable evilness of matter and the complete goodness of spirit.[76] This position had the logical advantage of removing the scandalous possibility that God himself had created evil. Hence, God is pure spirit and had nothing to do with a physical creation, which was the result of a clash between the goodness of spirit and the evil force of the material world that had encased and entrapped some spirit in fleshly matter. This clash was behind the creation of all living, spirit-filled things—plants, animals, and humans.

The Manichaean worldview thus conflicts with the biblical account of creation by God, in which every physical creature is made by God and pronounced by him to be "good" (Gen 1:1–31). In addition, it has the much more problematic liability of making God seem utterly passive and weak, an innocent but ineffectual bystander as pieces of his own spiritual being and goodness are broken off and enslaved by the "realm of darkness" (*Conf.* 7.2.3). The Manichees basically sacrificed God's omnipotence to maintain his goodness intact.[77] But we needn't be judgmental of either their logic or their orthodoxy, since the exact balance between God's goodness and omnipotence always remains problematic, even to Christians. If anything, more logical and personal problems are raised by the orthodox Christian idea that God did not create evil, and that God is all-powerful and therefore could at any time destroy evil, but does not do so. Augustine himself struggled with these problems long after he rejected Manichaeism.[78]

But as this quotation from Augustine shows, the main problem with the Manichaean explanation of evil is not in some logical inconsistency or in some disagreement with the account given in Genesis. Such problems are far too theoretical, abstract, and remote to be the real reason someone would opt for or against a religious belief. Augustine himself saw the logical problems in Manichaeism long before he disavowed the religion: "Mounting doubts came to beset him. . . . How could one properly worship a deity so powerless and humiliated?"[79] "Long after he had begun to appreciate the intellectual difficulties in the Manichaean system, its moral attitude still attracted him."[80] As Augustine can finally confess, this "moral attitude" held on to him so long, not because of an intellectual error, but because of his "pride." It is essential to the bad kind of pride that it constantly looks outward and seeks to evaluate, own, and appropriate for its own use and aggrandizement everything it sees. "Not only external factors hindered his sight. His pride also got in the way. Augustine's sense of himself as an expert in the forms of outward things . . . prevented him from looking within."[81] Or, more accurately, it prevented him from looking within honestly and truthfully, for Augustine, like all of us, wanted desperately and constantly to be able to look within himself and see something utterly and entirely good:

> The elaborate avoidance of any intimate sense of guilt would later strike Augustine as the most conspicuous feature of his Manichaean phase. . . . Augustine as a Manichee could enjoy the very real consolation, that for all his intense ambition, his disquieting involvement with his concubine, the pervasive sense of guilt that came so often to cloud his relations with his mother, at least the good part of him remained throughout, unsoiled. . . . For Augustine, the need to save an untarnished oasis of perfection within himself formed, perhaps, the deepest strain of his adherence to the Manichees.[82]

And in the sixteen centuries since Augustine, the only thing that has changed is the vocabulary used by our pride to try to excuse our sins. We might not blame the "realm of darkness" for our sins, but we would eagerly blame peer pressure, bad upbringing, or just a simple mistake or emotional stress. We frequently see others engage in this kind of rationalization—with which we are much less tolerant—but this only shows how universal is the urge to excuse oneself.[83] Pride draws us to this most stunted form of "confession"—the admission of sin only as an accident, an external and temporary impediment that can be discarded, or at worst, a bad and long-standing habit. At the same time, pride beguiles us to look for our perfect, beautiful, sinless "self," which is beyond and above such earthly stains, seducing us to ignore the fact that the stains as well as the beauty are what we really, fundamentally are. Augustine well appreciates and warns us of how such a prideful outlook or blindness can render sin inescapable: "And that sin was made more incurable, insofar as I judged myself not to be a sinner" (*Conf.* 5.10.18).

For Reflection: Ambition Traps Us—*Confessions* 9.4.7

> The day came, on which I was actually freed from my profession of teaching rhetoric, as I had already been freed in my mind. And so it happened: You loosened my tongue, as you had loosened my heart, and I blessed you, rejoicing as I departed for the country estate with my whole company. . . . But when could there be enough time for me to record all

your great, generous acts toward us at that time, especially now that I am hurrying on to other, greater matters? My recollections call me back to that time, and it is sweet to me, Lord, to confess to you by what inner stabbings you conquered me, how you made me into a level plain by laying low the mountains and hills of my mind, how you made my twisted ways straight and my rough parts smooth. (*Conf.* 9.4.7)

Here Augustine describes how he gave up an exceptionally successful career, and he was enormously glad and grateful for giving it up. It wasn't even a blessing in disguise. It would be more accurate to say that his previous life of ambition had been one big curse in disguise, and his new life was unambiguously a blessing, a gift from God. But what does it mean to call a "successful" life a failure, or to call a life of sitting around thinking a "success"? These things don't quite match up with our expectations, so some reflection seems necessary to understand Augustine's insights here.

Ambition is corrosive of relationships and community, which I don't think requires that much sensitivity to see amply illustrated all around us. How many couples or friendships of which we have been a part were ruined because we spent too much time on our careers? How many times have we neglected our loved ones, especially our children, because of our careers, or snapped at them because we were tired or frustrated because of work? And to see how ridiculous and unbalanced we have become, consider the almost complete absence of the other extreme: How many relationships have we been in that ended because one member prayed too much? How often have we spent time with our children, then later wished that we had spent that time on work? And ironically, we almost always justify pursuing our careers and neglecting our family, friends, or God by saying that we are doing it only so that later we will be "secure"—no one ever wants to be "rich," just "secure." When secure, we intend to mend or even improve those relationships. But "security" is elusive and long in coming, whereas the damage to our relationships is present and constant. Striving to be happy in the future while ignoring or ruining the opportunities for happiness in the present is one of the pervasive symptoms of ambition. It is an almost sure way to guarantee one's unhappiness.

Nonetheless, it would be hard to imagine a lesson from Augustine that is more difficult to square with modern values than this on ambition.

Even more than pride, we ourselves are unapologetically ambitious, thinking to avoid the pitfalls of "too much" ambition, but enthusiastically pursuing what we deem the "right" amount. And at the same time, we honor and admire others who are ambitious, while we usually look with contempt on those who are not. Unlike Augustine, few of us have the insight to choose rightly between a happy beggar and an unhappy lawyer. But we should recognize, as we did when considering the possible opposites of pride, what Augustine is advocating here as the alternative to ambition. He is certainly not rejoicing at being able to live a life of laziness or lethargy, for the rest of his life was almost manic in its level of activity, activity that was particularly purposeful and determined. After his conversion and ordination, Augustine remained as driven as ever.[84] A look at the sheer volume of his literary output, which he began writing while "resting" at Cassiciacum, will attest to how busy his life of "leisured" contemplation really was. Here again, it seems mostly a matter of outlook or attitude. Ambition is striving to get ahead *on one's own*, almost always with little or no consideration for others, usually even hostilely competing with them. Contemplation is devoting oneself to truth, a goal that is more effectively pursued together with others than by oneself, a goal that is beyond ownership or competition. Even if we deemed it finally vain, it would at least make sense to strive to be a better golfer, or singer, or author than anyone else, while it would simply be nonsensical to strive to love truth more than anyone else. Contemplation is also finally above or beyond one's own ability to "earn" it, always acknowledging God's role in enlightenment. Augustine "never suggested that true ideas are inherent or innate within the soul. They always appear as the Creator's gift."[85]

Further, we should observe that the same "success" may be pursued out of ambition, or out of love of truth. By the usual standards of earthly success, Augustine was a huge "success," for he became one of the most influential men who ever lived. But he did it without, I think, being ambitious. To think of him toiling away in his study and in his pulpit so that he could "beat" Jerome or Chrysostom as "Greatest Church Father" goes beyond cynicism into mere ridiculous satire. In similar terms, Gandhi and Lincoln were at least as successful as political leaders as were Hitler or Stalin, but their motives and goals were so different that we can rightly call the former noble or holy, and the latter base or damned. What would go for church or world leaders would surely apply equally to church members, college professors, athletes, or insurance underwriters. Ambition is, in short, trying to make our own selves happy, while contemplation is acknowledging that the only happiness we can achieve comes when we pursue God together with other people, whatever our career, vocation, talents, or station in life. Any activity can be ambitious and entrapping, and any activity can be contemplative and liberating. This is one of the essential insights of Zen Buddhism and why it has been so popular among Westerners, even Christians, who appreciate its simultaneous embracing and transcending of mundane activities, even without wholly accepting its theology or worldview.

While I certainly believe that all of one's life activities can be a kind of contemplation of and devotion to God, there is still the practical question of how much time we should spend on the narrower kind of contemplation, meditation, or prayer. This is the kind everyone would recognize as a silent, introspective time devoted exclusively to contemplating God directly, and not doing anything else. If the "right" amount of ambition is difficult or impossible to determine and pursue without harm to one's personal and spiritual life, is the "right" amount of contemplation any easier to calculate? Probably not, though I would still guess that almost all of us err on the side of too little, rather than too much. But perhaps we can gain some guidance from another religious tradition—the Jewish observance of the Sabbath, the example that Augustine himself uses extensively in the *Confessions*,[86] as well as in *City of God*.[87] The Sabbath is a practice that seeks to regulate and make mandatory the benefits of contemplation, as well as to curtail and limit the negative and pervasive effects of ambition. It is believed to be a cyclical period of rest built into creation by God himself. It is even observed by God and allows humans a recurring opportunity and duty to imitate God, to live briefly as God does, above the mundane pursuits of everyday life, and come closer to God's holiness and rest. Whatever one's religious tradition—or even if one wished to pursue it purely for reasons of physical, let alone spiritual, health—all of us would surely benefit from such a frequently recurring break from the competition, anxiety, and stress that normally characterize our lives. For a time it would give us a chance to forget that we are teachers, or accountants, or even parents, and just to enjoy being playful children of a loving Father.

For Prayer: Real Knowledge, Real Rest—*Confessions* 1.1.1

> You have made us for yourself, and our heart is troubled, until it rests in you. (*Conf.* 1.1.1)

This is an oft-quoted sentence from the first paragraph of *Confessions*.[88] In it Augustine anticipates and already condemns all the restless, frantic activity that he will describe in his *Confessions*, showing how utterly futile such activity is at either procuring or holding on to happiness. As long as the heart loves and follows other things instead of God, it is troubled, restless, never happy. So why shouldn't we just leave our jobs and families and pray all day? Augustine was influential in encouraging and spreading the monastic movement, and he himself seemed to prefer being left alone so he could contemplate.[89] But he also knew well the positive value of human relationships, earthly loves, and mundane pursuits, as well as his duties toward other members of the church, the body of Christ. Just because such things are finite and mortal does not make them expendable or trivial. "A good Platonist, he might agree that the physical presence of the friend was a 'tiny thing': but he had the courage to admit how much he 'greatly craved' this 'tiny thing.'"[90] We should love people and things other than God, and we should pursue activities other than direct worship and prayer, but unless these other loves and activities are directed toward God, they only burden and enslave us. On the other hand, if these other loves are experienced as a part of loving God, then they are liberating blessings to us. "Blessed is the one who loves you [God], and his friend in you, and his enemy for your sake" (*Conf.* 4.9.14).

This little quotation about real rest is a wonderful balance between the negative restlessness we have all known, and the calm and assurance Augustine has come to know. In this, the prayer sounds much like many of the Psalms, which are quoted constantly throughout *Confessions*, beginning with the first line, a reference to Pss 48:1; 96:4; 145:3. Many of the Psalms sound this same note, lamenting the sorry state into which we have sunk, but expressing hope and complete confidence that God can and will remedy the situation, even make it better than ever it was. The sorrow and joy of the Psalms echo much of Augustine's own journey in the *Confessions*: "The Psalms . . . catch up together his entire odyssey."[91] Like the psalmist, Augustine can be sure that our heart will find rest; because God has made us for himself, he has made us to find rest. So ironically, all our restlessness and dissatisfaction are ultimately positive as well as painful. The only way we would not feel restlessness in this world would be if we were not fallen—regrettably not the case, and this is what causes us pain—or if we had fallen so far as to be incapable of redemption—thankfully not the case, and this is what gives us hope and joy.[92] Our restlessness in this fallen world shows us that it is not our true home, but it fills us with hope for our true home and our true heavenly Parent.

This sentence also prayerfully answers a petition Augustine expresses throughout his writings, beginning with almost the first thing he wrote, *Soliloquies* (ca. 386): "God, who is always the same, may I know myself, may I know you."[93] Although Augustine would later criticize such early works as still tainted with "scholarly pride,"[94] knowledge of oneself and of God is a fair summary of his spiritual quest, or of anyone else's, for that matter. He repeats this petition for knowledge in the heart of *Confessions*: "May I know you [God], the One who knows me; then I will know, even as I am known" (*Conf.* 10.1.1). And as Augustine begins his *Confessions* with a praise of God and an acknowledgment of the fallen, exiled state of our restless heart, he has come to know the truth about God and himself. God is our Creator and our Sustainer on the journey back to him, and we are his lost children. He is our only Source and should be our only Goal. Until we realize that, or whenever we forget it, then nothing makes sense and nothing can bring us happiness and fulfillment. Once we realize this truth, everything makes sense and nothing can completely take away our happiness, because we are finally fulfilled, at peace with God and ourselves. But as simple as this truth is, we all know that the moments when we can hold on to it with complete certainty are fleeting, easily dispelled by another interruption, another irritation, another disaster, or even another "opportunity" to pursue something other than God, and off we go again, chasing something that cannot satisfy us. Augustine's prayer offers us reassurance in our restless world, helping to remind us of the truth about ourselves and God during weakness, doubt, distraction, and temptation.

For Further Reading

Augustine. *Augustine of Hippo: Selected Writings.* Translated by M. T. Clark. New York: Paulist Press, 1988. Selections from many of Augustine's works, including *Confessions* and *City of God*.

Brown, Peter. *Augustine of Hippo: A Biography.* Rev. ed. Berkeley: University of California Press, 2000. An excellent introduction to Augustine's life and thought, weaving biography with analysis of themes from his texts.

Paffenroth, Kim, and Robert Kennedy, eds. *A Reader's Companion to Augustine's Confessions.* Louisville: Westminster John Knox, 2003. A collection of essays to help guide readers through Augustine's most famous work.

Notes

1. Biographical facts and dates are taken from the useful introductory material in J. K. Ryan, *The Confessions of St. Augustine* (New York: Image Books, 1960), especially the list of dates on 39–40. See also the chronological tables in P. Brown, *Augustine of Hippo: A Biography* (Berkeley: University of California Press, 1967), 16, 74–77, 184–87, 282–85, 378–79. (All my references to this work are to the original edition.) For more biography, see also H. Chadwick, *Augustine* (Oxford: Oxford University Press, 1986), reissued as *Augustine: A Very Short Introduction* (Oxford: Oxford University Press, 2001), and the excellent website maintained by J. J. O'Donnell: http://www.georgetown.edu/faculty/jod/ (site visited January 9, 2004).

2. Cf. Brown, *Augustine of Hippo*, 31: "What Augustine remembered most vividly about his parents, was a subterranean tension. . . . Both parents, however, had one quality in common: determination. . . . Augustine was able to make this quality his own. It is no mean feat to have done so. We can see the result, above all, in the manner in which he hounded his ecclesiastical opponents, and stuck firmly to his own ideas: Patricius and Monica, one feels, were highly-suitable parents for a Catholic bishop in fourth-century Africa."

3. *Conf.* 3.4.7, my translation, as are all subsequent quotations from *Confessions*, unless otherwise identified.

4. Cf. S. A. Cooper, *Augustine for Armchair Theologians* (Louisville: Westminster John Knox Press, 2002) 62: "A pagan work, then, one that presented wisdom itself as the goal of philosophy rather than a particular philosophical school, set Augustine to reading the Bible!"

5. Chadwick, *Very Short Introduction*, 36, 38. For a thoroughgoing analysis of Augustine's continued commitment to Platonism, see P. Cary, *Augustine's Invention of the Inner Self: The Legacy of a Christian Platonist* (Oxford: Oxford University Press, 2003).

6. His time with the Manichees is variously calculated as nine years (Brown, *Augustine of Hippo*, 46), ten years (Chadwick, *Very Short Introduction*, 14), and eleven years (Ryan, *Confessions*, 39).

7. Brown, *Augustine of Hippo*, 32.

8. K. Adam, *Saint Augustine: The Odyssey of His Soul*, trans. D. J. McCann (New York: Macmillan, 1932), 5.

9. Chadwick, *Very Short Introduction*, 4.

10. On Augustine's friendships, see my essay "Friendship as Personal, Social, and Theological Virtue in Augustine," in *Augustine and Politics*, ed. J. Doody, K. Hughes, and K. Paffenroth (Lanham, MD: Lexington Books, 2005).

11. Brown, *Augustine of Hippo*, 32.

12. On Monica, see my essay "Book Nine: The Emotional Heart of the *Confessions*," in *A Reader's Companion to Augustine's Confessions*, ed. Kim Paffenroth and Robert Kennedy (Louisville: Westminster John Knox, 2003), 137–54.

13. See Brown, *Augustine of Hippo*, 30: "Augustine, a man of many significant silences, will pass over him coldly. . . . Augustine, who will soon experience and express deep grief at the loss of a friend, will mention his father's death only in passing"; Chadwick, *Very Short Introduction*, 11: "Augustine betrays no sign of having felt close to him [his father]."

14. On the acceptability of this arrangement, see Brown, *Augustine of Hippo*, 62: "Concubinage of this kind was a traditional feature of Roman life. Even the Catholic church was prepared to recognize it, provided the couple remained faithful to one another."

15. See Chadwick, *Very Short Introduction*, 46: "The Thagaste community was not called a monastery. The 'society of brothers,' as they were called, shared property, lived in frugal simplicity, but had no formal vows, no identical clothing, no fixed rule and requirement for obedience. They were far more intellectual than most later monasteries. This was in practice the first monastic community in Latin Africa."

16. On Augustine's unwilling selection, see Brown, *Augustine of Hippo*, 138–39: "The incident was a common one in the Later Empire. It passed over quickly: in a sermon, the bishop, Valerius, spoke pointedly of the urgent needs of his church; the congregation turned to find, as they expected, Augustine standing among them in the nave; with the persistent shouting required for such a procedure, they pushed him forward to the raised throne of the bishop and the benches of the priests, which ran around the curved apse at the far end of the basilica. The leading Catholic citizens of Hippo would have gathered around

Augustine, as the bishop accepted his forced agreement to become a priest in the town." See also Chadwick, *Very Short Introduction*, 58.

17. See Chadwick, *Very Short Introduction*, 1–3: "Through his writings, the surviving bulk of which exceeds that of any other ancient author, he came to exercise pervasive influence not only on contemporaries but also in subsequent years on the West."

18. Cf. Cooper, *Armchair Theologians*, 16: "First and foremost, however, the book is the story of a spiritual journey."

19. Ibid, 10: "Rather I take my lead from Augustine because I believe that his theology, a theology of grace, develops from a specific story—his story—of being set free."

20. Ibid, 48: "What he means by pride should not be confused with what we would call self-esteem."

21. J. F. Procopé, "Initium omnis peccati superbia," in *Cappadocian Fathers, Chrysostom and His Greek Contemporaries, Augustine, Donatism and Pelagianism*, ed. E. A. Livingstone, Studia patristica 22 (Leuven: Peeters, 1989), 315–20, esp. (quotation from) 316.

22. See P. J. Weithman, "Toward an Augustinian Liberalism," *Faith and Philosophy* 8 (1991): 461–80, esp. 471: "The proud person . . . is inclined to attribute to herself goods, including moral goods, that she does not have; the vainglorious person seeks a reputation for goodness of one sort or another. The hypocrite ties pride to vainglory by trying to secure a reputation for qualities pride leads her to affect or exaggerate."

23. See Weithman, "Augustinian Liberalism," 466: "Rather acts of pride are primarily motivated by an undue desire for *preeminence* or *superiority*. This undue desire for preeminence or superiority can . . . be accompanied by contempt for those over whom superiority is sought" (emphasis in original).

24. See R. A. Markus, "De ciuitate dei: Pride and the Common Good," in *Augustine—Second Founder of the Faith*, ed. J. C. Schnaubelt and F. Van Fleteren, Collectanea Augustiniana (New York: P. Lang, 1990), 245–59, esp. 253: "At the heart of this there is a duality: government seen as domination and government seen as guardian of the common good. Pride as the original sin has produced a fallen, dislocated society in which all human bonds were necessarily strained. . . . In this way Augustine could drive a wedge between the Empire itself and the traditional ideological basis of Roman rule; what was wrong was not what the Romans did, but that they took credit for it."

25. Cooper, *Armchair Theologians*, 48, 50.

26. W. M. Green, *Initium omnis peccati superbia*, University of California Publications in Classical Philology 13 (Berkeley: University of California Press, 1949), 421. This is a wonderfully full and helpful treatment.

27. D. J. MacQueen, "Augustine on Superbia: The Historical Background and Sources of His Doctrine," *Mélanges de science religieuse* 34 (1977): 193–211, esp.

203. But cf. Green, *Initium*, 428–29, where he discusses the alternative position of Reitzenstein, that Augustine is somehow always guilty of pride.

28. All point to some ambivalence by Augustine as to the sense in which pride is the "origin" or "cause" of sin. See Green, *Initium*, 412: "Pride, or self-love, here seems a principle vast enough to explain all evil, in heaven and on earth. In other passages we are told that pride is the cause of all human vices, diseases, and sins. In his controversy with Pelagius, however, Augustine found it necessary to qualify his position"; Procopé, "Initium," 319: "Pride he saw as 'the origin of all sin' in more senses than one"; Weithman (who interprets Augustine through Aquinas), "Augustinian Liberalism," 465: "He therefore thinks that every sin is, in effect, a failure properly to subject oneself to God; he concludes that *every* sin however motivated and whatever its object is, in effect, a sin of pride" (emphasis in original).

29. On the pear tree incident, see my essay "Bad Habits and Bad Company: Education and Evil in the *Confessions*," in *Augustine and Liberal Education* (ed. K. Paffenroth and K. Hughes; Aldershot, UK: Ashgate Books, 2000), 3–14; also J. Cavadini, "Book Two: Augustine's Book of Shadows," in *A Reader's Companion to Augustine's Confessions*, ed. K. Paffenroth and R. Kennedy (Louisville: Westminster John Knox Press, 2003), 25–34.

30. Nietzsche would return to mock Augustine many times; on this particular passage, see Friedrich Nietzsche, *Nietzsche Briefwechsel: Kritische Gesamtausgabe* (Berlin: W. de Gruyter, 1982), 3.3.34.

31. Cf. Cooper, *Armchair Theologians*, 46: "Because Augustine saw truly into his motivation for this relatively minor crime, he was able to plumb the depths of evil. Not all transgressions reveal the structure of sin so clearly. But still, it is all too easy, even in our moments of critical recollection, to come up with some supposed good we sought in actions we now believe to have been altogether wrong."

32. MacQueen, "Augustine on Superbia," 201; cf. J. Burnaby, *Amor Dei: A Study of the Religion of St. Augustine* (London: Hodder & Stoughton, 1938), 119–20: "The 'perverse imitation of God' is the sin of pride, in which the individual soul constitutes itself its own end, seeks 'to become and to be the principle of its own existence,' putting itself in the place of God; and this results, by the necessary operation of the divine law, in the subjection and enslavement of the soul which has rebelled against its own Master, to the external and material nature which is properly its servant."

33. Augustine, *Sermons* 330.3; 96.2; quoted by Burnaby, *Amor Dei*, 120.

34. On Sirach, see chapter 1 of my *In Praise of Wisdom: Literary and Theological Reflections on Faith and Reason* (New York: Continuum, 2004); also the full commentary of P. W. Skehan and A. A. Di Lella, *The Wisdom of Ben Sira: A New Translation with Notes* (New York: Doubleday, 1987).

35. On the differences between the Latin, Greek, and Hebrew of the verse, see Green, *Initium*, 413; Procopé, "Initium," 315; Skehan and Di Lella, *Ben Sira*,

221–26. On Augustine's frequent use of the verse, see Procopé, "Initium," 315–17.

36. Translation from Skehan and Di Lella, *Ben Sira*.

37. *City of God* 14.13, trans. H. Bettenson (New York: Penguin Books, 1972); all subsequent quotations are from this translation. On the passage, see Green, *Initium*, 413–16; Procopé, "Initium," 316–17. See also M. Baasten, "Humility and Modern Ethics," *The Reformed Review* 38 (1985): 232–37, esp. 233: "Augustine calls pride the beginning of sin, because it is both first in time as the sin precipitating the Fall and first in origin as the vice serving as the root of other sins."

38. Procopé, "Initium," 316.

39. P. Cary, "Book Seven: Inner Vision as the Goal of Augustine's Life," in *A Reader's Companion to Augustine's Confessions*, ed. K. Paffenroth and R. Kennedy (Louisville: Westminster John Knox Press, 2003), 107–26, esp. 118.

40. Cf. Green, *Initium*, 419: "It was from 'certain books of the Platonists,' more particularly described as 'a very few books of Plotinus,' that Augustine learned to think of evil as a corruption, or privation of good, a movement in the direction of non-being. For both Plotinus and Augustine this movement constituted the fall of the soul, a voluntary turning from the good toward the evil."

41. Cf. Burnaby, *Amor Dei*, 119: "Plotinus describes the fall of the soul . . . as an act of 'audacity' or 'self-will,' as the 'desire for standing apart,' for 'self-ownership.' . . . Augustine often uses very similar language; but what he is concerned to explain is not the existence of the material world but the existence of spiritual evil, of sin itself; and this gives a turn to the thought which we do not find in Plotinus"; Chadwick, *Very Short Introduction*, 41: "Although Augustine dissented from Plotinus' opinion that evil begins in matter, he agreed that the prime consequence of the soul's mistaken choice is that it has become obsessively attached to the body"; Green, *Initium*, 419: "Plotinus states that the beginning of evil for souls is the audacity (τόλμα) in which they turn toward the world of change (γένεσις) and wish to be differentiated and independent. Rejoicing in their power of self-movement they run away from the Father from whom they sprang, and forget him and their own true nature as well"; Markus, "Pride and the Common Good," 248: "This is nothing other than Plotinus' *tolma*, the 'audacity' which makes the soul forget its true place and thus to dissipate itself"; Procopé, "Initium," 317: "In turning to itself from him who supremely is to something of lesser reality, a 'conversion' which can only be called 'pride,' the creature is going against the order of nature. . . . Implicit in this doctrine are metaphysical notions which Augustine derived from Plotinian Neoplatonism."

42. Cf. J. P. Burns, "Augustine on the Origin and Progress of Evil," *Journal of Religious Ethics* 16 (1988): 9–27, esp. 20: "[Augustine] surmised that before she was tempted by the demon, Eve had already sinned, through pride. God allowed the devil to tempt her to an open transgression in order to manifest and correct that first, hidden sin."

43. Cary, "Book Seven," 119.

44. Green, *Initium*, 416–17.

45. Burnaby, *Amor Dei*, 70.

46. G. W. Schlabach, "Augustine's Hermeneutic of Humility: An Alternative to Moral Imperialism and Moral Relativism," *Journal of Religious Ethics* 22 (1994): 299–330, esp. 318.

47. J. N. B. Van den Brink, "Humility in Pascal and Augustine," *Journal of Ecclesiastical History* 19 (1968): 41–56, esp. 52.

48. R. D. DiLorenzo, "Augustine's Sapiential Discipline: Wisdom and the Happy Life," *Communio* 10 (1983): 351–59, esp. 356.

49. Cf. Baasten, "Humility and Modern Ethics," 233–34, who points to three elements of humility in Augustine: humility is "a willingness to acknowledge that all good deeds come from God" (233), it is to "become aware of [our] own basic unworthiness and weakness" (234), and it is "obedience" (234).

50. This is especially important and is stressed by Augustine in the case of clergy: see L. F. Bacchi, "A Ministry Characterized by and Exercised in Humility: The Theology of Ordained Ministry in the Letters of Augustine of Hippo," in *Augustine: Presbyter factus sum*, ed. J. T. Lienhard, E. C. Muller, and R. J. Teske, Collectanea Augustiniana (New York: P. Lang, 1993), 405–15.

51. Van den Brink, "Humility in Pascal and Augustine," 51.

52. Cf. Baasten, "Humility and Modern Ethics," 234: "Viewed as obedience, then, humility represents 'an ordered submission and orientation of the will to God'"; Bacchi, "Theology of Ordained Ministry," 406: "Augustine also demonstrated this ontological humility by describing the ordained ministry as an instrument of divine grace. God is the source and goal of all ministry in the church, and the ordained minister is but an instrument through which the Lord works."

53. Burnaby, *Amor Dei*, 71.

54. Burns, "Origin and Progress of Evil," 24.

55. Van den Brink, "Humility in Pascal and Augustine," 52.

56. See J. P. Kenney, "Saint Augustine and the Limits of Contemplation," in *St. Augustine and His Opponents, Other Latin Writers*, ed. M. F. Miles, E. J. Yarnold, and P. M. Parvis, Studia patristica 38 (Leuven: Peeters, 2001), 199–218, esp. 205–6: "[Augustine] is conceding both the validity of pagan Platonic knowledge about God and the soul, while also indicating the failure of the Platonists to recognize the incarnation of the Word. . . . Augustine subtly suggests that Platonists have been misled by their monstrous pride. . . . Platonists, by the force of their fall into embodiment, have failed to exercise the virtue of humility necessary to recognize the incarnation, and thus to grasp fully the nature of God. Thus was Platonic wisdom made foolish." Even Cary, "Book Seven," 119–20, underscores the fact that the Platonists could not accept the incarnation, though he then concludes with the incredible assertion that Augustine "never suggests that anything about Platonism kept him from believing in Christ" (Cary, "Book Seven," 120).

57. *Sermon* 188.3, quoted in Van den Brink, "Humility in Pascal and Augustine," 52.

58. See D. K. O'Connor, "The Ambitions of Aristotle's Audience and the Activist Ideal of Happiness," in *Action and Contemplation: Studies in the Moral and Political Thought of Aristotle*, ed. R. C. Bartlett and S. D. Collins (Albany: State University of New York Press, 1999), 107–29, who shows this concession to ambition by both Plato and Socrates, as well as Aristotle.

59. Cf. Burnaby, *Amor Dei*, 71: "The soul's cleansing is a journey—in the phrase of Plotinus a 'voyage to the fatherland'—but it is a journey which we could not make, had not the Way itself come down to us"; also J. P. Kenney, "St. Augustine and the Invention of Mysticism," in *Augustine and His Opponents, Jerome, Other Latin Fathers after Nicaea, Orientalia*, ed. E. A. Livingstone, Studia patristica 33 (Leuven: Peeters, 1997), 125–30, esp. 129: "For the Platonists—at least on Augustine's account—were prone to overestimate the soul's natural capacity for *theoria*, based on their doctrine of the soul's undescended aspect. But for Augustine, *theoria* cannot succeed salvifically because of the profound moral weakness of the soul. It is this theme that dominates the final sections of book seven: while contemplation has demonstrated to the pilgrim the reality of the transcendent world, it has also, in its brevity, underscored how little claim the fallen soul has on eternity"; also J. V. Schall, "Plotinus and Political Philosophy," *Gregorianum* 66 (1985): 687–707, esp. 688: "Yet, as St. Augustine knew from Pelagianism, philosophy could not enable man by his own intellectual efforts to reach the One. This was merely pride."

60. On this theme, see the classic treatment by L. Ferrari, "The Theme of the Prodigal Son in Augustine's *Confessions*," *Recherches Augustiniennes* 12 (1977): 105–18.

61. On the philosophers' belief in the superiority of contemplation, see Schall, "Plotinus and Political Philosophy," 694: "The active life as such could not satisfy man's ultimate desires because these desires were found, not made, by man. In other words, the active life needed the contemplative even if it is to remain active. . . . Excessive emphasis on the practical life finally ended in degradation for the masses and a seeking on the part of nobler souls for some contemplative philosophy which would enable them to leave the world to itself by immersing themselves in the absolute."

62. Cooper, *Armchair Theologians*, 49.

63. Kenney, "Limits of Contemplation," 204.

64. G. R. Evans, "*Alienatio* and Abstract Thinking in Augustine," *Downside Review* 98 (1980): 190–200, esp. 193.

65. Cf. W. A. Smith, "The Christian as Resident Alien in Augustine: An Evaluation from the Standpoint of Pastoral Care," *Word and World* 3 (1983): 129–39, esp. 136: "One way in which Augustine urges contemplation is in focusing on the beauty and harmony of creation—to look at God's creation for the

'traces of the trinity'. . . . For him, creation is good, nature is good and, as far as the person is nature then, in spite of corruption, that person, as created by God, is good (*City of God* XI.22). He eloquently describes the beauty of the things in God's creation and the pleasure that this provides for the beholder. In creation he truly sees the goodness of God."

66. Ibid., "Resident Alien," 136.

67. Cf. DiLorenzo, "Augustine's Sapiential Discipline," 355: "Any advance in the knowledge and love of wisdom must increase humility simultaneously, thus directing the soul ever more gratefully to the humility of the Incarnation"; B. J. Francis, "The Mysticism of St. Augustine," in *Prayer and Contemplation*, ed. C. M. Vadakkekara (Bangalore: Asirvanam Benedictine Monastery, 1980), 95–108, esp. 100: "Humility, recognition of the weakness of our hearts, a transcending of corporeal images and a looking beyond the passing goods is necessary to come to this contemplation of the total Good"; also E. J. Stormon, "The Spirituality of St. Augustine," in *Christian Spiritual Theology: An Ecumenical Reflection*, ed. N. J. Ryan (Melbourne: Dove Communications, 1976), 129–44, esp. 137–38: "Through [the Platonists] he learned to lift his mind towards the invisible things of God by the things that are made. . . . But what he did not understand at that time, and what his neo-Platonist authors did not tell him—for they did not understand it themselves—was that the way to God lay through a mystery of humility, the Word that was made flesh and dwelt among us."

68. Cf. Stormon, "Spirituality of St. Augustine," 131, 139: "Again, in spite of this strongly intellectual element in Augustine's contemplation of God, there is a certain development in his awareness of his fellow-man, of his membership in the community of the Church, that marks off later descriptions from the earlier. . . . Subsequent and more varied experience brought home to him that the Christian life is a corporate one. If we walk by faith (*fides*) to that point where we have sight of the reality (*species*), as, in the wake of St. Paul, he is so fond of saying, we do so in the company of many brethren."

69. Brown, *Augustine of Hippo*, 120; cf. also Francis, "Mysticism," 107: "St. Augustine also insists on the fact that contemplation is possible for all and not just for a select few."

70. This is a necessary corollary to Augustine's ideas on original sin and original perfection: see J. A. Bernstein, "Ethics, Theology and the Original State of Man: An Historical Sketch," *Anglican Theological Review* 61 (1979): 162–81, esp. 163, "Original perfection not merely intensified the doctrine of original sin. It also tended to stress man's dependence upon God more radically than a doctrine which pointed to a human power of self-elevation from an initial bestiality. Second, original perfection expressed an attitude which tended to place contemplative values over moral ones."

71. On Manichaeism, see Brown, *Augustine of Hippo*, 46–60; Chadwick, *Very Short Introduction*, 12–15; Cooper, *Armchair Theologians*, 64–73.

72. See Chadwick, *Very Short Introduction*, 14: "Church people could be especially impressed by the fine parchment and calligraphy of Manichee sacred books and by the special solemnity of their music."

73. Cf. Cooper, *Armchair Theologians*, 63: "Augustine was put off by the Bible he read in the clunky and literal Old Latin translation then available. Compared to the exalted character of Cicero's writing, where a great matter was appropriately expressed in a great style, it seemed unworthy of further attention."

74. See Chadwick, *Very Short Introduction*, 14: "By a bizarre twist, he [Mani] presented his lush, partly erotic mythology with the claim that it was a rational, coherent account of revealed truth, in strong contrast to the simple faith of orthodox Christians who believed on mere authority."

75. Ibid.

76. See Brown's thorough analysis of the Manichees under the two categories of "Dualism" and "Gnosis": Brown, *Augustine of Hippo*, 46–60. For some reason, the label "Manichaean" has caught on among American liberal critics of the Bush administration, who seem to use it a little uncritically to mean simply "people who believe good and evil are easily distinguishable, and who believe that they themselves are unambiguously on the side of good." This broadly, the label would apply equally to Manichees, the Bush administration, Islamic extremists, and most liberal American critics of the administration.

77. See Brown, *Augustine of Hippo*, 51–52: "The price which the Manichees had seemed to pay for this total disowning of the bad, was to render the good singularly passive and ineffective. As a bishop, Augustine will emphasize this aspect of Manichaeism: for it is the one element in the Manichaean system that he would come to reject most forcibly."

78. See Burns, "Origin and Progress of Evil," 16–17: "The narrative of the *Confessions* and the writings of the period immediately after his conversion indicate that Augustine had indeed reached an understanding of the nature of evil. None of these writings, however, presents or even claims to present an answer to the more perplexing question: the origin of that evil"; cf. Cooper, *Armchair Theologians*, 119: "Many people find the question concerning the relation of God to evil a difficult and thorny thicket. Christianity traditionally affirms the omnipotence of God, human free will, and the reality of evil. What you think of one issue frames the manner in which you conceive the others."

79. Chadwick, *Very Short Introduction*, 15.

80. Brown, *Augustine of Hippo*, 51.

81. Cooper, *Armchair Theologians*, 121.

82. Brown, *Augustine of Hippo*, 50–51.

83. Such hypocritical dodging of responsibility in relation to current crimes and crises is wonderfully pilloried by Frank Rich, "It Was the Porn That Made Them Do It," *New York Times*, May 30, 2004; online: http://www.nytimes.com (accessed May 30, 2004).

84. Cf. Stormon, "Spirituality of St. Augustine," 144: "It is evident from Augustine's life that contemplation did not mean withdrawal from the duties and the activities of his state, but rather gave him the strength and the inspiration to carry these out."

85. Chadwick, *Very Short Introduction*, 51.

86. On Augustine's extensive use of the image of the Sabbath throughout the *Confessions*, see the excellent treatment of R. McMahon, *Augustine's Prayerful Ascent: An Essay on the Literary Form of the Confessions* (Athens, GA: University of Georgia Press, 1989).

87. *City of God* 22.30; see Stormon, "Spirituality of St. Augustine," 144.

88. It is only part of a sentence in the Latin original.

89. See Chadwick, *Very Short Introduction*, 58: "At one stage he seriously considered withdrawal to desert solitude. . . . His contemplative endeavors were abruptly ended, but he could not refuse. He sat down with his Bible to equip himself for a calling to which he felt unfitted by temperament, inclination, and physical health."

90. Brown, *Augustine of Hippo*, 161.

91. William Mallard, *Language and Love: Introducing Augustine's Religious Thought through the Confessions Story* (University Park, PA: Pennsylvania State University Press, 1994) 173.

92. This is exactly the same point made so powerfully by the seventeenth-century French philosopher and theologian Blaise Pascal, throughout his book *Pensées* (Thoughts): see chapter 4 of my book *In Praise of Wisdom*.

93. *Soliloquies*, trans. K. Paffenroth, ed. J. Rotelle (Hyde Park: New City Press, 2000), 2.1.1.

94. *Conf.* 9.4.7, my translation: *superbiae scholam* is more literally "the school of pride," as in Ryan's translation.

3

DANTE
Different Loves

Introduction

Dante Alighieri (1265–1321) was born in Florence, Italy, to a noble but no longer wealthy family.[1] In 1295 Dante entered politics and thereby became involved in the bloody struggle between the Guelphs and Ghibellines, two political parties that had been feuding in northern Italy since the end of the twelfth century. This conflict also provides the historical basis on which Shakespeare based his *Romeo and Juliet*,[2] a moving depiction of the senseless misery the feud brought to all of Italy for generations. The general difference between the two parties was that on matters of the relative power and influence of the church and the state, the Guelphs favored the papacy and the Ghibellines favored the emperor, though the battle also had class strife behind it, as the Guelphs tended to be the rising middle class, and the Ghibellines were the ancestrally wealthy.[3] By Dante's time, the Guelph party was ascendant, but then it too split into two warring factions—Black Guelphs and White Guelphs. Dante himself was a White Guelph. In 1302 the Black Guelphs came to power in Florence with the help of Pope Boniface VIII. As a result, Dante was expelled from his hometown under pain of death, and he spent the rest of his life in exile, a fate that practically defined the rest of his life and work, "an exile in both the social and religious senses."[4]

Dante was filled with anger at the destructiveness and madness of secular leaders, and with disgust and disappointment at the corruption
of the church. Though he would always maintain the legitimacy and
sanctity of the papacy and the church, he inveighed bitterly against
those who used the church and its offices for their own selfish and evil
ends—hurting, corrupting, and misleading those whom they had
been entrusted to serve, help, and save.[5] Dante traveled throughout
Europe, possibly as far as Paris and England, until his death in
Ravenna, Italy, in 1321.

When he was about twenty, Dante married Gemma Donati, and the
couple had several children. Nonetheless, throughout his life Dante
considered his inspiration and spiritual guide to be Beatrice, a mysterious woman he met when he was only nine years old and she was either
eight or nine; she died in 1290. While we might raise our eyebrows at
such a situation, it is necessary to recognize Dante's context to understand his feelings for the woman at the center of his life and work. Dante
was writing at a time when marriage was regarded, especially among the
nobility, as a practical arrangement whose main products were peace
and progeny, not love.[6] Dante's own marriage was probably arranged by
his father before Dante was twelve.[7] And love outside marriage was celebrated in the tradition of courtly love and troubadour poetry, but all of
this was considered a rather embarrassing concession to human weakness, a throwback to paganism, and hardly to be compared to Christian
charity or agape.[8]

Many critics have attempted to avoid this embarrassment by elevat-
ing or reducing Beatrice to an allegorical figure because of the unsavory
and pagan associations of courtly love. However, I think this misreads
and misrepresents Dante.[9] What is surprising in Dante is not that he
chose to write about someone other than his spouse as the embodiment
of love, but that he showed how a love between a man and woman—
ordinary, human love, whether married or not—could be capable of
transcendence, beauty, and truth. I am not saying that Beatrice is *not*
symbolic, only that she is not *merely* symbolic. She is a real, human
woman in whom Dante saw a divine, transcendent meaning, a dual role
we overlook only to our own detriment and diminishment: "Indeed, for
Dante, literalism in the reading of texts, or of life, is one of the most fundamental human deformations."[10] I think all serious readers struggle
with how to interpret Beatrice. But in the end, are Dante's feelings for

her really that different from what we feel and intuit in our own relationships, which often go way beyond or beneath the surface, literal experience of them? Nicole, the first girl I kissed, and Greg, a childhood friend who died right after high school, hold much greater significance for me than my brief time with them more than twenty years ago would lead one to expect. I think of them both much more frequently and deeply than many other people I see on a regular basis, even if I couldn't explain why to another person, at least not in a rational way. Dante has introduced me to Beatrice, a similar person in his life, and his experience resonates with truth and honesty, if not logic. Dante's genius and his value to us as a spiritual guide are in his eloquent defense of human loves, showing us how they raise us up to the divine love that validates and makes possible all such other loves.

Dante wrote of his love for Beatrice in an early work, *La vita nuova* (*The New Life*, ca. 1292), and he makes this love the guiding principle of his greatest and most famous work, *The Divine Comedy*, over which he labored between 1308 and 1321. In Dante's usage "comedy" does not mean "funny," but refers to any story that has a happy ending and therefore is not a tragedy. Since his story is one of salvation for himself and others, it is the happiest of all.[11] On the one hand, the work is quite simple to explain: Dante is allowed to journey through the three realms of the Christian afterlife—hell, purgatory, and heaven—and he describes to us in great detail what he saw there of the damned, the penitent, and the saved. But within this seemingly simple and huge journey, Dante pauses to give complicated discussions of a huge number of topics—not just theology, but history, politics, numerology, biology, meteorology, astronomy, and many more. While some of these discussions seem merely curious to us, the one overall topic that Dante returns to in so many guises remains utterly compelling—a complex, comprehensive, and nuanced analysis of sin and redemption, showing how each process works within ourselves, within our society, and within the world. Expressed in the most beautiful and sensual language, Dante's analysis is one of the best examples and defenses of how art sometimes expresses intellectual and spiritual truths with greater clarity and power of conviction than a theological treatise could,[12] because it does so by giving vivid, concrete expression to intensely personal, subjective experiences: "The universality of the poet, as differentiated from that of the theologian, cannot but take its starting point from the singularity of personally lived experience."[13] Dante's poetry is not a rational argument, but it has even more persuasive force than such a presentation, because it brings its readers into an "affective engagement, . . . a kind of reasoned conversation with our own ideas."[14] Like any great author, Dante transcends the time in which he lived to converse with us in ours, but what is especially surprising is how modern his analysis often seems. His insights often come quite close to modern ideas of psychology and personality,[15] and he eloquently reminds us to have wonder and appreciation for our lives: "At any moment a new strangeness of beauty may be there and gone; the activity of our minds must be ready for that contemplation. The pageant of this medieval Italian poet is not really as alien to our most intimate life as we choose to think."[16]

Dante's special insight into sin and redemption is in how he shows that both—indeed, how all being and action—are instances of love: "Son . . . the Creator, nay / the creature too, was ne'er devoid of love."[17] Dante's discussion therefore takes us beyond an analysis of sin based on (dis)obedience, purity, or social cohesion and makes our reflections on sin and redemption into an all-encompassing theory and experience of all our actions. He asks us to consider what and how we love, and the effects that the objects and types of our love have on us. We will consider our loves in two categories, each of which presents us with a good and bad side. One type of love is appetitive or acquisitive, usually directed toward objects, and can addictively take over our lives when unrestrained, but can be properly enjoyed when it is controlled and directed through reason. The other type of love seeks to enjoy other people and God, and is malice and evil when it is the love and enjoyment of harming others, but is selfless and self-fulfilling love when it seeks the good of others. And what is so beautiful in Dante is that he does not dwell only on how all bad loves lead to misery—though he shows this clearly enough. Instead, he constantly brings our attention to the overwhelming joy that good loves bring: "Dante . . . is the supreme poet of joy."[18] For Dante, love is an essential fact of all life, and joy can be a part of every love, and every life.

Appetite and Reason

As Dante begins his journey through hell, readers are struck by how he has organized the infernal regions. Instead of having all the damned thrown together indistinguishably into a lake of fire (see Rev 19:20; 20:14–15), the genius of Dante's hell is in how it distinguishes between different sins. Dante has ordered the many sinners according to what he regards as the relative severity of their sins, and his order is often surprising.[19] The sins are not ordered according to our more normal sense of the amount of damage these sins do to others, so murder is not the worst sin in Dante's hell. Rather, they are ordered according to how much damage they have done to the perpetrator, how hellish and irredeemable the sins have made him or her. Sin is not merely a crime, but a deliberate disordering and disease of the soul. With this definition of their severity, Dante ranks sins of appetite or incontinence as the least damning. These are sins in which a normally healthy appetite for something has become obsessive—lust, gluttony, avarice (greed), prodigality (wastefulness), wrath, and probably sloth (depending on how one identifies the sinners of the fifth circle). In other words, these are the seven deadly sins, minus envy and pride, and adding wastefulness as the complement or flip side of greed. Although his later categorizations may surprise us, his ranking of these sins as the least evil is fairly easy to understand: these desires are sinful only in their quantity and violence, not in their object. All these sins are desires for something normal, natural, and good—sex, food, possessions, righteous anger, and leisure. For all these sins, the proper enjoyment of their object is part of a saved and blessed life, part of the soul's journey to God.[20] This is especially clear in the case of lust, whose proper expression is human love, one of the highest, most transforming, most salvific of experiences. These sins are only addictions, not perversions. They are not sins of hate, but of excessive love, and that makes them the least evil. It also makes them the most poignant, since the people who indulged in them came so close to ordering their loves and lives rightly.

How close these sinners came to living rightly is shown by another group in hell that does surprise most readers. Surprisingly, Dante is not led through his whole journey by Christian figures. Instead, he is led through hell and purgatory by the spirit of the Roman poet Virgil (70–19 B.C.E.), and the first place they come to after passing through the gates of hell is the limbo where he and the other virtuous non-Christians reside. Dante populates this limbo with a variety of famous authors, political leaders, philosophers, scientists, mythical characters, and even Muslims; Virgil himself mentions that the souls of unbaptized infants also reside here. These spirits suffer no punishment, and they live in a beautiful castle that includes all of the things that are absent in the rest of hell—light, flowing water, green grass, and most of all, community, friendship, and enjoyment with one another.

This limbo is shocking from two different perspectives. First, from a more conservative or traditional perspective, we have to ask why the adults among this group are here, unpunished, free to do whatever they please within their castle, even though this is hell. Dante answers this by repeatedly insisting that these non-Christians—much like the unbaptized infants—lived their lives without ever committing a sin; therefore, they cannot be punished for and by sin, as all the other inhabitants of hell are. So Dante, unlike many Christians, believes it is possible for humans to avoid committing any sin their whole lives. This is because Dante—much like Socrates or Confucius—has a very high opinion of the value and power of human reason: exercised rightly, even without divine aid or revelation, he believes it can guide one to live without sin. For Dante, those who sin and are damned have "lost the good of the intellect."[21] They are either stupidly, immaturely, or bestially unrestrained, as are the less guilty sinners; or they have lost intellect and reason by insanely embracing falsehood and violence, as are the worse sinners deeper in hell. According to Dante, sinning is a disorder of the mind and soul, but it is a disorder into which we need not fall, for God has given us the faculty of reason to order our loves and control our desires rightly.[22] While Dante's estimation of human nature may seem a bit optimistic, if we consider how obviously stupid and self-destructive many sins are, his counsel to use our reason to help us avoid sinning seems eminently practical. Even if we disagree that this could work in every case for an entire lifetime, we would have to admit that it would often work, and it would make our world and our lives much better than the sinful messes we make of them.

Yet from another perspective—the more ecumenical or liberal perspective, toward which Dante himself seems to be leaning in his generous estimation of the power of human reason—the image of limbo bothers us because the virtuous non-Christians are still in hell, even if unpunished. If they have lived without sinning, why are they not in heaven? The short answer is that they're not baptized and therefore still suffer the effects of original sin, but I think this answer reduces Dante's insight to a mere technicality. We will address this more fully in the next section, when we consider the non-Christians whom Dante meets in heaven. But something can be said here about the role of reason in attaining salvation. The one thing the virtuous non-Christians in hell share with all the rest of the damned is their seeming sense of satisfaction, of completeness or wholeness. Everyone in hell gets exactly what they desire and love: "They desire to be where they must be."[23] "It is love and love alone that keeps the souls in Hell."[24] With the rest of the damned, Dante shows this love by his choice of punishments. These penalties are not the opposite of the sinners' desires—such as starving the gluttonous, tying up the wrathful and keeping them from hitting each other, dangling riches before the thieves that they cannot steal— but are exactly a hideous, eternal indulging in their sins. Thus, the obese gluttons are rolling in rotten food, the wrathful are forever tearing each other apart, the thieves are stealing from each other over and over and over again. None of the people in hell really have a punishment inflicted on them by God or devils. Instead, God allows the unrepentant to embrace sin and abandon him forever. "Sinners do not suffer because a heteronomous force decrees, for legalistic or even mysterious reasons, their eternal damned state. That force, rather, validates what they have made of themselves by decreeing they will live forever in ways that manifest with startling clarity who they actually are."[25] Surprisingly, beautifully—and perhaps most of all, frighteningly—Dante's *Comedy* is not really about what happens to us in the afterlife, but about what we are doing to ourselves right now.[26]

And on this point, the virtuous non-Christians are exactly like the other inhabitants of hell. They are what they have always been, and they have what they have always desired, except that unlike the other souls in hell, what the virtuous non-Christians desire, love, and eternally possess is not at all vicious or ugly. They eternally embrace life, goodness, reason, honor, beauty, human truth, and human companionship. They live in a city that is not merely better than any other part of hell; it is more perfect and peaceful than any city on earth ever has been.[27] Although reason can lead them to the highest kind of merely human life and accomplishments, it cannot lead them to anything beyond or above the human realm. Worldly success based on reason lifts us above sin, which Dante believes is inherently unreasonable. But such success can then become entrapping, for it can keep us from believing in other unreasonable realities that Dante believes are necessary for salvation, such as the incarnation and the atonement that it brings: "It is the practical man, the politician, the husband and father, the scholar and poet— . . . it is such a man who is blinded and lost. This is the danger."[28] This is the sad, incomplete life in which the virtuous non-Christians are forever trapped, but it is the rightly attractive, successful life that all of us pursue, even as we Christians acknowledge and long for something more.

Another difference between the virtuous non-Christians and the other souls in hell is how they seem capable of some motion and change, while the sinners are not. Like us on earth, the virtuous non-Christians live normal lives, conversing and moving about, shown most vividly in how Virgil is capable of even moving out of hell into purgatory. But the sinners are trapped in their individual places, incapable of movement or change, and totally uninterested in conversation or interaction with one another. Even though no one forces them to do so, all they can do now and eternally is sin, hurting themselves and preying on others. Ironically, although we often associate sin with change and excitement—having sex with people other than our spouses for a change, doing something different and naughty, imbibing substances that make us feel different—Dante shows how sin finally results in an existence that is "infinitely unchanging, . . . monotonously the same."[29] It is ultimate, eternal addiction, no longer capable of stopping the sinful behavior, or even recognizing it as sinful, or even conceiving of any other kind of behavior. As much as change frightens us with its unfamiliarity and its possibility of mistake, there is hope for us so long as we retain the possibility of change.

One of the most striking and powerful illustrations of unchangeability, endless repetition, and loss of reason is found near the bottommost depth of hell, in a scene that leaves an indelible impression on most readers. Even though this is where malice and treachery are punished, it is also the epitome of all sinfulness. In the final circle of hell, Dante encounters Ugolino, an Italian count who had betrayed his city in one of the struggles between the Guelphs and Ghibellines. Count Ugolino is frozen in ice, with only his head protruding, but he leans over to bite the head of the man frozen next to him, Bishop Ruggieri. The count's hatred of the bishop is highly understandable: the bishop had had Ugolino and his sons and grandsons walled up in a tower until all had starved to death. As the count pauses from his bloody gnawing long enough to recount the horror to Dante, he tells of how the ordeal was

75

worsened by the fact that he was physically stronger than his sons and grandsons, and therefore suffered through seeing them all die before him. He also hints that, before expiring, he himself may have resorted to the further horror of cannibalism. Dante even embellishes the story by making it seem that Ugolino's grandsons were younger than they actually were. Having told his story, the count immediately resumes munching on his neighbor and enemy, an activity he will apparently continue throughout eternity—not because of compulsion by some outside force or demon, but because it's exactly what he wants to do, and will always be. Here is the perfect example of understandable human feelings—hatred, revenge, anger—being indulged in and fostered until they grow so strong that nothing else can ever get in the way of their practice or "enjoyment." Anger is sometimes healthy, and measured retaliation is probably necessary sometimes. But when guided by reason, both ultimately have a goal—the righting of an injustice and the eventual repair of relationships. Any reasonable person who pursues anger or retaliation beyond these goals would grow bored with them and stop. For Dante, this is the simplest, most basic sense of virtue or repentance, possible for all people just by the exercise of their innate faculty of reason, even without God's direct help or the gospel. If someone fails to become bored with sin and stop it, it is because one has abandoned reason and lost sight of any real purpose in life, pursuing only mindless, numbing, repetitive activity. They have condemned themselves to live in "a dog-eat-dog world in which cannibalism replaces communion, in which the atrocities of earth are allowed to play themselves out for eternity."[30] While Ugolino's relentless pursuit of eternal spite may strike us as extreme, Dante has shown us how every sin is a step away from reason, away from changeability, and toward this kind of perfected, adamantine, unchangeable irrationality.

Malice and Love

As Dante and Virgil journey deeper into hell, they go beyond the sins of mere appetite and into what Dante considers worse sins, the sins that damage and punish us more. These sins are not just normal appetites for good things that have gone beyond reasonable bounds: they are appetites for things that people were never meant to desire or pursue. They are even things that people probably find unpleasant at first—

unlike the sins of appetite—but which, like all sins, gradually become easier and more pleasurable the longer they're practiced. These worse sins are not only addictions; unlike the lesser sins, they are perversions, deliberate twistings of the human will toward objects it should naturally find repulsive.

In the lower circles of hell the two broad categories of sin are violence and fraud, for according to Dante, people naturally desire peace and truth, so violence and deceit are unnatural pursuits, which people would avoid unless they forced themselves to participate in them. Dante shows once again that his ordering of the severity of sins is not based on the harm they do to others, for he ranks violence as less sinful, less damning than fraud. His reasoning, as he has Virgil explain it, is that by behaving violently, people are acting like beasts: much like the sins of appetite, they are giving in to base, animal urges. In short, they are acting subhuman, denying and degrading their higher faculties, especially reason. But fraud is something humans are uniquely capable of—unlike humans, animals practice deceit and subterfuge only against members of other species, not their own—and fraud does not deny reason, but uses it to deceive and do harm to others. It is, therefore, unlike any of the other sins in hell, not a "giving in" to any urge, but a deliberate directing of the will toward things that no one finds attractive and no one tolerates or excuses when they're done to oneself—falsehood and harm. Such sins are not from a subhuman lack of reason, but a perversion of the highest human faculties of reason and love, misusing both to create and pursue a love of utter negativity, without truth or reality. Unlike violence, fraud does not seem to have any possibility of creativity, for it can only destroy trust and love between people. In most cases, we would rather a loved one hit us than lied to us, for the latter would poison the relationship more thoroughly and would be harder to detect, forgive, or fix. Violence sometimes can even bring about an end to itself by satisfying the urge to violence, but fraud perpetuates both itself and violence much more than do the other sins; more insidiously, it can even turn into self-deception, till the sinner can no longer distinguish the truth even to himself. Though seemingly a surprising categorization at first, the idea that fraud sickens our soul and dissolves our society more thoroughly and cancerously than any other sin turns out to be frighteningly accurate.

Dante shows this not only in his ordering of the sins, but also in the punishments for the sinners. In the circles of the violent, the punishments of heat and fire we normally associate with hell are prevalent—walls and sepulchres glowing with heat like a furnace, a river of boiling blood, a wasteland of burning sands, a rain of fire from above. Violence has at least the semblance of a perverted, subhuman passion, and therefore it is associated with heat, with life and dynamism.[31] But in the final circle of hell, Dante and Virgil make their way across an enormous frozen lake, in which are embedded those who have lied to and betrayed their family, country, guests, and masters. In this frozen lake they finally meet Satan, who is not really the ruler of hell, but only the worst of its inhabitants, the worst traitor and sinner, trapped in the very center of hell. This final image of sinfulness is one of the most brilliant in Dante, both because it surprises us with its lack of flames, and also in its final depiction of the worst depth of sin. With an image of ice instead of fire, we can see again that sin only appears to be dynamism and change, but really results finally in complete unchangeability and ossification in one's sinful ways, as one is "fossilized into the fixed pattern of perverted voluntary affirmations."[32] And not only does the ice's frozenness graphically convey unchangeability. It also vividly depicts the other qualities of sin at its extreme—impotence, sterility, death, immobility, silence— qualities that again would not be noticed if Dante were surrounded by flames and the screams of the damned. Satan, who once was the most beautiful in heaven and powerful enough to vie with the Almighty, can not hinder or even speak to the humble Dante. With Virgil's guidance Dante escapes from hell by rudely climbing down Satan's side until they emerge into a cavern at Satan's feet and climb up to the surface on the other side. "The silent Satan . . . is a once splendid being . . . from whom all personality has now drained away, . . . even the ability to move about, that modest prerogative of animal life, is now beyond him."[33] Even though sin is "intended by the sinner to be an assertion of self, . . . sin in Dante's eyes is the ultimate denial of self, the immobilizing of personality."[34] As powerful as sin appears in our fallen world, it finally gives no real power to its practitioners. Instead, it only saps their strength until they're incapable of doing anything except just barely existing—sad, motionless, and mute.

Another way to look at the image of the frozen sinners at the bottom of hell is how it is the epitome of loneliness that we see throughout hell. The other sinners cut themselves off from others by focusing on their sin, and therefore their punishment is to wallow eternally in their sin while ignoring everyone around them. The traitors' sin was to harm and deceive others and thereby to destroy their relationships with them. So their punishment is also to get exactly what they had worked for—the complete destruction of their relationships with others and complete isolation and insulation from God or any other person. Damnation is, once again, getting exactly what one wanted and worked so hard to get—an aggrandizement of self and a complete ignoring and abuse of others until they have no way to contact, communicate, or change you. "In hell, the self is sovereign, cut off, frozen in obsession and monomania, always alone no matter how dense the crowd."[35] No matter how much sin in this life requires others as victims and coconspirators, it constantly erodes our relationships with others, even our fellow sinners, until we are as cut off from one another as the sinners frozen in the infernal lake. A lifetime of treating others as objects has made the sinners into horribly self-enclosed subjects, totally cut off from the outside, and with nothing left inside themselves to love or contemplate. A lifetime of treating others as unimportant, interchangeable tools for their own sinful ends has made the sinners indistinguishable and utterly uninteresting to others or even to themselves.[36] And what a lifetime of such behavior finally and horribly perfects in hell, it begins in this life— one little lie, one little betrayal, one damaged relationship at a time.

But if complete loneliness and isolation is the final vision of hell, Dante sees the joyous alternative as soon as he sets foot on the mount of purgatory and begins his ascent. Even for those Christians who do not believe in purgatory, Dante's depiction there of Christian love and community is utterly relevant and beautiful, for the idea of purgatory is that it is a place in the afterlife where one continues the process of penitence and healing already begun in this life. It is the realm of the afterlife that is most like our earthly existence, because change, improvement, and penitence go on there.[37] The only difference between purgatory and our earth is that the souls there are now assured of salvation: however long it may take them finally to cleanse themselves, they know they will be successful. So even if one no longer believes in purgatory, one can see in Dante's description a beautiful image of how we are to behave in this life, and a wonderful, life-giving alternative to the deadly loneliness of hell from which he has just emerged. Everywhere Dante goes in purgatory, the souls are eager to talk with him. They even ask his assistance for themselves—to pray for them when he gets back to Italy, and especially to ask their loved ones and family members to pray for them. The penitents also offer their own prayers to Dante and to their loved ones in exchange and in humble gratitude. Exactly opposite to how the damned destroyed their earthly relationships, the penitent and the saved continue, foster, and enjoy them in the afterlife, typified by Dante's meeting with his great-great-grandfather in paradise.

This joyous community has a salutary effect on Dante's own feelings, since several of the characters he meets in purgatory are members of the rival faction of the Ghibellines (e.g., Manfred, in *Purg.* 3.112; Buonconte, in *Purg.* 5.88). Dante was frank enough to make it clear that he believed his hated nemesis Pope Boniface VIII would one day burn in hell for his corruption and the misery he brought to Dante and all of the church. Yet, he shows in purgatory that his theological vision is not merely an excuse to pillory his enemies and praise his friends and relatives.[38] He had already partly shown this by placing some of his friends in hell, most notably his beloved teacher Brunetto (*Inf.* 15.30–120). But Dante's feelings toward his damned friend and his saved enemies show another wonderful contrast between hell and purgatory. Dante talks to Brunetto with great kindness, still praising and thanking him for his life, which was "gentle and paternal; . . . you taught me how man makes himself eternal."[39] Although Virgil scolds Dante elsewhere for showing sympathy to the damned, he does not criticize his tender words to Brunetto. Springing from love and not pity, they are not just permissible, but also humane and just. For all loves that have helped to bring us closer to God "must be remembered, willingly praised, and ardently published before earth and heaven. Any who have been at all our source and derivation deserve, for ever and ever, no less."[40] But while love lasts forever, surviving even eternally damning sin, Dante's kind, respectful conversations in purgatory with his former enemies show how we can outlive our sinful, earthly hates to live in loving community with everyone.[41]

If Dante experiences and shares such joyful, community feeling in purgatory, how much more so is it felt in heaven: "And it is communion, carefully and sometimes painfully learned in the *Purgatorio*, that becomes the sublime play of paradise."[42] Here we see how people freed from sin behave, as they frolic and play with one another in God's presence: "Was there ever a heaven so full of nods and becks and wreathed smiles, so gay and dancing?"[43] Exactly as the damned embrace their sinful, earthly loves eternally, the saved also go right on embracing their virtuous, earthly loves, for Dante believes that it is always love that guides us. The saved continue and perfect the loves they began in this life, because these loves are what guided them to God. And Dante believes that the special love that led him to God was the love of Beatrice.

How Dante thinks his love for Beatrice was salvific and not sinful greatly enhances our understanding of love and redemption. No gnostic or dualist, Dante believes in the value and God-centeredness of creation, that God made all creatures so that he could love them, and they could love him and one another. Dante's view of the universe is "sacramental; . . . he holds to the notion that all things reflect the glory of God, that God speaks to man not only by things but in things."[44] Creation and love go hand in hand, and neither is the result of sin or lack: "The Many—the diversity, the fragmentation, the otherness of the world—is there precisely as a consequence of God's will and not as some after-effect of a primal fall."[45] It is therefore not merely appropriate to take pleasure in creation, especially in our fellow human creatures; it is also the absolutely necessary and only Christian response: "And still his ingrained sense of life is totally opposed to the 'pagan' sense, with its disparagement of the miserable, blind body."[46] Dante offers us a deeply Christian view of the value and delight of creation that is a helpful corrective to the often-dour caricatures many have of Christianity.

Even more outrageously, Dante makes passionate, human desire the result and the only right reaction to this sacramental, God-centered world. No ascetic or prudish scold, Dante believes in the value of his real, human, physical love for a woman. "I could catch the daring, even dangerous truth of what Dante was attempting in the figure of Beatrice: how *eros* could be transfigured into *caritas* without turning its back on the body."[47] Dante's human, sexual love is transfigured—perhaps subsumed is a better image, since it seems to be a part of a larger reality—into divine love, but it is not denied or regretted.[48] Most surprisingly, this human desire does not go away, even in paradise, though it there becomes a beautiful paradox, "a union of peace and ardor, tranquility and passion, a passionate tranquility in which desire finds rest without in some sense ceasing to be desire."[49] Beatrice's love could lead to God precisely because it pointed to and contained something beyond and above itself. This keeps Dante from idolizing her—making her into a false goddess distracting him from the real God—and allows him instead to love her as an icon—seeing in her the human image of God and joyfully following that image back to its source. And this right ordering of his love for Beatrice not only directs it toward God; it also makes the love fulfilling and rightly ordered in itself, allowing Dante to miss so many of the pitfalls of an ordinary, human love affair. He does not love Beatrice because he longs for her—the confusion of lust for love that is seen in the circle of the lustful and that we will see epitomized with Paolo and Francesca. He longs for her because he loves her—the right subsuming of normal, physical attraction to a higher, nobler, more humane, more divine feeling.[50] He does not love her because he has idealized her—the deceptive mistake of fantasy, which is bound to make one resent the real beloved when he or she falls short,[51] as is done tragically in Shakespeare's *Othello* and many other works of imaginative fiction. Instead, Dante idealizes Beatrice because he loves her, and such idealization is really only a "joyous recognition"[52] of her for who she really is—a beautiful creature of God, providentially sent to allure, love, and save him.

In the experiences of love the differences between the three realms of the afterlife also affect the souls' feelings of satisfaction. In exactly the opposite way from how the damned were all so satisfied—though unhappy—with their lot, the penitent in purgatory are, of course, profoundly dissatisfied with how they are, even as they rejoice at God's mercy and love. They are sinful, and they want nothing more than to be cleansed of their sin. While the sinners in hell madly and dumbly embrace their sin—which thereby becomes their eternal punishment—the penitent in purgatory gladly and enthusiastically embrace their punishment, which cleanses them of their sin. Though the penitents are so happy to see Dante and talk with him, each of them is also eager to get back to his or her punishment, even though these punishments sometimes seem more horrible than their hellish counterparts—starvation for the gluttonous, being crushed under massive weights for the proud, being engulfed in flames as hot as molten glass for the lustful, and (the one that often makes my students' skin crawl) weeping with eyelids sewed shut with steel wires for the envious. Unlike the sinful, the souls in purgatory look back on their earthly lives with regret and shame, so they want nothing more eagerly than to fix the harm and heal the wounds they inflicted on themselves and others by their sinning. The sinful in hell look at the earth as an awful place that they blame for their own sinfulness, and their lack of remorse condemns them. Those in purgatory and heaven look upon the earth with love for all the God-given goodness it contains, and sadness and even anger for how they and others have turned it from a paradise into a virtual hell.[53] While the impenitent are obsessed and trapped in their past lives and sins, the penitent in purgatory often refer to themselves in the past tense, because the sinful self they once were has been left behind, or is in the process of being finally and eternally transformed. And once this trans-formation is complete in heaven, the souls can then look back on their mortal lives with joy and not regret. "Yet here repent we not, but feel delight / not for the sin, which none remembers now, / but for God's overruling and foresight."[54] Satisfaction or complacency with this sinful life leads to eternal misery. But dissatisfaction or even anger at our sin leads to repentance and longing for God, which then bring eternal joy and peace as we see God's wisdom at work in every life and love, and thank him for turning even sin and evil to his perfect, loving purpose.

The most shocking and uplifting example of this dissatisfaction with earthly life and value is vividly shown when Dante sees in paradise two men—the Roman emperor Trajan and the Trojan hero Ripheus—who could not have been baptized or belonged to the Christian church in their lives: "More startling, more inebriating still, is the revelation that a Trojan hero is present" in paradise.[55] Just as the virtuous non-Christians in limbo are perhaps the most interesting and surprising part of Dante's hell, these two are the most interesting and surprising inhabitants of Dante's heaven. Unlike the characters from the Old Testament who appear in paradise, these two cannot be explained away as having had some messianic expectations that would allow them to be counted as "Christians." One might dismiss them as some inscrutable exception because there are only two of them. But Dante is clearly so obsessed with order, organization, and consistency that had he wanted to do so, he could have excluded any exceptions to the rules he was making. On the contrary, these two are more probably like every other person Dante encounters in all three realms—symbols or particular instances of more general rules of how sin and redemption work. "Dante the poet exalts him [Ripheus]—as a symbol—like the unknown soldier—of countless others."[56] The rules that would explain how this seeming incongruity can occur are given by the heavenly host of which these two seeming non-Christians are a part (*Paradise* 19.103–111). No one enters heaven without faith in Christ, yet some are saved who did not know Christ, suggesting that it is possible to have faith in Christ without knowing him. I cannot pretend to explain exactly what this might mean, but some clarity may be lent by the observation that these two must be different from the virtuous non-Christians who were not saved but condemned to limbo. Although Trajan and Ripheus were known for their righteousness, so too were the people in limbo. The one similarity between the inhabitants of limbo and the sinners in the rest of hell was their satisfaction with their eternal lot and their inability to conceive of anything beyond the merely human—merely human reason for those in limbo, merely human sinfulness for the rest of the denizens of hell. Hence, it seems reasonable to think that this is the point at which both would differ from these saved men. These two saved pagans must have felt that there was something more to life than what they could achieve on their own or conceive with their own human minds and wills. It would be something they lacked, which therefore made them dissatisfied with their lives and long for help from a God who could give them this knowledge and peace. Put in such general terms, it does seem possible that a person who has never heard of the Bible—a person who does not "know" Christ, who does not "know" the story of how Jesus lived and died—could come to this dissatisfaction and longing on one's own. I think Dante may have in mind something as minimal as this: God could bring a person to himself if that person had ever knelt down and prayed, "I want to be with God, and I know I can't accomplish that on my own. But I know that God can do this, and I put my hope and trust in God that he will provide a way." Such a feeling of limitedness, dissatisfaction with what we can accomplish on our own, and total dependence on God is not a bad definition of the beginning of redemption, of what makes redemption possible and conceivable to us, and which makes us long for it.

Dante has shown how all sinful loves trap us in unchangeability and degrade us to the point of near nonexistence. But he has also proclaimed how the right love for God and for other people changes us into what we were supposed to be all along—a loving community worshiping and praising God. Let us turn now to specific instances of that process in the *Comedy*.

For Study: Desire Is Not Love, but Love Is Desire—
Inferno 5.100–106

> Love, quick to kindle in the gentle heart,
>   seized this one for the beauty of my body,
>   torn from me, (How it happened still offends me!)
> Love, that excuses no one loved from loving,
>   seized me so strongly with delight in him
>   that, as you see, he never leaves my side.
> Love led us straight to sudden death together.[57]

One of the most memorable incidents in all of the *Comedy* is in canto 5 of *Inferno*, in the circle of the lustful, where Dante meets an Italian noblewoman, Francesca. The story of her sad death was current at the time, and Dante uses it as a rich and evocative basis for his analysis of lust, and of sin in general. Francesca is the representative spokesperson in the circle of the lustful, instead of more famous sinners such as Helen of Troy, Cleopatra, or Achilles. We must be careful to analyze the details of her story and the way she tells it in order to understand Dante's point here.[58] Trapped in a loveless, arranged marriage, Francesca fell in love and had a long-standing affair with her husband's younger brother, Paolo.[59] She tells Dante of their first love-making, as they sat reading the story of Lancelot and Guinevere, and how they were so overcome by the story's similarity to their own situation that they succumbed to temptation. Later, her husband surprised them during another tryst and murdered both of them, and now the two lovers are forever together in hell. Dante is deeply sympathetic to her story, so overcome with pity that he faints as soon as she finishes speaking. But he also shows how his reaction, while understandable, is flawed and incomplete: "Dante the poet presents the story in a way that shows us the error of both our own and the pilgrim's reactions."[60] Since Francesca is the epitome of lust, there must be something in her speech and in her situation that is to teach us about lust and sin, and not just to elicit our sympathy: "Hell means something of which she must be an intentional expression. . . . She is one figure in a dialogue which as a whole is planned to tell us something about the action of love."[61] There are several points in her speech that show us the difference between sinful and pure love, which is, in a concentrated form, the difference between damnation and salvation, between hell and heaven.

First, there is the way Dante has so carefully crafted Francesca's manner of expression. On the one hand, it is clearly "warm and personal,"[62] "charming, . . . appealing, tender, . . . tempered by sweetness and feminine grace,"[63] and "vital and engaging."[64] But at the same time, she is a little too solicitous: she is far too familiar with the stranger Dante for us to believe it is completely sincere.[65] Francesca is seductive and entrancing, thereby recalling Eve,[66] the first human sinner and seducer, here at the beginning of Dante's journey through all sin and falsehood. Francesca is unctuous and insincere in her greeting. Since all of Dante's encounters are supposed to be representative or typical of the people he meets, we are to assume that her overwrought speech must be how she manipulated others and ingratiated herself to them during her whole life. And insincerity turns into outright dishonesty as she tells her story, for she changes the details of the story of Lancelot and Guinevere to fit more closely her situation with Paolo.[67] She misremembers the story so as to blame it for her sin, just as she blasphemously misrepresents God's love and justice. Francesca does this by accusing God of having too little love, and she only approves God's justice insofar as it will punish her murderous husband worse than herself. Thus, she blames God for her condition. But worse than lying to Dante or us, she has told such lies to herself so often and avoided blame for so long that she is thoroughly "self-deceived,"[68] and therefore "frozen in self-pity,"[69] incapable of repentance.[70] She quite rightly blames her husband and pities herself for her death, but that is the only blame, the only bad thing that she sees in what happened. And since she sees nothing wrong in what she did, like all the other sinners in hell, she will go right on doing it forever, trapped with the lover she chose, though he no longer brings her any joy or pleasure.[71] This is not external punishment from a wrathful God—as Francesca would have us believe and as she has convinced herself. It is simply the way she is: "Hell is, so to speak, the place that takes seriously enough the actual characters of people to allow them to be that way forever."[72] God, more than any other being, respects people's choices.

Even though Francesca's empty words are distasteful to us, and her self-deception keeps her from repentance, it is important that she is in the circle of the lustful, not in any of the circles where the deceptive are punished.[73] So her story is supposed to be more directly about lust:

What was it in her love that was defective, that needed repentance, that made it lust and not love? As with the technicality of the nonbaptism of the virtuous non-Christians condemned to limbo, the mere fact that she and Paolo were both married to other people would not seem totally to explain Francesca's damnation.[74] It certainly would not explain why Dante would make her the spokesperson or epitome of all the lustful. Her prominence seems to show that she did not just love the wrong man or at the wrong time, but somehow that she loved in the wrong way. As she describes it in the lines above, it becomes clearer how her love was wrong.

First, Francesca describes her experience of love as far too passive. Love "seizes" her and Paolo; it is something done to them, not something they do.[75] This passivity cannot be explained away as Dante's medieval ideal of womanhood.[76] Besides the fact that Paolo also displays this kind of passivity, Dante fills all three realms of the afterlife with powerful, commanding female figures, chief among them Beatrice, who is idealized for her strength, purity, and *active* love toward Dante. Dante praises or values passivity in no one. Passivity is a descent into a merely animal existence, as shown by the bird imagery in this canto, which depicts the souls as wheeling and swooping in a way that is both beautiful, but also uncontrollable, violent, and chaotic.[77] As we will see in the next section, Francesca is essentially describing desire, the first stage of love but not its totality. Her love is real but incomplete, stunted, and therefore twisted and hellish: "Their love is beautiful, moving, faithful: what is wrong with it? Only the prolongation of the self-indulged moment. Love is lazy. But that laziness, though it is the most touching in hell, is yet the very opening to all hell."[78] Partly we can tell how wrong her love is by how easy, almost effortless it was to act upon it. Real love is difficult and painful right from the beginning, but offers us eternal enjoyment. Francesca's lust was all too easy to begin, and only painful now and eternally. She is "in love with love,"[79] or perhaps worse, "in love with Paolo's love for her,"[80] making her love vicarious as well as passive. Such a limited, immature, lazy kind of love traps her and Paolo at the level of mere attraction to bodies and delight in them, but this kind of delight cannot last or satisfy on its own. It is "the first rung of the ladder of love, pointing the way forward to other steps, but in itself perilous to cling to, and fruitless."[81] As sad as her death was, her kind of love could never have brought Francesca eternal joy, even if her husband had not murdered her. That is her tragedy, self-destruction, and damnation.[82]

Perhaps even more damnable than the passivity of Francesca's love is its self-centeredness and possessiveness. Besides discounting the feelings of either her husband or Paolo's wife—perhaps a fairly understandable oversight, under the circumstances—Francesca's love turns ugly in how it overlooks Paolo's feelings, his person, and his fate. She is in love with love; she loves and clings to the way Paolo makes her feel—even now, in hell—and not Paolo himself. She is not "in love with a person who has an integrity apart from her reactions to him."[83] She shows no concern or interest in him, "no trace of authentic tenderness."[84] Instead, her love is the antithesis of real love—complete "self-indulgence . . . [and] selfishness."[85] Swinging wildly to the opposite extreme from passivity, her love is an idolatrous glorification of her own will and domination of another person, "the human will intent, according to nature, upon the good of the subject, alone."[86] All of this is also shown simply but loudly in her manner of speaking. She never mentions Paolo by name, even though he's right next to her, for he is only a pronoun, an object, a possession to her.[87] Ironically, of course, such possessiveness and objectification are exactly how her family and her husband had treated her—as a possession to be sold off in a politically motivated marriage, an object to be used to continue a family line and guarantee future alliances. In perhaps the saddest and most ironic lines of the *Comedy*, we see here how a woman took the temporary, bad situation of being trapped and objectified by her husband and society, and turned it into her own eternal state of enslavement to sin. Francesca did this by deceiving herself and willingly practicing a kind of love that could never give her real companionship and enjoyment of another person, but only complete self-absorption and loneliness, eternally isolated from her lover, even with him right beside her. She is eternally cut off from God, even though he always loves her and is ready to forgive her.[88]

For Reflection: How Love Works—*Purgatory* 18.55–60

> Therefore, no man can know whence springs the light
> > of his first cognizance, nor of the bent
> > of such innate primordial appetite
> as springs within you, as within the bee
> > the instinct to make honey; and such instincts
> > are, in themselves, not blamable nor worthy.[89]

In cantos 17 and 18 of *Purgatory*, Dante has Virgil launch into a long discourse on the nature of love. Numerically, it is the center point of the entire *Comedy*. Geographically and cosmically, Dante is halfway through his journey, exactly halfway up the mount of purgatory. At this significant midpoint Dante puts an examination of the subject that is at the heart of his art and message—how love works, for good or bad.[90] Besides its beauty, it is the subtlest and most complex description of love that I know, for Dante makes love a confusing interplay between "innate primordial appetite," reason, and free will. As we reflect on this description, I think we also see how it is a quite accurate account, bringing out the aspects of pleasure, pain, compulsion, choice, and finally fulfillment that all of us have felt in our various loves. Dante enriches our understanding of love, taking it far beyond our often-debased ideas of lust, attraction, and even sentimentality.

Dante knows well the mystery of the beginnings of love, the impossibility of explaining how it begins, and why it is drawn to some objects or people and not to others. At its most positive, this mysterious attraction shows us the otherness, mystery, and beauty of the things and people we love, and how we appreciate and surrender to them with joy. "Yet this response of love is not something a person creates nor something one can will by and for oneself. Rather it comes from a source outside oneself. Love comes from the Other."[91] But as beautiful as this experience of love can be, it complicates things for Dante a good deal, for it appears to leave out the two major human faculties he highlights throughout his poem—reason and will. Dante knows he cannot distill love down to a pure act of will. He knows that we do not really choose to what or to whom we are initially attracted, the things and people with whom we automatically feel pleasure. And Dante is equally and accurately adamant that love does not spring from reason.[92] Our reason cannot object to the beginnings of love, and we cannot convince ourselves rationally to love someone, or to stop loving a person. A love based on reason would not really be love; it would lack "the passion, the 'madness,' and the ecstasy of love. These 'irrational' dimensions transport the human soul out of itself into a world beyond the merely rational world—a transcendent world."[93] If Francesca's love is an example of stunted love that is beneath reason, there is also a love that goes beyond reason, "the 'madness' of ecstasy or rapture, a rapture which involves the intuition of truth not fully understood."[94] The honesty and accuracy of

Dante's description are exactly what makes it so compelling: it matches our experience, as messy, confusing, and inconvenient as that may be.

But while Dante knows the inaccuracy of making love into just an act of either the will or reason, I think he also knows better than many others the inaccuracy and danger of making love merely a function of innate, uncontrollable desire. He knows that love is cheapened and twisted by talking of it solely in terms of desire, or by using images like Cupid's arrow or the bite of the love bug to describe it. Even the common language of falling in love trivializes the experience, reducing it to an unavoidable accident. His critique of such a description has the sound of a convert's zealousness, for Dante had earlier in his poetic career subscribed to such a view of love. "Dante is reacting against a strain of fatalism in the courtly love tradition, a fatalism he had himself encouraged in some of his lyrics."[95] Such fatalism is literally pagan, making love into a capricious and sometimes malevolent trick played on us by a minor deity, basically equivalent to catching a disease. It is not even a willing and glad surrender, but an unwilling and terrible affliction. If that is how love is, then it could never be fulfilling, but only burdensome, an addiction that not only doesn't connect us to other people, but even alienates us from ourselves,[96] since we seem to have lost all control over ourselves, becoming mere spectators or bystanders to our most intimate and often painful actions. If love is the right word to describe our highest and most noble attachment to the one, true God and to other people, then it cannot be a completely instinctual, compulsive action. Our will and reason have to play some part in it, as experience shows they do. Even though we do not choose our impulses, we choose whether or not to act on them, and they almost always can be tamed or habituated. We acknowledge this in the negative case of acquired tastes like tobacco and alcohol, but often overlook it in the acquisition of better habits, like kindness, politeness, and generosity, for example, all of which often do not come "naturally," but which do become second nature and even enjoyable through practice. We may not be rationally able to convince ourselves to love this or that thing or person, but we can acquire better habits of an open, loving nature. As mysterious as this interplay between desire, reason, and will may be, I think once again that it is an accurate description at the same time as it is a valuable warning. For although love is not merely desire, if we let ourselves believe that it is, then we will never experience real love.

Sexual attraction is one of the most powerful of these mysterious, innate, and instinctual appetites that can lead to something more. Rightly understood and experienced, sexuality can be an essential part of the soul's journey to God, not an obstacle on that path. "Sexual attraction, like everything else, is providential."[97] For Dante, physical beauty and our natural attraction to it are discernible clues or allurements to bring us back to God. They are some of the teeth with which God bites us, in one of Dante's graphic physical images (*Paradise* 26.55). Even though they often turn our staid world upside down, attraction and love are in a sense the ultimate example of order, not disorder, for they discern beauty and react to it rightly. "Because reality shines with God's presence, one has only to open one's eyes to love it; and particularly the eye of the mind; which discerns, through the sensible beauty of bodies, the rational beauty of order, the divine design."[98] Love only becomes sinful when this natural progression—from bodies, to the beauty of bodies, to beauty itself, to the Author of all beauty—stops before its final goal. As we saw with Francesca and Paolo, this is when natural attraction does not go beyond itself, but remains trapped and stunted at the first stage of love. It is a kind of laziness and self-indulgence—"the sin of indulging oneself in love instead of devoting oneself to the duty of love"[99]—and it is surely significant that Virgil's discourse on love is given while they are among the slothful in purgatory. Such immature love we have all felt as teenagers, and it is utterly forgivable in teenagers, who are just beginning ineptly to feel romantic love and sexual attraction. Such love is infatuation, the love of being in love, "a desiring merely to desire."[100] Essentially, it is to fall in love with attraction, rather than to let attraction develop into love. It barely deserves the name of "love": it is merely the relentless, restless, painful, and self-destructive pursuit of an object.

But just as Dante believes it is possible for reason to overcome every sinful behavior, he also believes it is possible for reason and will to bend any attraction—no matter how strong, dangerous, or destructive—into a positive experience. We are not responsible for our urges, as these are not fully or finally under our control, but we are responsible for our acting on them, for our cooperation and consent are under our control.[101] At least, reason and will could restrain the desire and gain practice in patience and self-control. Perhaps this is what Paolo and Francesca needed in their particular, unfortunate situation, so that they could have loved chastely and innocently, not lustfully and fatally. But again, Dante is not primarily about self-denial or even self-control: he is all about enjoyment, "a full-blooded attachment to a genuine, pleasure-giving goal."[102] And in many, many instances in our lives, it is possible not merely to restrain and control our desires for other people; it is also possible to experience them fully and in the right way, a way that brings satisfaction and enjoyment to both lover and beloved. "It . . . is but the normal made infinitely profound. . . . Eros . . . has a right to his delights; they are a part of the Way. The division is not between the Eros of the flesh and the Agape of the soul; it is between the moment of love which sinks into hell and the moment which rises to the in-Godding."[103] Even if it started as gross, physical attraction that only wanted to grab and possess, such an attraction can turn into something quite different— indeed, almost the opposite.[104] This is when love becomes a longing only to serve and benefit the beloved, when it is a love that denies the self and accepts rather than pursues the beloved, when it is experienced equally by both partners in a way that does not jealously diminish or threaten their other loves, but instead actually increases all the loves of both part-ners. This is a true love that can be practiced and enjoyed by both part-ners eternally, and shared and celebrated by those around them, as we see among the souls throughout Dante's paradise. This is part of Dante's beautiful lesson on love: that we should be honest and admit that innate, unavoidable attraction begins our love, but we can finally see how only true, selfless love validates and makes meaningful our attrac-tion. It is not a matter of doing whatever feels good—our ugly, selfish debasement of love—but of discovering that what feels good is a neces-sary but incomplete part of ultimate goodness. Pleasure and attraction are not sinful, but they are only means, not ends or goals. The end is love, and the goal of all who love truly is God.

For Prayer: Loving All—*Paradise* 26.64–66

> I love each leaf with which enleaved is all
> 　　the garden of the Eternal Gardener
> in measure of the light he sheds on each.[105]

In canto 26 of the *Paradise*, St. John asks Dante the pilgrim more about love, especially the problem of how one can properly love things other than God. These lines from Dante's response capture the rapturous experience of this kind of love for creatures that can finally be fully embraced without detracting or misleading from the love of God. They show with such clarity all the implications—for oneself, for one's beloved, and for God—of such a love. I am deeply grateful to Dante, for his poetry has helped me understand how my friend Greg, despite his early death, was richly blessed by God. This has helped me experience my love for him as pointing to the God who blessed him, rather than making me bitter toward the God who took him away.

First, to love properly, one must have one's sin ever before oneself, even at the same time as one constantly reminds oneself of God's infinite, redemptive love. Dante makes this clear in the lines leading up to those quoted above, in which he praises the death God died for us. It is only that death and the love that prompted it that free us to love rightly (26.58–63). A person without the experience and acknowledgment of sin cannot understand or believe in Jesus' life and death. At the same time, one who does not believe in the possibility of redemption also cannot believe in or draw sustenance from Jesus. Jesus and his sacrifice cannot heal a heart that does not know its sickness, nor can they heal one that despairingly believes its sickness is terminal. Jesus cannot make whole a person who does not know she or he is missing a fundamental part of oneself, nor can Jesus fulfill one who regards one's own spiritual incompleteness as permanent and irreparable. Virgil and the other virtuous pagans are sad examples of people without sin who are also uncomprehending of God's sacrifice and love: they are forever locked in the real but incomplete beauty of human reason and love. All the other sinners in hell are pathetic or despicable examples of people so devoid of reason and love that they can no longer perceive the ugliness of sin, nor imagine any alternative to it. They are forever trapped within the ugly, stunted beings they have made of themselves. As we pray to have the right kind of love for all of creation, let us remember that we have all sinned, we have all faltered in our belief, we have all had times when we forgot the love of God. At the same time, we all know and love unrepentant sinners, and perhaps even more poignantly, we all know and love virtuous people who are unbelievers. In our prayers to God, let us express our love and care for such people who have wandered from the way, even as we joyfully repent for our own misguided wanderings. We can perfect and increase our love by remembering that God throws unexpected, undeserved, but wonderful detours into everyone's journey. The most unexpected and undeserved of these expressions of God's love was the cross, together with the often circuitous and frustrating paths by which God has led each of us to put our faith and trust in such an infinite, sustaining, shocking love.

Second, one loves properly when one loves the things and people to which one is attracted by loving them as gifts from God. This kind of love makes our loved ones into finite gifts that point us to their infinite source; it properly directs our love toward God, even as it allows and demands that we love God's creatures. And loving creatures in this way overcomes their finitude and ours. It overcomes one of the most painful and constant challenges to human life and love—the challenge of death, the sign and terrible symptom of our finitude and sin. This is beautifully shown in Dante's love for Beatrice, who is gone from his earthly eyes for a time, but eternally present and more fully alive to him than ever.[106] Loving people as gifts from God can also overcome any imperfection in the love. Like all human things, our loves are necessarily imperfect. But by directing our imperfect love toward the perfect, loving God who gives the gift, our love and its object become perfect and complete, offering us satisfaction, fulfillment, and healing in place of our restlessness, emptiness, and brokenness. Beatrice again shows this. Although Dante blames himself for weaknesses or lapses in his love, since Beatrice directs his love toward God, she and God can nonetheless forgive and overcome such imperfections and joyfully embrace Dante. And from the sinful perspective of human lust, nothing could be more imperfect than Dante's love for Beatrice, as it offered no consummation or gratification. But from the right perspective of a love that leads to and includes God, such earthly signs of love are seen for how trivial or even sinful they are. Our loves become holy, pure, and eternal when they transcend the signs of love—sexuality, favors, status, even earthly presence—to love the person for who he or she really is—a creature, gift, sign, and fellow-lover of God.

Finally, and perhaps most difficultly, these lines point to an opposite problem with love—not the problem of loving our friends and lovers too much, but loving our enemies too little. Every leaf in God's garden is to be loved according to the grace that God sheds upon it. This would mean that even Satan and the rest of the damned have to be loved, for they have the minimal grace of existence given to them and sustained by God. The same, or even more, would have to be said of every human being still alive, no matter how loathsome they may seem to us, or how wretched and wicked they may have made themselves. The bare fact of their existence demands that they be loved. Dante has thereby given us a beautiful, poetic expression of the command to love our enemies. Yet, he has also rather skillfully found a way in which not only are our special loves validated and pointed to God, but the differences between our loves—loving some people more, some less—are also shown to be (sometimes) appropriate. Let us not jump to the conclusion that our particular likes and dislikes are an automatic reflection of the person or object's relative goodness: this would be the height of arrogance and folly, to assume that our perspective matches God's. But this does not invalidate all preferential love. For example, it should come as no surprise that I love the three teachers to whom I have dedicated this book much more than other teachers I have had. But I should not therefore assume that those others are less good or less beloved by God, and it does not excuse me from loving them and being grateful for what they have taught me. On the other hand, Dante shows throughout his work that it's all right if I don't dedicate books to all my teachers, only to the ones I really love, just as he loves and follows Virgil and Beatrice, not any of the millions of other people he might have. Indeed, such signs of love are not just all right; they are also the kind of grateful, joyous celebrations of special loves that make our lives not just virtuous, but also delightful. If loving people goes beyond the signs of affection they can give us, it joyfully demands that we show our affection for them in all the usual ways. We surely can and often do love someone or something less than we ought, but a difference between our loves is acknowledged here as natural, beneficial, and part of God's plan to draw us to himself. This allows us to love our friends with passion and commitment, at the same time as it demands that we love our enemies with humility and respect. For our enemies also come to us from God and direct us to God, even in spite of themselves, and especially in spite of our own sinfulness and blindness.

For Further Reading

Collins, J. *Pilgrim in Love: An Introduction to Dante and His Spirituality*. Chicago: Loyola University Press, 1984. Remarkably clear, untechnical prose reveals how relevant Dante's theological vision is to our time.

Musa, M., trans. and ed. *The Portable Dante*. New York: Penguin, 2003. Excellent translation and notes for both the *Divine Comedy* and *La vita nuova*.

Williams, C. *The Figure of Beatrice: A Study in Dante*. New York: Boydell & Brewer, 1994. A very personal and moving analysis of Beatrice and how such love is ennobling to all of us.

Notes

1. See the biographical sketch in J. Collins, *Pilgrim in Love: An Introduction to Dante and His Spirituality* (Chicago: Loyola University Press, 1984), 1–16.

2. See C. Williams, *The Figure of Beatrice: A Study in Dante* (New York: Boydell & Brewer, 1994), 154: "The Pope and the Emperor both neglect their offices; the Montagues and Capulets are in wretchedness and fear. . . . *Romeo and Juliet* becomes a little darker, for the play itself—there and for us—is a sudden vignette of that all-Italy upon which Dante is invoking the judgement and pity of God."

3. See Collins, *Pilgrim in Love*, 8–9.

4. L. H. Yearley, "Selves, Virtues, Odd Genres, and Alien Guides: An Approach to Religious Ethics," *Journal of Religious Ethics* 25 (1998): 127–55, esp. (quotation from) 133.

5. Cf. Williams, *Figure of Beatrice*, 131: "Boniface VIII is in hell, but all heaven shudders at the outrage done to his office in his person. The office and function is always to be honoured."

6. See the description of P. Fiorini, "Beatrice, That is, 'On Fidelity,'" trans. M. Hickin, *Communio* 24 (1997): 84–98, esp. 91: "He loved Gemma as his spouse, who bore him children and with whom he experienced, at least for a certain length of time, the peace of family life."

7. Collins, *Pilgrim in Love*, 8.

8. Cf. K. Foster, *The Two Dantes, and Other Studies* (Berkeley: University of California Press, 1977), 36: "Yet the currents of thought that formed this enclave [courtly love] moved from principles which, so far as they were truly rational and human, no Catholic philosopher can allow himself to abjure; for we must believe that all that is authentically human can be brought within the sweep of grace. . . . When all is said, courtly love was an effort to bring sex into harmony with the spirit; it was an aspiration to refinement and, as such, part of that general aspiration towards intellectual, emotional and spiritual refinement which marked the wonderful century in which it was born." See also Fiorini, "Beatrice," 84–86.

9. See I. Brandeis, *The Ladder of Vision: A Study of Dante's Comedy* (Garden City, NY: Doubleday, 1961), 103: "For there is nothing to be gained but falsification and diminishment of Dante's poetry by interpreting Beatrice as an allegorical representation of Theology or Divine Revelation, or any other abstraction of the sort"; Collins, *Pilgrim in Love*, 5, agrees that she is probably historical;

Fiorini, "Beatrice," 90, cautions against "reducing Beatrice to a mere allegory"; and Williams, *Figure of Beatrice*, 101–2, also insists on her "mortal identity." Foster, *Two Dantes*, 51, calls her "quasi-symbolic."

10. L. H. Yearley, "Genre and the Attempt to Render Pride: Dante and Aquinas," *Journal of the American Academy of Religion* 72 (2004): 313–39, esp. 326.

11. Cf. W. Fowlie, "Faith and Narrative in Dante," *Notre Dame English Journal* 15 (1983): 67–76, esp. 71–72: "Tragedy is the literary imitation of an action, written in an elevated style, that ends in disaster. Comedy is written in the common, even coarse, speech of the vernacular, and represents an action that ends happily. Comedy for Dante is thus synonymous with redemption in the Christian sense: the struggle in life that ends happily." See also the fuller discussion of R. Hollander, "Tragedy in Dante's Comedy," *Sewanee Review* 91 (1983): 240–60.

12. On this dynamic, see the comments of P. S. Hawkins, "'What Is Truth?': The Question of Art in Theological Education," *Anglican Theological Review* 76 (1994): 364–74. This does not mean that the *Comedy* is a theological treatise disguised as a poem, but it is a poem with a deeply theological meaning. See the discussions in Brandeis, *Ladder of Vision*, 11–14; R. Hein, "Divine Imagination," *Christian History* 20, no. 2 (2001): 11–16; and Yearley, "Genre and Pride," 313–39.

13. Fiorini, "Beatrice," 98.

14. Yearley, "Alien Guides," 127–28.

15. Cf. Fowlie, "Faith and Narrative," 70, who identifies Dante's "modern awareness of individuality, of 'character as destiny.'"

16. Williams, *Figure of Beatrice*, 177.

17. Dante Alighieri, *The Divine Comedy* (trans. G. L. Bickersteth; Oxford: Blackwell, 1981), *Purgatory* 17.91–92. Cf. Foster, *Two Dantes*, 39: "For Dante, as for St. Augustine and Freud, love was the absolutely central topic. At the heart of his thought, and so of his poetry, is a conception of the soul as appetitive, as *attracted*" (emphasis in original).

18. B. Reynolds, "Dante, Poet of Joy: A Celebration," *Theology* 97 (1994): 265–75, esp. 266, quoting Dorothy Sayers.

19. On the ordering of the sins, see M. Cogan, *The Design in the Wax: The Structure of the Divine Comedy and Its Meaning* (Notre Dame, IN: University of Notre Dame Press, 1999), 1–19; Foster, *Two Dantes*, 5; R. J. Payton, *A Modern Reader's Guide to Dante's Inferno* (New York: P. Lang, 1992), 63; T. K. Swing, *The Fragile Leaves of the Sibyl: Dante's Master Plan* (Westminster, MD: Newman, 1962), 9–13.

20. See Foster, *Two Dantes*, 47: "Thus man as appetitive has a different natural relation to God from man as cognitive. As appetitive we are attached to God directly and from the start."

21. Dante, *Comedy* (trans. Bickersteth), *Inferno* 3.18.

22. Cf. K. Foster, "The Mind in Love: Dante's Philosophy," in *Dante: A Collection of Critical Essays*, ed. J. Freccero (Englewood Cliffs, NJ: Prentice-Hall,

1965), 43–60, esp. 56: "And pulling against this attraction from beauty to order goes the reverse movement of egoistic cupidity, whose symbol is the Siren or the Wolf or money or simply 'earth.' Hence, after Dante's dream of the Siren, half-way up the Mount of Purgatory, sounds the ringing voice of Virgil's imperious reason, the recall to order."

23. Williams, *Figure of Beatrice*, 117.

24. J. M. Deschene, "The Divine Comedy: Dante's Mystical and Sacramental World-View," *Studia Mystica* 4 (1981): 36–46, esp. 42.

25. Yearley, "Alien Guides," 144.

26. See ibid.: "The *Divine Comedy* can be seen as a work that 'demythologizes' the notion of states after death."

27. Although I have yet to find a Dante scholar to support me, I will confide in you my own theory of the final fate of the virtuous non-Christians. When purgatory has fulfilled its function and every repentant sinner has ascended up through it into heaven, it will then be empty. The virtuous non-Christians will be allowed to live in the earthly paradise at its top, for this is where sinless people—Adam and Eve—were meant to live at the beginning.

28. Williams, *Figure of Beatrice*, 105.

29. Ibid., 115, 120.

30. P. S. Hawkins, "Dante: Poet-Theologian," *Princeton Seminary Bulletin* 16 (1995): 327–37, esp. 334.

31. Though it is true that some of these images in the circles of the violent also carry implications of sterility, as observed by Williams, *Figure of Beatrice*, 129–30.

32. Ibid., 114.

33. C. Ryan, "The Theology of Dante," in *The Cambridge Companion to Dante*, ed. R. Jacoff (Cambridge, UK: Cambridge University Press, 1993), 136–52, quotation on 143.

34. Ibid.

35. Hawkins, "Poet-Theologian," 334.

36. Cf. Williams, *Figure of Beatrice*, 121: "A separation from others has become a resentment at others. No one of them is recognizable, nor does Virgil permit Dante the effort."

37. See H. Hatzfeld, "The Art of Dante's *Purgatorio*," in *American Critical Essays on The Divine Comedy*, ed. R. J. Clements (New York: New York University Press, 1967), 64–88, esp. 71–77.

38. Cf. Hawkins, "Poet-Theologian," 336: "Some have dismissed the *Comedy* as an extended grudge against Florence, as if writing well were Dante's best revenge against the city that exiled him."

39. Dante Alighieri, *Inferno*, trans. J. Ciardi (New York: Penguin Books, 1954), 15.82–84.

40. Williams, *Figure of Beatrice*, 131.

41. Cf. Hawkins, "Poet-Theologian," 334–35, "One also begins to imagine human community as it might be, if grace were given the upper hand. Gone are the operatic soloists of *Inferno*—each of them singing his or her life song, but nobody listening to anyone else—and in their place are individuals discovering what it means to be members of a choir, to move in procession as well as to make music together. Communion, in other words, becomes a way of life."

42. Ibid., 335.

43. Reynolds, "Dante, Poet of Joy," 267, quoting Dorothy Sayers.

44. Deschene, "Dante's World-View," 36.

45. Ibid., 38.

46. Brandeis, *Ladder of Vision*, 128.

47. Hawkins, "Poet-Theologian," 331.

48. Cf. Foster, *Two Dantes*, 45: "*Amor* here is *eros* in the wide trans-sexual sense already noted. But as Virgil's discourse develops into the argument about free will, a specific sexual reference is discernible—naturally so, given that Dante was a man of the world before he turned to theology, and a poet of sexual love before he set out to sublimate *amor* into *caritas*." Again, I would stress more continuity and inclusion than sublimation, but all critics are struggling for the right word for what Dante is imaging here.

49. J. A. Mazzeo, "Dante's Conception of Love," in *American Critical Essays on The Divine Comedy*, ed. R. J. Clements (New York: New York University Press, 1967), 140–57, esp.154.

50. Cf. H. Chadwick, *Augustine: A Very Short Introduction* (Oxford: Oxford University Press, 2001), 48: "While the symmetry and proportion of the human body were indeed measurable in mathematical terms, Augustine added, with what may seem to the modern reader extraordinary romanticism, 'Adam did not love Eve because she was beautiful; it was his love which made her beautiful.'"

51. Cf. Williams, *Figure of Beatrice*, 166, who paradoxically calls such stunted love an "Ideal Gratification" that relentlessly pursues earthly delights and then wallows in despair over their imperfection, rather than gratefully enjoying them as God intended.

52. Brandeis, *Ladder of Vision*, 128.

53. Cf. Reynolds, "Dante, Poet of Joy," 270–71, "I am always surprised to recall that Schiller found the *Paradiso* boring; and the reason surprises me still more; because it contained, he alleged, all praise and no blame. This is far from being the case. The higher Dante ascends and the more ecstatic his joy becomes on beholding the perfection of Heaven, the model of what the Kingdom of God could be on earth, the more fiercely he denounces those who betray that ideal."

54. Dante, *Comedy* (trans. Bickersteth), *Paradiso* 9.103–105.

55. Reynolds, "Dante, Poet of Joy," 270. There was a legend that Trajan had been resuscitated and baptized, but this again would seem to reduce Dante's ideas to mere technicalities.

56. Reynolds, "Dante, Poet of Joy," 270. Cf. M. P. O'Connor, "The Universality of Salvation: Christianity, Judaism, and Other Religions in Dante, *Nostra aetate*,

and the New Catechism," *Journal of Ecumenical Studies* 33 (1996): 487–511, who thinks Dante does not believe in the salvation of people of other religions. His analysis is simplistic and incomplete, only quoting *Inferno*.

57. Dante Alighieri, *Inferno*, trans. M. Musa (New York: Penguin Books, 1984), 5.100–106.

58. On her role as representative and not individual, cf. M. Musa, *Advent at the Gates: Dante's Comedy* (Bloomington, IN: Indiana University Press, 1974), 14: "Finally, Virgil has tried to teach him that, among the damned, the individual does not count: the damned are a mass in which individual differences are unimportant blurs."

59. For a detailed analysis of the historical and social context, see T. Barolini, "Dante and Francesca da Rimini: Realpolitik, Romance, Gender," *Speculum* 75 (2000): 1–28.

60. Yearley, "Alien Guides," 142; cf. Musa, *Advent at the Gates*, 1, 14–15: "As a result, they may attribute to the latter, to the artist-theologian, certain all-too-human attitudes that could only belong to the weak, confused, inexperienced Pilgrim. . . . It is obvious that he has learned nothing that he should have. His mood toward Francesca is that of tenderness and compassion for her fate, and sympathetic association with her feelings—an expansive, one might almost say, self-indulgent pity to which he has subjected his reason."

61. Brandeis, *Ladder of Vision*, 23.

62. Ibid., 28, adding that her words "suggest in Francesca a rather quick compliancy. And this compliancy is the very nature of the soul that goes by her name, and the root of her sin."

63. Musa, *Advent at the Gates*, 1, 19.

64. Yearley, "Alien Guides," 143.

65. Cf. Musa, *Advent at the Gates*, 22: "That the caressing words that open her address are inspired by gratitude for his expression of compassion, and for the invitation he extended to the lovers, already suggests, if only slightly, her hunger for appreciation, her pleasure at having been singled out for consideration from among the many others flying there. . . . Again, as evidence of her graciousness, I have already mentioned her readiness to comply with the Pilgrim's invitation, . . . her words flowing forth so freely. But surely this flow, this effusiveness is slightly ridiculous."

66. The wonderful identification made by Musa, *Advent at the Gates*, 35: "Is not Francesca Eve? And not content with having seduced Paolo in the flesh, this *figura Evae* has attempted successfully to seduce the Pilgrim, who is Everyman, into committing not the sin of lust itself but what has been defined as the essence of Lust: the subjection of reason to emotion."

67. See ibid., 27–29; R. Poggioli, "Paolo and Francesca," in *Dante: A Collection of Critical Essays*, ed. J. Freccero (Englewood Cliffs, NJ: Prentice-Hall, 1965), 61–77, esp. 71.

68. Yearley, "Alien Guides," 143; cf. the more charitable evaluation of Musa, *Advent at the Gates*, 28: "Perhaps Francesca, like so many persons concerned with

their own prestige, has developed the ability to remember past events in a way that redounds to her credit."

69. Collins, *Pilgrim in Love*, 93. Though his analysis of the episode is as insightful and eloquent as elsewhere, it contains two minor factual errors: Francesca was not guilty of just one indiscretion with her brother-in-law—the affair apparently went on for years, and her husband was not yet dead at the time the poem is supposed to take place.

70. Cf. Musa, *Advent at the Gates*, 30: "We have already seen that Francesca in her two confessions takes every means possible to excuse her sin by presenting it as caused by forces beyond her control, and of course we could not possibly have expected to find in her words any indication of repentance."

71. Cf. Brandeis, *Ladder of Vision*, 31–32: "What hurts Francesca in Hell is not an external tempest, but the inner tumult of her painful choice, the storm of sensual desire closed in upon itself, . . . the storm of remorse turned inside out: not for her sin against life, but for the only things she knows how to feel concern with—her own death, Paolo's death, and the ending of the embrace. . . . That *amor* of which Francesca says 'even now it leaves me not,' has become through their living embrace utterly barren"; Musa, *Advent at the Gates*, 32: "In the first place eternal togetherness in itself is not necessarily a cause for exultation, it may also be the cause of deepest anguish. . . . And how could it make Francesca happy—or, rather, how could it alleviate her suffering—to know herself never to be free of the naked body of her dead lover, this constant reminder of passion spent, of the sin that condemned them, of shameful exposure and death? Rather, their inseparability may well be the bitterest aspect of their punishment."

72. Yearley, "Alien Guides," 144.

73. Cf. Musa, *Advent at the Gates*, 34: "But it was not for vanity, or emptiness, or phoniness, or any other flaw in her personality that Francesca was condemned to Hell; she was condemned to the Second Circle for her lust."

74. Cf. Brandeis, *Ladder of Vision*, 33: "Facing Francesca, he is aware of no fault whatsoever in her, except possibly the technical one of the adultery."

75. Cf. Barolini, "Dante and Francesca," 9: "Francesca's passivity is a function—as also etymologically—of her passion; her passivity reflects her sinful refusal of moral agency"; Musa, *Advent at the Gates*, 25: "At each step she presents herself as the victim of an irresistible force."

76. See the perceptive counterpoint made by Brandeis, *Ladder of Vision*, 28: "Some readers may not accept this association of compliancy with sin. Says F. De Sanctis, speaking of Francesca: 'The poetry of womanhood lies in being conquered.' Such a view, however popular, cannot be found in Dante." Poggioli, "Paolo and Francesca," 75, also attacks De Sanctis's reading as making the episode merely sentimental and pathetic.

77. See the discussions in Brandeis, *Ladder of Vision*, 25–26; Musa, *Advent at the Gates*, 16–17; L. Ryan, "Stornei, Gru, Colombe: The Bird Images in *Inferno* V," *Dante Studies* 94 (1976): 25–45.

78. C. Williams, *Outlines of Romantic Theology*, ed. A. M. Hadfield (Grand Rapids: Eerdmans, 1990), 100.

79. Yearley, "Alien Guides," 143.

80. Brandeis, *Ladder of Vision*, 29.

81. Ibid., 30.

82. Cf. ibid., 27: "Since not all, even of these, died as a consequence of love, we must assume that the poet meant that the life of each was spoiled by love— love always as desire dominant over reason. The implication is that love, pitted against reason, inevitably destroys."

83. Yearley, "Alien Guides," 143. Cf. Deschene, "Dante's World-View," 42: "Her love, however, has never learned the importance of the Other."

84. Fiorini, "Beatrice," 88.

85. Collins, *Pilgrim in Love*, 93.

86. Brandeis, *Ladder of Vision*, 26, quoting M. Casella.

87. See Fiorini, "Beatrice," 88: "Francesca does not mention her lover by name"; Musa, *Advent at the Gates*, 32: "She never turns to him, even for a brief moment, to address him. . . . She does not call him by his name or by any endearing term"; Yearley, "Alien Guides," 143: "Francesca refers to Paolo never by name but always as an object."

88. Cf. Deschene, "Dante's World-View," 42: "For Francesca, Hell is to love and yet to be wholly incapable, by a radical refusal, of moving toward the Other or the one loved. Even in Hell, God is present, but the place is Hell precisely because His love is not accepted on its own terms."

89. Dante Alighieri, *Purgatorio*, trans. J. Ciardi (New York: Penguin Books, 1957), 18.55–60.

90. This observation is often made, as in Collins, *Pilgrim in Love*, 146: "It is literally the mid-point in the soul's ascent of the mountain and the mathematical center of Purgatory and of the whole *Comedy*. . . . Cantos XVII and XVIII contain Virgil's discourse on the nature of love, the central theme of the *Comedy*"; Foster, *Two Dantes*, 39: "It is no accident that the numerically central cantos of the *Comedy*, *Purgatorio* 17–18, contain Virgil's discourses on love"; Mazzeo, "Dante's Conception of Love," 149: "The main discourse on love is elaborated in the *Purgatorio* (XVI–XVIII) at the very center of the *Divine Comedy*. It is at the center because love itself is the 'central' revealer of the universe, it is the heart of things in both the actual universe and the universe of the poem."

91. Deschene, "Dante's World-View," 41.

92. Cf. Foster, *Two Dantes*, 50: "The gist of the sonnet, stripped of its grand imagery, is that the poet knows by long experience that reason is powerless against love, that where love is at work free will is extinguished and all deliberation useless."

93. Collins, *Pilgrim in Love*, 148.

94. Mazzeo, "Dante's Conception of Love," 144.

95. Foster, *Two Dantes*, 50, who continues: "The best and briefest way to bring out his mature critique of this fatalism is to contrast the denial of free will

contained in that sonnet with the assertion of it in the central discourse of *Purgatorio* already in part analyzed. For in effect the latter text recants the former." See also Fiorini, "Beatrice," 88: "But likewise Francesca's rhetoric is none other than Dante's own. . . . It is not simply a rhetorical expedient in order to change the argument and move on, it is the . . . physical perception that such an evil belongs not to another, but is his own; and that grace alone, and not his own merits, has preserved him from it."

96. Yearley, "Alien Guides," 138: "Mencius [Confucian writer, 4th century B.C.E.] and Dante share, that is, the connected beliefs that we usually are strangers to ourselves. . . . They also think, however, that capacities and powers are present that can aid us."

97. Foster, *Two Dantes*, 48.

98. Foster, "Mind in Love," 56.

99. Williams, *Outlines of Romantic Theology*, 101.

100. Foster, *Two Dantes*, 54.

101. Cf. ibid., 41: "The 'primary desire' is not within our control because we cannot deliberate about it. What we do deliberate about is our appetitive reactions and responses to particular experiences precisely as such."

102. Yearley, "Genre and Pride," 333.

103. Williams, *Outlines of Romantic Theology*, 111.

104. Cf. Fiorini, "Beatrice," 88–89, "Desire-love (eros) is now called to go beyond itself, precisely in order to be faithful to the beloved; it is a call to self-denial in order to continue in being, not 'dialectically,' however, but 'theologically,' in an experience of crucifixion which is the surrender of the beloved into the arms of a destiny which only faith (rediscovered or, at last, experienced) can see as love (agape)."

105. Dante Alighieri, *Paradise*, trans. M. Musa (New York: Penguin Books, 1986), 26.64–66.

106. Cf. Fiorini, "Beatrice," 88: "Taken away from before his mortal gaze, Beatrice is now in 'high heaven' wherein she was from all eternity 'beloved.'"

4

FLANNERY O'CONNOR
The Kingdom Comes with Violence

Introduction

Flannery O'Connor (1925–64) was born in Savannah, Georgia, a devout Catholic in a predominantly Protestant South. After a brief period in Iowa, New York, and Connecticut, she returned to Georgia in 1950 and lived there until her death, an intellectual isolated on a rural dairy farm, a locale that nonetheless proved to foster and focus her religious and literary genius.[1] O'Connor suffered her whole adult life from lupus, until it killed her, as it had her father. Both apparently suffered this affliction with uncommon patience and dignity,[2] making their suffering into an occasion for meaning and strength: "And though the vicissitudes of her own life might well have made her bitter, she did not seem to be so. . . . She seemed rather to have turned on her own life the same searching glare she gave the world in her fiction, found what was good, what was bad, and accepted it all as reality."[3] The experience of her father's death clearly seems to have influenced O'Connor's fiction, for she populates her stories almost exclusively with mothers,[4] but not fathers, as though the latter relation is "sacrosanct."[5] His long suffering and death may have influenced her theology as well: though for most of us, God the Father summons up images of authority and power, O'Connor's main associations with God are mystery, love, persistence, and suffering, all qualities usually associated with the other persons of the Trinity.[6] Such qualities may have been easier for her to associate with a father figure, based on her own painful but revelatory experience.

In her evaluation of her non-Catholic neighbors (and her irreverent, often unappreciated use of them as material for her stories), she showed a similar graciousness in turning challenges into opportunities for enlightenment and spiritual improvement. "There was nothing narrow or sectarian about her."[7] "She wanted her stories to transcend religious boundaries, to transcend even regional and social boundaries."[8] Where lesser souls would have felt either persecuted or bigoted, O'Connor instead saw in southern Protestants an imperfect but salutary counter-balance to the evils of modern society, and thought that Catholics should have as a goal the "reclaiming from the biblically rooted Protestant South the twin antidotes of existentially grounded faith and religious passion."[9] Although adamantly and unapologetically Catholic throughout her life, she saw both branches of Western Christianity as locked in an urgent battle "against the well-intentioned unbelievers, the liberals, the educated, the social workers and teachers, who even in their effeteness cause such havoc in her tales."[10]

In her disease, her ecumenism, her religion, and of course in her writing, there is the deepest appreciation and reverence for human and divine immediacy and sacredness. And this sacredness cannot be taught; it must be experienced in its immediacy. She saw her fiction as her particular spiritual gift for helping others to achieve this experience: "Like *zen koans* [paradoxical stories from the Buddhist tradition], O'Connor's works exist not so much to be answers as to be experienced in their peculiarity."[11] Her stories "invite the reader to experience one's own moment of radical unknowing."[12] Or as O'Connor would describe her stories, they are "an experience, not an abstraction."[13] And this woman wrote with such breathtaking power that the moments of grace in her stories are nearly as powerful and ineffable to her readers as those we experience in our own lives, haunting us and making us smile or cringe years after first reading them.

But as hopeful and faithful as she was, O'Connor's work is deeply suffused with the horror, power, and inescapability of sin. Here again was something that she felt her Protestant neighbors intuited more deeply than her fellow Catholics: "O'Connor felt that the doctrine of Original Sin had been overlooked by contemporary Catholics, but not

by the Southern Baptists she lived among."[14] She depicts sin so graphically that first-time readers of her stories are often put off by their violence, brutality, depravity, and grotesquery. But O'Connor's fictional
world is never unrealistic or unbelievable, and to dismiss it as such
reveals our own naïveté: "Realistic fiction only appears 'grotesque' to the
modern eye. . . . This is because our 'vision' of human society is con-
strued wholly from fantasies and wishful thinking about human motive
and behavior."[15] Nor is her grotesquerie ever gratuitous, as is so much of
violence and ugliness in other modern culture. While others seek
merely to shock, O'Connor's writing seeks to shock people into seeing
an uncomfortable theological truth—the reality and power of sin in
their own lives: "What is surprising in O'Connor's stories is how she
upends and indicts . . . the trivialization of violence, . . . to restore to a
largely jaded audience the capacity for shock and with that, the possibility of recognizing evil, our involvement in it, and our need for redemption."[16] And sometimes in her stories, grotesquerie and violence need not
be ugly and sinful, but only unexpected, an unusual occurrence from
which to gain insight, not to look away from: "For O'Connor, faith pro-
ceeds from a recognition of what was already there; hers is a sacramental vision. Acquiring the eyes of faith is not a matter of discovering a
new secret level of existence, but of discerning the true nature of this
life."[17] The unexpected within the ordinary is a fundamental part of
Jesus' parables, and O'Connor seems to have used it in a similar way,
making her tales of bizarre individuals into parables of universal applicability.[18] All the ugly or unexpected things and people in her stories are
utterly realistic, dramatically necessary, and theologically revealing.[19]

O'Connor's work provides a fitting conclusion to our reflections on
both sin and redemption. We started with the unfamiliar worlds of
ancient Israel and Rome. Now O'Connor's stories move us into the
familiar but strange world of modern American Christianity, a world
that confronts our faith with new challenges: atheism, individualism,
alienation, materialism, consumerism, secularism, relativism, a complete loss of the sense of the sacred and the transcendent, even ration-
ality and objectivity taken to their extremes. O'Connor saw all these
worldviews as essentially idolatrous, almost hellish: "There is no common cause to be made, O'Connor discovered, with a culture bent on the
denial of transcendent grace and judgment."[20] They are all different
worldviews ultimately derived from the sinful feeling of self-sufficiency

that has grown to monstrous proportions in the modern world. It is a "royal consciousness"[21] that impotently usurps God's power, a "Promethean willfulness"[22] that rebels and steals from God, but that finally turns out to be the "most ludicrous aspect of our fall from grace, to wit, our persisting and sentimental refusal ever to acknowledge that we had [fallen]."[23] O'Connor saw these sinful worldviews as so pervasive that they were not only manifested overtly in atheism, but also implicitly even in most Christians. "In fact, she traces world views equally crippled by belief or disbelief. For . . . the same claustrophobic fatalism circumscribes the creeds of both her agnostics and Christians."[24]

Her calling as a writer and a Christian was therefore to help her readers break free of these worldviews and this sin, calling them to a real experience of religion. "Her business as a writer, then, was to 'pulverize' the idolatrous minds of her characters and readers through force. If she could not entirely restructure the modern idolatrous mind, she would at least open it to new ways of seeing by shattering the many false hierarchies her culture had given itself over to."[25] Her mission was a prophetic one,[26] and specifically that of an apocalyptic prophet. Like John the Baptist, who proclaimed, "Repent, for the kingdom of heaven has come near" (Matt 3:2), O'Connor "wants to stun her readers into an apocalyptic recognition of how late the hour is."[27] She believed that "the duty of the prophet is . . . to reveal to arrogant oblivious listeners their fallen state."[28] And this mission was not only personal and spiritual, but also social and political, "a one-woman war against the age's moral blindness,"[29] "a pervasive critique of religious, economic, and social structures."[30] This prophetic calling also further explains her use of the grotesque, violent, and unexpected, telling people things they have no interest or willingness to hear. "If any writer is to fulfil a prophetic office he will accentuate the violent and grotesque, having learnt that his own society seldom looks into a mirror."[31] In the beauty, horror, and profundity of her work, most of her readers would say that she fulfilled this prophetic mission with a personal courage and a God-given grace as powerful and effective as they are rare.

I have chosen to analyze two closely related sins in O'Connor's stories—self-deception and self-righteousness. They should not be taken at all as mutually exclusive, for these two bad qualities are very similar and often coincide in her characters and in ourselves: self-righteousness is a false and falsifying evaluation of ourselves, and self-deception is usually in the direction of overestimating our own goodness and righteousness. But what I think makes the distinction useful is when we consider the salvific or life-giving alternatives to these sins. When we are primarily self-deceived, what we really need is to learn the truth about ourselves. The problem is mostly one of understanding and knowledge, and we need a revelation that leads us out of the ignorance and falsehood in which we have lost ourselves. But self-righteousness seems more willful and emotional than intellectual. It is an attitude that one feels rather than thinks, and the terms closely related to it are even more explicitly about feeling—smugness, complacency, arrogance, disdain. So the solution to self-righteousness is not new knowledge: we cannot be shown or convinced that we are not righteous on our own, but we must come to know it in the ancient sense of an intimate, powerful experience within us. And O'Connor shows us how this antidote to self-righteousness comes through unexpected, unprepared-for experiences of God's grace, when he puts into the hearts of her characters an overwhelming appreciation of their sinfulness, together with a passionate longing for his loving, forgiving presence. O'Connor shows how revelation and grace clear our self-deluded minds to know him, break our stubborn and proud spirits to follow him, and free our wounded and enslaved hearts to love him.

Self-Deception and Revelation

O'Connor was masterful at depicting self-deception in all its ugliness. She also knew the urgency of unmasking this power: "O'Connor was preoccupied with the delusions we adopt to avoid reality.... Reality, for O'Connor, meant acceptance of the self as given.... An admission of one's limitations is a sense of one's dependence upon God."[32] As seen in Dante and in O'Connor's stories, as well as in figures from popular culture like Hannibal Lechter in *Silence of the Lambs* or the killer in the movie *Seven*, even in the most complete and sadistic evil there can be some integrity, something whole and honest: there is still some sense of a self behind the evil, blinded and locked in by it, but still there, maybe even still struggling to get out. But to deceive oneself is to give up integrity and honesty at the deepest level, letting sin and deceit into one's innermost self and utterly surrendering to and identifying with them. Dante showed this by categorizing deceit as the worst sin; it is to lose oneself more completely than any outwardly directed sin or crime ever could. If God is all goodness, truth, and beauty, then the complete alienation from God would not just be total evil; it would also be inescapable, undetectable deceit and nauseating ugliness.

But as dire as this sin is, it also seems to be one of the most pervasive, ubiquitous as it is destructive at every level of society, from those who lead lives of quiet desperation at the bottom of the economic pyramid, to kings and emperors with their delusions about new clothes and so many other foolish things.[33] As the story of the emperor's new clothes shows, self-deception is among the funniest of sins, that the grotesque beings we turn ourselves into bring a certain uneasy laughter, usually first at others, then more importantly and helpfully at our own expense. With her caustic and self-deprecating wit, O'Connor frequently used this grotesque humor to great effect, and she is said to have laughed uncontrollably whenever she read her stories out loud, with their ridiculous (but utterly believable) characters.[34] This laughter helps point us to human inadequacy and sinfulness. "The very concept of the grotesque, which implies not only horror but a certain grim humor, seemed for her rooted in a realization not only of man's presumption but also of his sheer *folly* in trying to live on any terms but God's. Man is, finally, not only sinful but just plain silly."[35] It is much the same perspective that moved medieval architects to put such ugly but humorous gargoyles on their cathedrals, or Dante to make the demons in the eighth circle of hell so slapstick. O'Connor's stories are full of such menacing but laughable, gargoyle-like people, staggering through their sinful antics.

Part of the essence of self-deception is taking ourselves far too seriously. When a mirror is held up to our self-importance and unmasks it, there is first disgust at how we have wasted our lives and hurt others. But then the laughter cannot help but break forth at how foolish we have been, what a grand and silly joke we have played on ourselves for so long. "Furthermore, the grotesque's ultimate purpose is therapeutic: it is comic shock treatment. Even at its most menacing, it seeks to liberate."[36] It is laughter filled both with grateful joy and regretful relief that our delusion is now beginning to be over. O'Connor even used this grotesque but therapeutic humor on herself; some of her ugliest, most unlikable characters are self-deprecating parodies of herself.[37] She could even laugh at the intense pain that her lupus caused her, spurning either bland, Christian pieties or heroic, Stoic endurance. Instead, she portrayed a laughing acceptance that could put sickness and death—two of the more debilitating offsprings of sin—in their place as fleeting but nonetheless horribly real experiences of human life.[38]

But O'Connor's steadfast realism demanded that revelatory moments often come too late—not too late in an ultimate sense, for any revelation is surely better late than never, but too late for the person to change his or her life and live happily ever after. This is the essence of tragedy, where the scene of recognition or revelation is constitutive of the tragedy, as is the fact that it comes too late to save the characters from their doom. And this is also the almost unbroken pattern of O'Connor's stories, where most of her characters clearly see the light of truth in the penultimate paragraph, and are usually brutally killed in the last paragraph.[39] While this may seem unduly depressing to some, the sudden violence in her stories is just as realistic and completely nongratuitous as the other grotesquerie. First, it is an accurate depiction of human nature, showing that we are more likely to ask for and receive God's grace in moments of crisis and shock, as O'Connor observed: "Some kind of loss is usually necessary to turn the mind toward faith. If you're satisfied with what you've got, you're hardly going to look for anything better."[40] The violence in O'Connor's stories is never meaningless and random. It is always part of "ultimate conflicts—sin vs. salvation, faith vs. unbelief, grace vs. condemnation, life vs. death,"[41] conflicts in which we painfully find the meaning of our lives, conflicts that change us for the better. "Grace is about change and change is painful, causing disorientation and a letting go of the darkness of sin."[42]

Further, O'Connor's violence is an urgent reminder to remain receptive to revelation and grace. The violence in O'Connor's stories usually explodes when someone resists God's grace and stubbornly lashes out at those who bear this unwelcome challenge. "Thus, caught in a fundamental misrelation to their true being, they experience grace as a threat, a violence to the self, and they resist."[43] We are so used to sin that we would rather kill or be killed than give it up for God's unexpected grace, and it is this addiction to sin that O'Connor warns us of, not the violence that it entails. O'Connor even believes that God often uses such violence to break down our resistance to him.[44] Evil is not—as my students often assert—ultimately necessary for the existence of good, but in our fallen state, the experience of evil is often necessary for our understanding of good. Evil does not have an ultimate existence, but it

does have educational value: O'Connor insisted on "the epistemologi-
cal role of evil . . . as a means to attain self-knowledge."[45] God is in no
way reliant on violence and evil, but our fallenness makes *us* reliant on
them in order to fulfill God's saving purpose for us.

Perhaps the most loathsome and humorous of O'Connor's self-
deceived characters is General Tennessee Flintrock Sash in "A Late
Encounter with the Enemy."[46] He is a 104-year-old Confederate veteran
of the Civil War. Everything about him is false: his name, rank, and uniform were all bestowed on him twelve years before the story as part of
the publicity surrounding the premiere of a Civil War movie (an obvious parody of *Gone with the Wind*). But he finds these Hollywood trappings so much more grand and impressive than reality that he readily
and eagerly believes in them. But the posturing has an unexpected outcome, for the trappings now define and own him, tormenting him more
than his physical ailments, and bringing him as much pain as satisfaction in his life. He is dressed in his fake uniform and carted to a museum
each year in his wheelchair for people to look at, the way they look at
other dead and decaying objects from the past. The action of the story
takes place at a similar outing, where the General is wheeled onstage at
his granddaughter's college graduation and dies there of a stroke.

But as breathtakingly vain as he is, these outings really don't satisfy
him at all, for they are just more annoying intrusions of mundane reality into his fantasy of glamour and beauty. In his daily interactions with
people, he can only "snarl" or curse at them; at best, he tells them about
the premiere of the movie, not about the actual war itself. With the
character of the General, O'Connor deftly shows how self-deception
goes hand in hand with complete alienation and loneliness. One cannot
love or be loved unless one is real and has something real to offer. And
even or especially if the something real is a meager and wounded self,
it's better than the dead, static phantoms into which we try to make
ourselves—physically, mentally, or spiritually sculpting ourselves into
the image we want to project, not the fallen image we must accept.
But whereas most of us let our vanity go unbridled only at irregular
intervals—in the gym, or the classroom, or the pulpit, depending on
one's inclination—the General lives in this self-imposed hell of vanity
every minute of every day.

Even though his life is hardly worth living because of his vanity, this
vanity brings with it an odd sense of immortality or invincibility.

Despite his age and ailments, the General has no concept of death. He not only doesn't think of it, he also apparently *cannot* think of it, and never has. Having made himself into an animate corpse, he has given himself a painfully immortal, wraith-like existence. The fear of death is an ironically salutary thing for most of us, and the General's lack of it is another way he has cut himself off from others, and anesthetized himself from our common, human pain, without removing the source of that pain.

But the "enemy" of the story's title is not death, even though the General's vision of the truth is fatal.[47] His real enemy is not the death that is in the future and that is coming to meet him in the present. Though we might think that someone at his age would live in the past, the opposite is true: he has no more concept or recollection of the past than he has of death. As he sits on stage, dying, it is his past, which he has falsified and obliterated, that slowly consumes him. This is the real enemy that he has avoided for so long and to whom he must now surrender. But, of course, one's past shouldn't be one's enemy: the General has made his past into a torment by his falsification of it. If he had held on to his real memories of the Civil War and of his whole life—good and bad, pleasant and painful, noble and base—then he might have gotten some satisfaction in the intervening years from sharing these with others, even some satisfaction from brooding about them alone, if it came to that. Instead, he has relied on the manufactured and packaged memories of his fake sword and uniform, and these are as dead and unsatisfying as they are false. As with most of the epiphanies that O'Connor grants to her doomed characters, it is not clear what the General makes of his final vision, whether he accepts it or rejects it with his last gasp. But it is clear that the truth does finally overwhelm him when he sees his wife, son, and mother, whose memories he had betrayed and denied for so long. Whether or not the General is saved, such a truthful vision of the past, together with all the confusion it painfully dredges up within us, is the absolutely necessary prelude for anyone to be saved. It is "a moment of unknowing, . . . a sense of infinite openness, confusion, . . . that functions as a pre-evangelical moment."[48] All of us frantically run from our pasts, and the General shows us how futile and self-destructive this race is, and what a salvific victory it will be when we finally let ourselves lose it, losing our vain, false selves and winning back our loves and our lives in truth.

Much more appealing than the General, there is Mrs. May in the story "Greenleaf." She is more appealing because her self-deception is not so comical and overt as the General's, and because she is obsessed with hard work and self-reliance, qualities that are generally considered good. O'Connor frequently writes of women characters who have these qualities in abundance, not for typically feminist reasons of showing that women are as strong as men, but for the theological purpose of showing that women are as sinful as men, and just as likely to take such virtues to sinful extremes.[49] The target of O'Connor's prophetic harangue is not patriarchy, but modernity, "the contemporary cult of the self, rather than any disadvantage within the dynamics of this process unique to women."[50]

Mrs. May has run a farm and raised two sons by herself for fifteen years after her husband died. Her children are among O'Connor's most obnoxious characters, unbelievably rude and nasty to their mother, vicious and violent to each other. In a way opposite to the General, Mrs. May lives in a fantasized future, imagining indignities that will be perpetrated against her in the future and envying people for things that they have not yet gotten. In fits of self-pity, she scolds her sons with the prospect that they'll appreciate her when she is dead, while inside she thinks to herself that she will die only when she decides to do so. Again, a strange sense of immortality, or denial of mortality, goes hand in hand with a sick, sinful dissatisfaction, sadness, and anger at real, mortal life.

Mrs. May's special kind of self-deception is in her evaluation of her own goodness, and her comparison of it with the lack of goodness she sees so clearly displayed in others. The particular focus of her judgment and fantasies of persecution are her tenant farmers, the Greenleafs. Mr. Greenleaf does her bidding, if not enthusiastically or efficiently, at least obediently, and she therefore regards him as not so bad. The ugly falseness of her evaluation of others is shown in how it usually relates back to her. If not nearly as vain as the General, Mrs. May's particular kind of narcissism expresses itself as valuing, owning, and judging others based on their relation to her. "Creation exists as so many objects to which she affixes the possessive *her*. . . . The world and its freeloading inhabitants stand guilty before her."[51]

But it is Mrs. Greenleaf who most offends and disgusts Mrs. May, not because Mrs. Greenleaf really does anything to Mrs. May, but just because of who she is and how she lives, which Mrs. May simply cannot understand or tolerate. Mrs. May values "respect" for religion (without believing or practicing any of it) and, of much more importance, she values propriety and cleanliness above all. Therefore, religion is only important to her insofar as it promotes these values; it is only "a mark of social decency."[52] But Mrs. Greenleaf has a totally different set of values: Neither she nor her children are especially clean (though one always has to figure in Mrs. May's exaggeration and imagination; when she meets Mrs. Greenleaf's grandchildren, even she has to admit that they're not as dirty as she expected). They practice the dirty (but not immoral) habit of dipping snuff. Most scandalous of all, Mrs. Greenleaf worships God in a most unusual, but sincere and heartfelt way. Every day, she cuts out all the articles in the newspaper that are about pain and injustice—rapes, prison escapes, children being burned, trains and planes crashing, movie stars getting divorced—and buries them in a hole in the ground. Over that hole she then flings herself, praying and writhing ecstatically for the people's healing. At first seemingly random, her choice of articles seems quite deliberate. It includes both the fatal and the trivial, acts of moral depravity as well as natural disasters, and includes all ages, genders, and social classes. In her own way, Mrs. Greenleaf knows that pain is the common lot of all people, and all pain—even the seemingly frivolous and fleeting discomfort of Hollywood starlets—demands our attention and calls us to feel it and alleviate it in any way we can.[53] As strange as it may seem to Mrs. May (or us), Mrs. Greenleaf feels real and total compassion, loving and suffering in a most Christlike way as she takes on his suffering and the suffering of all people. "With raw abandon this woman tries to love as Jesus loved by hurling herself deep into his misery."[54] "She loves by assuming the affliction of each victim."[55] This is what Mrs. May cannot understand or accept. Even more than her judgmental feelings of superiority, it is her complete inability to appreciate compassion—let alone feel it— that makes her ugly, sinful, and utterly miserable. It is hard, painful, but exuberantly enlivening to feel compassion; it is hard, painful, and depressingly deadening not to feel it. Feeling pain lets you know you're alive, and it can give meaning to your life.

But the action of the story only indirectly involves the Greenleafs. It is a bull belonging to their sons that conflicts with Mrs. May. The bull has broken out of its field and is now impregnating Mrs. May's cows, threatening to dilute the stock with his supposedly inferior genes.

Predictably, the staid and orderly Mrs. May cannot tolerate this. She asks Mr. Greenleaf to take care of it, but he doesn't move quickly enough. She then goes to ask his sons to capture the bull, but they are nowhere to be found. Finally, she takes Mr. Greenleaf with her in her car and demands that he shoot the bull. However, as Mr. Greenleaf walks off in search of the animal, Mrs. May is left alone in a field. The bull happens upon her, charges, and gores her to death. Only then does Mr. Greenleaf belatedly shoot the bull and kill it.

As usual with O'Connor, the violence is as comical as it is shocking, but I think this story is meant to do more than shock or amuse. O'Connor herself labored long on the ending of this story and felt that she finally got it right.[56] She makes it clear that Mrs. May sees something in her final moment, just like the General. "She had the look of a person whose sight has been suddenly restored but who finds the light unbearable," and she slumps over the bull, as if she were "whispering some last discovery into the animal's ear."[57] As with the General, it is unclear whether or not Mrs. May accepts this new knowledge or rejects it,[58] but there is no question that something is revealed to her.

The content of her revelation is more ambiguous than the General's, but it can be found by looking back over the story. O'Connor specifies that when the bull gores Mrs. May, his one horn encircles her in an embrace while the other pierces her heart. On the one hand, it would be hard to miss the sexual images of the whole story and of the ending in particular. The bull and the Greenleafs clearly represent an earthy power of fertility and virility before which the lonely and repressed Mrs. May is powerless. But the sexual imagery is not just to show the hollowness of Mrs. May's prudishness. Mrs. May needs, and the bull offers, something much more than just sexual, orgasmic ecstasy. Rather, Mrs. May's demise and her revelation show how intertwined are love, sexuality, suffering, death, and God.[59] This powerful and intertwined spiritual combination was invoked earlier in the story when Mrs. Greenleaf, writhing and groaning facedown on the ground on top of her newspaper clippings, shrieked, "Oh Jesus, stab me in the heart!"[60] Mrs. Greenleaf loves everyone and takes on their sufferings. She erotically revels in this loving agony, and she gives herself over to the awesome love of God that demands one's entire being, even as God offers himself in complete sacrifice. This powerful daily experience of God's love and sacrifice—even while rolling in the dirt of human misery—has lifted up

Mrs. Greenleaf and made her alive, fertile, joyous, and grateful: "Mrs. Greenleaf's heart and body are life-giving because she is pain-embracing."[61] Mrs. May, on the other hand, has selfishly exaggerated her own suffering, while ignoring God, Jesus, sexuality, other people, and their suffering. And while this may seem like the safer or more prudent life, it brings her only sadness and emptiness. When the bull brings all these unfamiliar experiences crashing into her unprepared body and soul at the end, it is fatal. We will inevitably love and suffer for others: our only choice is whether we do so willingly and joyfully, thriving in our joys and afflictions like Mrs. Greenleaf, or whether we do so grudgingly and resentfully, dying slowly and then suddenly in our miseries like Mrs. May.

Finally, let us consider a story in which what is revealed to the character is much less ambiguous, O'Connor's story "Revelation." It is one of O'Connor's last stories, written during her final months of pain and weakness, when she still unbelievably found the energy to write, and when her stories took a decidedly more hopeful turn. In these final stories she gives her characters their closest encounters with God, even as O'Connor knew and rejoiced that she herself would be meeting him soon.[62] The protagonist of "Revelation" is Ruby Turpin, a large, hardworking, generous, good-natured woman, happily married and much more cheerful and outgoing than Mrs. May. While she does not indulge in Mrs. May's self-pity, in many ways she is quite similar to Mrs. May, sharing her intense love of judging others while feeling good about herself and her own virtues. But Mrs. Turpin's judgment is much more complex, because it is more objective (it is not therefore more accurate, but definitely more complex). While Mrs. May really only has two categories of people—herself (victim), and everyone else (victimizers)[63]— and her judgments are totally subjective, Mrs. Turpin makes judgments about individuals into categorizations of the whole human race. She does so with scholastic fervor, building a complex system of human worth with many categories and criteria. When not judging those immediately around her, Mrs. Turpin daydreams about all the people she knows, and where they would fall in a hierarchy that is based on race, class, wealth, manners, and hygiene. This is even how she sometimes puts herself to sleep at night, considering all the subcategories of people until she falls asleep.

As ridiculous as this nightly exercise is, it nevertheless contains the imperfect shadows of truth that will allow Mrs. Turpin to receive a complete and nonfatal revelation at the end of the story. As flawed as her judgments are, her powers of observation are acute, just misdirected: "Ruby's intuitive powers prove to be her redeeming quality."[64] First, it is significant that, unlike Mrs. May, Mrs. Turpin does not put herself at the top of the hierarchy she is building, but squarely in the middle. In Mrs. Turpin's mind, there is a strange, imperfect sense of humility: her judgment of herself and others is terribly wrong because it is based on faulty, meaningless criteria, but not because it is motivated by the sin of pride. Second, the very complexity of her system sows in Mrs. Turpin the self-doubt that is so necessary to overcoming self-deception and the addiction to judging others. When judging people right in front of her, Mrs. Turpin relies on only one criterion—she looks at their shoes—and this makes her judgments as simple, sure, and irrevocable as the persecution fantasies of Mrs. May. But in her nightly categorizations, Mrs. Turpin confuses herself with conflicting criteria and overlapping categories—rich people with no manners, poor people who come from good families that used to be rich, and (most confusing of all to her) black people who have money. Thus, rather than smugly reassuring herself of her own worth and the accuracy of her evaluations, Mrs. Turpin's musings make her question her own place and the placement of others. The confusing complexity of her hierarchy even makes her doubt the project of constructing a hierarchy at all, for each night's categorization ends with all the people being jumbled together and killed, the common fate of all humans, the great leveler of all distinctions. As imperfect as her virtues are, Mrs. Turpin has humility, self-doubt, consciousness of mortality, and intuition of the equality that mortality implies. She has enough of these virtues that we could expect, even early in the story, that she, unlike most of O'Connor's protagonists, could learn and improve without being destroyed in the process.

The action of the story takes place in two movements. First, we find Ruby and her husband in a crowded doctor's waiting room. Mrs. Turpin goes through her usual process of sizing up everyone based on their footwear, most of them falling into the "white trash" or "common" categories. Ruby deems only one well-dressed woman worthy of conversation with her. Mrs. Turpin and the woman talk politely (by their standards), laughing at racist remarks and making subtle digs against the other occupants of the room. The woman's teenage daughter, however, scowls continuously at Mrs. Turpin, does not laugh at the racist jokes, and won't speak to Mrs. Turpin, leaving her mother to answer Mrs. Turpin's polite questions about the girl. And when Mrs. Turpin starts to thank Jesus for all the good things he's done for her, the girl hits Mrs. Turpin in the face with a book, then starts to strangle her. The doctor and nurse pull the girl off of Mrs. Turpin, and as they are sedating her with a shot, she says to Mrs. Turpin, "Go back to hell where you came from, you old warthog."[65] The comment shocks Mrs. Turpin, and she is left to ponder it in the second half of the story.

Later that day, while she is hosing off the hogs at their farm, Mrs. Turpin ponders the label put on her. Mrs. Turpin's hogs, of course, are kept scrupulously clean, cleaner than "white trash," she would add. Here again, her personal virtues, as flawed as they are, are nonetheless sufficient for the God of mercy to use them to help redeem her: "Her willingness to receive this hurtful attack as a message from Jesus opens her to the action of grace."[66] At first just shocked, then hurt, she becomes increasingly angry, calling out to God, asking why this message was given to her, why she was made to hear such an ugly and untrue thing about herself. She goes so far as to shout out to God, "Who do you think you are?"[67] But the question, sent by God to stun his imperfect follower Ruby with her own haughty question, echoes back to her. And again, Mrs. Turpin's salutary self-doubt works on her: she stands staring silently, another daydream of sudden, violent death enthralling her the way her nightly one does. She turns back to the hogs, who now are neither unhoggishly clean, as Mrs. Turpin imagined herself to be; nor are they irredeemably dirty, as she now fears herself to be. They are simply, beautifully, and fully alive: "A red glow suffused them. They appeared to pant with a secret life."[68] Finally Mrs. Turpin can see how she is herself a warthog from hell, but this isn't such a bad thing, for God loves and saves all his creatures, when they turn to him: "The hogs belong to God. Mrs. Turpin is a warthog from hell whose dark unconscious narcissism is allowed to exist in the presence of grace, . . . a hog and saved, too."[69] And this simple revelation then draws Mrs. Turpin's gaze upward, where she sees a vast throng of the saved making their way toward heaven, led by the dirty, insane, black, and deformed, while clean, respectable people like herself are in the rear of the group. The vision fades, but its memory lingers for Mrs. Turpin. We are left with the hope that she will live for years to come—awed, chastened, but also uplifted by this revelation (which was there all along). She will know herself to be a warthog beloved by God, and finally know and love all the other people, so dissimilar to herself, who are much closer to God than she is.

The story is one of O'Connor's most overtly religious, right from the title to the final vision. The religious and human implications are also concentrated in the girl who attacks Mrs. Turpin. She is named Mary Grace, and she is the instrument or bearer of God's gracious message to Mrs. Turpin, no matter what Mary Grace's own motives, which may well be as sinful as Mrs. Turpin's. Moreover, the book she hits Mrs. Turpin with is entitled *Human Development*, a sign that from a scientific perspective too, Mrs. Turpin's racism and evaluation of others also make no sense: her distinctions are not only sinful, they're irrational. And at the same time, the enlightened alternative is not just gracious or spiritual; it is also completely reasonable: spirit and matter coincide to teach us humility, human kinship, and divine origin.[70] Both divine grace and human reason undermine Mrs. Turpin's hierarchical and sinful imagination of others, and they help her accept herself as a flawed creature, even a warthog, who is being drawn up to God in spite of herself, entirely according to God's plan.

The story is also among O'Connor's most explicitly biblical. With the physical attack from a divine messenger on the protagonist, the story clearly evokes the story of Jacob wrestling an angel (Gen 32:22–32), an identification confirmed by O'Connor.[71] The end of the story, with its vision of a "bridge" full of people on their way to heaven, also sounds much like Jacob's earlier vision of a ladder to heaven (28:10–22). Although not as self-congratulatory as Mrs. Turpin, the patriarch Jacob is mostly known for his cunning self-sufficiency, his ability to get over on other people (almost always without God's direct help). He regards people as objects in a way not that different than Mrs. Turpin. But when Jacob wrestles the angel (or God; the story is ambiguous on this point), the heavenly being overcomes him and leaves him marked with a limp. Afterward, Jacob seems a little more contrite and humble in his dealings with God and with his brother, Esau. Similarly, Mary Grace leaves Mrs. Turpin marked with a blackened, swollen eye, having begun a process whereby Ruby's delusions about herself and others will disintegrate over the next few pages, ending with a new humility and faith. The Jacob and Mrs. Turpin stories are most similar in how they show the God of mercy and love using the main character's imperfect virtues—Jacob's physical and mental strength, Mrs. Turpin's acute powers of observation and organization—to bring them back to himself. God turns Jacob from predation to gratitude, and Mrs. Turpin from self-congratulation to humble awe.

Just as explicit is the identification of Mrs. Turpin with the Pharisee of Luke 18:9–14.[72] In the Gospel story, Jesus tells of a Pharisee who thanks God that he is a righteous, law-abiding man, and not a sinner, especially not a tax collector, among those considered especially sinful for collaborating with the Romans in economically exploiting the Israelites at the time. Although there is no hint in the parable that the Pharisee is hypocritical or guilty of some transgression, Jesus concludes that this is not a helpful way to pray: it expresses gratitude only by judging others negatively. Likewise, the final provocation that sets off Mary Grace's onslaught is Mrs. Turpin exclaiming how grateful she is to Jesus for making her the way she is and not some other way. Although not doubting the sincerity of Ruby's gratitude, God intervenes to show her the right way to be grateful. She should not be grateful for the things she has that others do not—in essence, not only being judgmental, but also being glad at others' supposed misfortune. Instead, she should be glad at the gift of being that God has bestowed. It is an awesome gift, as only God can give it, and not even God can take it away. He has bestowed it on all equally, so that the right kind of gratitude must include humility. "It is . . . the occasion for an intuition into the true nature of the gulf separating God and humanity: God as essentially giving, man as essentially receiving, to such an extent that all distinctions between individual humans based on possessions are reduced to nothing."[73] At this point the story turns from the parable of the Pharisee praying and begins to resemble the book of Job.[74] Ruby has been made to suffer in a much more gentle way, however, and she can accept back her life in true gratitude without having it first utterly destroyed, as in Job, or as in almost all of O'Connor's other stories. Like the prodigal son (Luke 15:11–32), Ruby can love and honor her heavenly Father only after she has been with the hogs and realized her place among them.[75] Like Job, her life with God will be more intimate and personal, even as it is less comfortable or complacent, as promised at the end of the book of Job: "I had heard of you by the hearing of the ear, / but now my eye sees you" (42:5).

O'Connor has brilliantly unmasked self-deception in several of its guises—vanity, self-pity, and false gratitude. As you read more of her stories, you will uncover many more that I have missed. All these sins

blind us to the goodness of others and to our own evil. They even per-
vert and diminish our own good. While they offer strange and stunted
feelings of immortality and self-worth, these turn out to be utterly hol-
low and unsatisfying. Only when our own sinfulness, incompleteness,
and mortality are painfully revealed to us do we realize our real worth,
which is also paradoxically the most humbling and most uplifting of
experiences. Only then do we find that God values us as his foolish,
ungrateful children, to whom he has given the whole world, and yet
who stubbornly remain ungrateful, unappreciative, and even accusatory. But once we realize our status as wayward children, God shows us
the way to real immortality, through his own love and sacrifice for his
unworthy children. "The mysteries of incarnation and redemption con-
found us. Yet it is precisely the operation of God's gratuitous love in the
violence of the paschal mystery that enables us to reach the faith conviction that God cares."[76] And once we realize the paradoxical, gratuitous
actions of this God, we can begin to follow his path to freedom and life
by willingly and faithfully, if always imperfectly, embracing our own
pain and dedicating our suffering to others. Thereby we take the fact of
our unavoidable, earthly trials and turn them into truthful and liberating sacrifices.

Self-Righteousness and Grace

O'Connor astutely depicts the related sin of self-righteousness with
slightly different implications. Although all the characters who are self-
righteous are also self-deceived, their misguided lives take different
turns than the ones we have examined thus far. In particular, O'Connor
uses this sin and its horrible consequences to mount a withering attack
against what she sees as two of the most awful perversions of human
beings in their relation to God and to each other. These are atheism and
the sinful, selfish manipulation of others, supposedly for their own
good. As mentioned, O'Connor saw atheism not as just another view-
point, not even as just an affectation of a tiny minority in Europe and
North America in the last few centuries. This is where I'd probably place
it, having borne such an affectation myself for the first half of my life.
Rather, she sees it as a sick virus that has permeated all of modern culture. Christians bear the deepest responsibility not just to respond, but
to fight it, as she described it: "If you live today, . . . you breathe in

nihilism. In or out of the church, it's the gas you breathe. If I hadn't had the Church to fight it with or to tell me the necessity of fighting it, I would be the stinkingest logical positivist you ever saw."[77]

As for the manipulation of others for their own good, I think O'Connor would say that the modern talk of "tough love" was all too often a sinful excuse and an oxymoron. She would say that there was a lot of toughness about it, but not a lot of love, and that the love it expressed was usually the practitioner's self-love and love of being right and dominating others. If everyone is sinful and flawed, then one of the most despicable and damaging things someone can do to another is to hurt that person in an attempt to teach him or her a lesson, as though someone had that right or ability, all the while claiming it is for the other person's own good, when really it is to satisfy one's own pride. In this way self-righteousness is much worse than self-deception. In these stories we see much worse violence, violence that seems nearly hopeless in its outcome. In the stories we examined above, violence and death from stroke, goring, and strangling could result in revelation, because these violent acts could ultimately bear grace to the victims. But when self-righteousness has obliterated the characters' need for and acknowledgment of God, then their violence breaks out into purely nihilistic, destructive acts—acts of abandonment, seduction, rape, murder, and suicide that leave no one enlightened, but only dead, empty, and hopeless. If the kingdom of heaven comes with violence, so too does the kingdom of hell, and in these stories O'Connor takes us on a harrowing tour of the hells we make for ourselves in our vain and stupid self-righteousness. Worse yet, these hells are inescapable, for the graced moments that are granted in these stories are always rejected or come too late.

The sinful and selfish manipulation of others is overt and grotesque in O'Connor's story "The Life You Save May Be Your Own." A wandering, one-armed handyman named Mr. Shiftlet shows up on the doorstep of an old woman named Lucynell Crater and her thirty-year-old daughter—also named Lucynell Crater—who is deaf and mentally retarded. As soon as he arrives, the mother and he engage in veiled but obvious negotiations for him to marry her daughter. From her side, Mrs. Crater selfishly sees an opportunity to get unlimited free labor around the house; from his side, Mr. Shiftlet immediately spots the real object of his desire—an old car sitting in a shed. While Mrs. Crater sentimentally gushes about how much she loves her daughter and Mr.

Shiftlet sermonizes on the beauty of nature and the mystery of the human heart and spirit, both are bargaining over a helpless woman's life without a thought for her. Their actions, though not as violent as in other O'Connor stories, are truly a "moral horror."[78] And our horror at their actions is intensified by their self-righteousness. Both think they are doing the young woman a favor, and both think it is the other who is wicked: "Both displace their base motives onto the other as though willing to grant the other a favor, and Lucynell serves as commodity for the trade."[79]

The negotiations continue as Mr. Shiftlet fixes up the house and the car. Mrs. Crater offers him increasing amounts of money, first to buy parts for the car, then for a honeymoon, on which Mr. Shiftlet insists as part of the bargain. Although Mrs. Crater repeatedly insists that her daughter is priceless, her final offer to pay for disposing of her is only "seventeen-fifty."[80] Mr. Shiftlet and Lucynell are married at the courthouse and leave on their trip. He drives a hundred miles and stops at a restaurant. As they sit at the counter, Lucynell falls asleep, and he abandons her there, speeding off in his new car. But Mr. Shiftlet has enough of a shred of goodness left that his plan gives him no satisfaction.[81] He is utterly empty inside, and when he's not distracting himself from this fact with cars and plans, he knows it thoroughly and painfully.

Like Mrs. Turpin, at the end of the story Mr. Shiftlet is given a chance to let his tiny bit of virtue grow and open up to God. As he drives along, he picks up a hitchhiker. Mr. Shiftlet works himself up into a fit of sentimentality, going on and on about his supposedly saintly mother. Since he has abandoned his helpless wife and stolen a car without any remorse, this sham of emotion fools no one—except Mr. Shiftlet himself.[82] It seduces him with a manageable, fake, and dulling feeling, rather than a real, uncontrollable, uncomfortable, and life-giving outburst of emotion: it is as sweet and fake as "saccharine,"[83] and finally as unsatisfying and bitter. The hitchhiker, a runaway from his own mother, lashes out at Mr. Shiftlet in a way similar to Mary Grace's attack on Mrs. Turpin, yelling at him, "You go to the devil!"[84] and then jumps out of the moving car. But unlike Mrs. Turpin, Mr. Shiftlet completely rejects this messenger and his offer of grace. Rather than admit that he is on a highway to hell, Mr. Shiftlet ends the story by self-righteously condemning the rest of the world for its corruption, while still steadfastly ignoring any responsibility for his own sinfulness.[85] As he speeds along, the only hope for Mr. Shiftlet is an apocalyptic storm of supernaturally huge raindrops that breaks over him, pelting his new car with the cleansing water that he himself had called down on the sinful world. Water can break down even stone, but Mr. Shiftlet speeds out of our sight before we can learn whether it will ever break down his "stony heart."[86]

A differently perverse seduction and abandonment take place in one of O'Connor's best-known stories, "Good Country People." Like Mrs. May, Mrs. Hopewell is a single parent, living with a grown, ungrateful child, and with farm workers who are an annoyance to her. Her daughter, Joy, had one leg shot off in a hunting accident when she was ten, and also has a heart condition, which keeps her living with her mother. When she grew up, Joy earned a PhD in philosophy and had her name changed to Hulga, just to spite her mother and assert herself. Joy/Hulga seems to derive no pleasure from her education, only using her intellect and knowledge to belittle her mother and everyone else, and to assert her own superiority and atheistic, secularized sense of her own salvation. Both her name change and her education are acts of defiance and deliberate self-laceration, attempts (like Mr. Shiftlet's overwrought sentimentality) to take control of unavoidable human pain and make it somehow manageable and uplifting, when pain really calls for honesty and submission. Joy/Hulga's "misguided intellect that eclipses the spiritual and emotional realities"[87] has made her sad and monstrous in a way that a physical wound never could. "By cloaking childhood shame in the adult garb of philosophy, she makes that shame more pronounced. Intellectual gambits not only keep the old wound of ten open, they render her unprepared at thirty-two to deal with life."[88] While trying to hide from or deny her pain, she has only made it worse, and opened herself up to the worse pain that will be inflicted on her in the action of the story.

Of the characters we have examined, Joy/Hulga is the first who loudly proclaims her atheism; she is also a self-conscious parody of the negative aspects of O'Connor herself.[89] Her atheism is associated with her hypertrophied intellect: "The perfect modern gnostic, Joy-Hulga is her own ultimate reality."[90] Joy/Hulga's belief in her own superiority and sufficiency make her vulnerable to real evil, which comes in the form of the lewdly named Manley Pointer. Manley is a Bible salesman who comes calling on the Hopewells. He seems simple and sincere. Mrs. Hopewell declines to buy a Bible—both from her own indifference and Joy/Hulga's hostility to its contents—but invites Manley to dinner. He seems so smitten with Joy/Hulga that they arrange to meet the next day. As she contemplates their impending "date," Joy/Hulga fantasizes that she will seduce this innocent, naive young Bible salesman, shatter his illusions about his false and imprisoning religion, and make him a better person—more like her, disillusioned and bitter. In its own way, her fantasies of domination and manipulation are as ugly and selfish as anything revealed in the last few pages of the story.

The next day as they walk to the hayloft, Joy/Hulga—and most first-time readers, I'm sure—mistake all of Manley's comments as merely innocent, or at most, playfully sexual. But as they are kissing, his comments turn overtly obscene and sinister when he asks to see how to take off her wooden leg. At first Joy/Hulga is shocked, but then the misguidedness and impotence of her mind overwhelms her as she incredibly mistakes his perverse interest in the limb for "real innocence."[91] The hardened atheist and cynic, who thought to seduce and destroy a timid and innocent Christian, instead finds herself falling in love with an innocence that she is only imagining. Joy/Hulga rightly and suddenly sees that the essence of love is vulnerability, but her stunted and immature emotional life means that she has unfortunately felt this for someone who has no interest in love or vulnerability. For once Manley has her leg off, he becomes more sexually aggressive and lewd. He produces liquor, condoms, and obscene playing cards from a hollowed out Bible, and shows that he perversely and somewhat impotently achieves sexual arousal only by looking away from Joy/Hulga and over at the detached leg.[92] When she becomes more frightened at his behavior and asks why he's doing this if he's a Christian, he snarls at her that he doesn't "believe in that crap,"[93] tosses her leg into his suitcase, and walks off, telling her that he has stolen many such things from women before.

Despite her final, shocking victimization, Joy/Hulga's earlier fantasies of destroying innocence and turning it into meaningless, hopeless emptiness make her as satanic as Manley: "In the haystack Hulga meets that satanic aspect of herself. . . . Critics have noted the resemblance between Hulga and Manley."[94] Indeed, in terms of intentions, Manley's appear the purer: he lusted after what he thought was another hardened atheist who shared his nihilism and perversity, while she thought to seduce and destroy an innocent young man. Both turned out to be totally wrong in their estimations of the other—or totally successful in their own disguises, even if only Joy/Hulga suffers directly for it. Perhaps more positively than Mr. Shiftlet, but less hopefully than Mrs. Turpin, Joy/Hulga's delusions about herself and the world are shattered. She had thought herself so smart, so tough, so unsentimental. But when faced with a true, hardened veteran of negation, evil, and diabolical intellect, she realized that she had only been playacting at atheism lite for decades. Her atheism really was just an annoying affectation and a sad, pathetic coping mechanism, while Manley's was the real thing—ugly, twisted, and violent. She had "impersonated herself,"[95] and when she saw a much better actor really being like she imagined herself, she recoiled in horror from the vision. While it seems a little optimistic to think that from this experience she will find "inner comfort, . . . true joy,"[96] it does seem like Manley has seduced her and then shoved her into the degrading, repetitive hell of her false life, and thereby pushed her to take the first step out of the shame and pain. Joy/Hulga found that she was not nearly as smart or as nasty as she wanted to be, and perhaps now she will value intellect and nastiness at least a little bit less. She finally realized that love is vulnerability. If she can ever recover from Manley's perverse degradation of her, perhaps she can love rightly once in her life—which is, I think, once more than most of us deserve.

The love that has gone terribly wrong is very different in O'Connor's story "A View of the Woods,"[97] in which it is not sexuality that has become twisted and destructive, but family attachments and dynamics. Mr. Fortune is a wealthy and successful seventy-nine year old man who lives with his one daughter and her family. She has married a man named Pitts, and Mr. Fortune detests the whole family, while they amply return the revulsion. But he makes an exception and loves his one granddaughter, Mary Fortune Pitts. The old man had at first not wanted his name associated with that of his hated son-in-law, but he relented when he saw the child's uncanny physical resemblance to himself. Mr. Fortune believes that this granddaughter is the only one in the family who is like him, who will carry on his vision for the family and the land. He has secretly made out his will so that all his possessions will bypass the rest of the family and go to Mary Fortune in trust.

But Mr. Fortune's vision for the family and the future is hardly one about which any normal person would get excited. Mr. Fortune sells off pieces of their property to developers who put up buildings of stunning practicality and ugliness on them. "His Eden consists of parking garages and huge monster machines,"[98] a "hodgepodge of newfangled petty enterprises."[99] The beginning and end of the story describe the earth-movers as huge monsters devouring and destroying the land, tearing it out from under them. The epitome of Mr. Fortune's idea of "progress" would seem to be the one developer we meet in the story, Mr. Tilman, who is described as bobbing up and down like a snake,[100] and whose store is a bizarre pastiche of everything from which one can make a profit. He runs a business that combines a general store, gas station, car dealership, junkyard, statuary garden (including tombstones, though these are displayed further back, so as not to depress more convivial customers), dance hall, and restaurant. It is one of O'Connor's most prescient and morbidly humorous parodies of American consumer culture run amok. Mr. Fortune thinks he has done a patriotic service by turning an idyllic land of pastures and forests into parking lots, trash heaps, and loads of cheap stuff to buy, while all the time stoking his own greed and pride at his supposedly grand accomplishment.

Despite Mr. Fortune's fantasies that his granddaughter is just like him, she does not really share his vision. This comes to a head when Mr. Fortune declares that he will sell a piece of land right in front of their house for a gas station. Mary Fortune leads the family in their objection to this scheme. But then the others turn on her and think that she has put her grandfather up to this latest whittling away at their property, bringing the ugliness of the modern world right up to their doorstep and obliterating their "View of the Woods." Pitts takes his daughter out to the woods for a brutal beating, something he frequently does, impotently and unjustly venting his anger against his father-in-law by abusing the old man's favorite grandchild. Mr. Fortune will not relent in his intention to sell the land, and when Mary Fortune continues to oppose him, he too tries to beat her like her father does. But although she is complacent to her father's beatings, perhaps understanding that she is only a proxy for her tyrannical grandfather,[101] she will not tolerate the injustice and hypocrisy of her grandfather. She refuses to take a beating from him, when she is defending the property that he is pulling out from under her family at the same time as he claims to be doing it out of love for her. Mary Fortune jumps on her grandfather—punching, kicking, and biting in a savage attack that overwhelms him until he begs for mercy. But then he momentarily regains his strength and dashes her head against a rock, killing her. He staggers away from this scene of horror and dies of a heart attack, staring into the woods he had sought to destroy. Mr. Fortune was oblivious to the beauty of the woods and to the needs of other people, actively pursuing the destruction of both woods and people. Therefore, the trees, like God,[102] can only be silent witnesses to his crime, death, and damnation.

Instead of the atheism and arrogant intellectuality pilloried in "Good Country People," Mr. Fortune indulges in another idolatry—the glory and supposed self-sufficiency brought by possessions and accomplishments. This idolatry is especially prevalent precisely because it is so acceptable and even encouraged by our society: "What is dangerous about material goods for O'Connor is not what they are but what they replace."[103] He is aptly named, always seeking his "fortune," always expecting others to be grateful to him for accumulating such a grand "fortune" to pass on to them, and resenting them when they're not. Contrast this with "Pitts," which suggests an emptiness, earthiness, and lowness that, while not admirable, are at least a more accurate reflection of human reality.[104] The two evil men are also contrasted anatomically. Whenever something goes wrong for Pitts, he is said to be on the verge of a stroke: there is something wrong with his head or mind. The anger he feels for Mr. Fortune is quite legitimate, but he irrationally and almost insanely directs it against Mary Fortune. Mr. Fortune, on the other hand, has heart trouble: there is something wrong with his emotions, with his ability to have immediate, soulful feelings, rather than postponed, desiccated calculations. So many years of being too reasonable, too focused on his plans for the future, have left him only with "mean-spiritedness, . . . emotional poverty."[105] Mr. Fortune can only destroy himself and Mary Fortune when her illogical but utterly passionate and humane attachment to the field threatens his deadly, empty schemes for the future.

Although this story is not one of sexual seduction, the selfishness, pride, and destruction are exactly the same as in the previous two stories. Mr. Fortune wants Mary Fortune to be a replica of himself, with no concern for her needs and desires. He has objectified her just as much as Mr. Shiftlet or Manley did their victims. He also goes just as far as they do in thinking that he's doing his victim a favor, giving his precious image and vision to her, when he is really taking away her own identity, and finally, her life. The added dimension to Mr. Fortune's use and abuse of his granddaughter is that—unlike Mr. Shiftlet or Manley, who simply move on to their next victim—Mr. Fortune's own self-worth is

completely tied up with his ability to shape and manipulate his granddaughter. When he fails at this project, he kills her out of rage against
the hated otherness and freedom that she now embodies for him, but
this loss kills him too, for without his narcissistic replica he has nothing
left for which to live. The ending is one of the bleakest in all of
O'Connor's stories, because the psychological and theological mistake
or disease is so much deeper. Mr. Fortune shows how self-righteously
manipulating others to give our lives meaning is simultaneously
betrayal, damnation,[106] deicide, and spiritual suicide.[107] The story is
another mysterious but profound call to let God live in our lives, rather
than trying to make someone else's life a sickened, enslaved shadow of
our own: it is once again to acknowledge our status as creatures, not
Creator. It is also a relevant warning to us. As much as we try to deny
any similarity between our lives and Mr. Fortune's violence, just as we
would deny any similarity to Mr. Shiftlet's callousness or Manley's perversion, there is no denying that we are similarly tempted. We are constantly faced with the temptation to live vicariously through our
children, or to put all our worth into the future of career and achieve-
ments, rather than to enjoy God's grace and peace now.

O'Connor produces terrifying results as she combines pseudo-
intellectuality, atheism, and intergenerational betrayal in "The Lame
Shall Enter First." The main character is Sheppard; despite his name bla-
tantly suggesting Christ, he is an avowed atheist who regards religion as
only for the ignorant or deranged. He instead tries to offer his own secular version of shepherding, working as recreational director for his
town, and then volunteering as a counselor at the reformatory on
Saturdays. Sheppard arrogantly and self-righteously regards his own
ability to help people as much more reputable and successful than that
of a priest. But his treatment of his own son, Norton, seems less than
healthful. Norton is ten years old, his mother having died a year before
the story takes place. Sheppard thinks Norton incapable of real feelings
and accuses him of selfishness and pettiness, while it is really he who is
incapable of compassion, ignoring the boy's real and obvious grief.
Sheppard looks down on the boy as a complete emotional and intellectual failure and therefore expends little energy on him. Like Mr.
Fortune, Sheppard only loves when there's a prospect of reforming the
loved person into an image of himself, and he foolishly disdains his own
son as too unintelligent for such a project.

But when Sheppard meets a diabolically intelligent boy, Rufus, at the reformatory, he immediately throws himself completely into the project of saving the boy—more secular attempts at Christlikeness. But such efforts are ineffectual because they unrealistically and arrogantly look forward to "a utopian future where sin and the poverty that attends it will be more than absolved by the priests—it will be eliminated by the scientists and social engineers."[108] Sheppard therefore creates here "another family doomed by a modern attitude."[109] Rufus is club-footed and violent. He steals, vandalizes, sets fires, and declares loudly that Satan has him in his power, but that Christ will save him if God so wishes. Although there is no sign of reform in Rufus, Sheppard steadfastly clings to the idea of saving him, only because of the boy's high IQ. He goes so far as to give Rufus a key to their home when Rufus leaves the reformatory. Rufus shows up at the house and terrorizes Norton, but Sheppard welcomes him in, ignoring his son's pleas that the intruder is not to be trusted, even beating his son when he quite understandably objects to Rufus sleeping in his mother's bed. Blindly favoring intellect, Sheppard lacks all appreciation of emotion or sacredness. Since Rufus is so intelligent, Sheppard believes he will eventually be able to lead the boy away from his bizarre, biblical beliefs and the violence that Sheppard believes only comes from the boy's shame about his deformed foot. But Sheppard is just as utterly naive toward Rufus as Joy/Hulga was toward Manley. The boy is committed to both his beliefs and his violence with complete deliberation and certainty. He never behaves with ignorance or shame, but with acumen, confidence, and power that are more than adequate to withstand the feeble attempts of Sheppard's psychologizing. Instead of Sheppard convincing Rufus of anything, Rufus works on the weak and distraught Norton, convincing him that his mother is in heaven; all Sheppard's statements of her simple nonexistence fall flat for the hopeless, impotent nihilism they really are. Sheppard embraces reason and science because he thinks they can fix everything by making a special shoe for a clubfoot, but he can't use them to confront the real, heartfelt anguish that is tearing apart what's left of his own family. Only God can help in that struggle, and Sheppard has excluded God from the conversation. In the heart-wrenching ending, Sheppard finally realizes his mistake, sees with complete clarity his own selfishness, and goes to embrace the son he has so neglected. But he only finds Norton's body hanging from a rafter; the boy has killed himself to be with his beloved mother and escape his neglectful father, seduced by Rufus's true but evil promises of immortality.

This contrast between goodness and rightness finally interprets the deadly conflict between Sheppard and Rufus, as Rufus observes of his opponent early on: "I don't care if he's good or not. He ain't *right!*"[110] Rufus and the devil he claims to follow are both correct in their knowledge of God and Scriptures, but evil in their intentions and actions.[111] Atheists like Sheppard are wrong in their ideas about God, and therefore can never be good, no matter how hard they try. Sheppard tries to be good, but so long as he denies the truth of God's existence and loving presence, there is no way for this goodness to be anything other than empty, self-serving, and self-destructive, as he himself finally realizes: "He had stuffed his own emptiness with good works like a glutton. He had ignored his own child to feed his vision of himself."[112] Like Joy/Hulga, an overreliance on reason has caused him to neglect emotions, will, and spirit. Rufus, on the other hand, intellectually accepts and vehemently defends the existence of God, but willfully rejects acting upon such knowledge. He knows that a person's will is so preeminent that it can deliberately contradict reason all the time, if it so chooses. With Rufus's complete victory, O'Connor makes it clear which one is right, if not good. Human beings really can steadfastly reject God's message forever, while intellectual disbelief will finally be unmasked for the utter emptiness and sadness it shamefully and ineffectually tries to hide. And either willful rejection or intellectual disbelief, or both together, are enough to kill Norton, the vulnerable, wounded, but hopeful child in all of us.

O'Connor has shown us the real torture and horror of self-righteousness. It is not at all humorous like self-deception, because the damage it can do is just too complete and too ugly to make us laugh. When only self-deceived, our relationship to God is "merely" wrong, like Mrs. Turpin's laughable gratitude, and our relationships to other people are more or less nonexistent, regarding others as nuisances or persecutors, but not really meddling with or harming them too much. But when fully immersed in self-righteousness, the reverse happens. Our relationship to God disappears, and it eventually becomes impossible for us even to have one, since we see no need for a God to make us righteous, for we think we already are so. Our relationships with other people become wrong in the most destructive and predatory ways, as we impiously try to remake them into our own image, robbing them of their worth as fellow subjects and human beings by making them into objects of our sick self-love. And as godlike as we try to be in our self-righteousness, the reverse again happens, and we are utterly abased in self-destruction. Only God possesses real righteousness, and to think that we possess it is not only grossly inaccurate; it is also frighteningly dangerous to our limited, sinful selves and to the people around us. The characters we have examined in these four stories—and most of us, most of the time—are completely trapped within themselves. They thus are blinded to their own sinfulness, their violence toward others, and their own vulnerability, as well as kept from seeing the power, evil, or goodness of others. If the stories of self-deception entreat us to turn inward, embrace our own suffering, and admit our sinfulness to God, then the painful recognition of our self-righteousness calls us to look at others, stop making them suffer, love them rightly, and stop sinning. Realizing the right relation to others, we will substitute real godlikeness for our sick attempts at divinity, and gain a real object for worship, instead of our stunted idolatry.

For Study: The Deception of Politeness— "A Good Man Is Hard to Find"

For a more in-depth study of O'Connor's style and her meaning, let us consider the last, intense page of her most famous story, "A Good Man Is Hard to Find." It is told from the perspective of a grandmother whose name is not revealed in the story. She lives with her son, Bailey, and his family. The family is planning a trip to Florida, and the grandmother tries to persuade them to go to Tennessee instead. She says this is because she fears an escaped criminal named the Misfit is on his way toward Florida, but the first line of the story reveals that she just doesn't like Florida and is trying to find excuses not to go there. They leave early the next day for Florida anyway, the grandmother having smuggled her pet cat in a basket. They stop for lunch at a barbecue place named The Tower that is run by Red Sammy, who agrees with the grandmother's estimation that the world is getting worse and it is hard to find a good man, though he also agrees with her flattery that he himself is a good man. Red Sammy's wife does not concur with this and gives the more pessimistic and orthodoxly Christian evaluation that no one is really good; while glaring at her husband, she declares that no one can be trusted, pointing to his self-righteousness and hypocrisy.

The family continues on their trip, and the grandmother tells the children that there is a plantation nearby, which has a secret panel with treasure hidden behind it. Although she knows the story is fiction, she cooperates with the obnoxious children in badgering Bailey into turning off the main road to look for the plantation. As they are driving, the grandmother suddenly realizes that not only is the secret-panel story fictitious, but also, the plantation she was remembering is nowhere near where they are. The thought shocks her so much that her feet jerk, thereby knocking over the basket with the cat in it. The cat leaps out onto Bailey as he's driving, causing him to lose control, and the car rolls over into a ditch. As they are standing by the car, another car comes along. Three men with guns get out and approach them. The grandmother blurts out that the leader of the three is the Misfit, thereby dooming the family.

As the Misfit calmly and politely orders his two men to take the family—first Bailey and his son, then the mother and the two smaller children—into the woods and shoot them, the real action and meaning of the story unfold in the extremely deep conversation between the grandmother and the criminal. On the surface, the conversation is just about the grandmother pleading for her life. Significantly, she pleads for none of the other family members, only for herself. But when the Misfit—unlike the hypocritical Red Sammy—disagrees with the grandmother's assertion that he is a good man, the conversation turns much more serious and abstract. As far as the Misfit is concerned, her death is determined, but his own goodness and badness is something much more mysterious and undetermined, a topic in which both of them are intensely interested, if for very different reasons. Like many other O'Connor characters, such as Mrs. Turpin or Mrs. Hopewell, the grandmother desperately wants to believe that the man's politeness and good hygiene translate into moral goodness—even as each gunshot informs her that another family member has been murdered at his command. And if the present, ghastly reality doesn't match up to her imagination of his goodness, she then seems to hope that she might be able to convince or trick him into believing in his own moral goodness so that he will refrain from killing her. She appeals to his upbringing, then to imaginations of how much better his life would be if he stopped his crimes, and then to religion. In all this, right up until the last page, there is no indication that the grandmother is thinking of anything other than her own self-preservation. She seems uninterested in the fate of her family or in anything the Misfit is saying; she is only focused on getting him to stop the shooting before it gets to her.

But the Misfit is self-centered in a way totally different from the grandmother. She is totally convinced of her own goodness, and naively but resolutely projects this assumed goodness on to others when it suits her selfish and vain purposes; he is completely unsure and wracked with doubt over the goodness or value of his life. While acknowledging his crimes, he gives an obviously heartfelt and well-thought-out rationale for not understanding how his crimes "fit" his punishment. Joining such literary luminaries as Job or Captain Ahab, the Misfit has clearly seen that salvation or damnation by works just doesn't make sense, for all too often the wicked triumph and the good perish. Indeed, he can see a glaring example of that right in front of him in the six innocent people—three of them children—murdered by his two accomplices, whom O'Connor goes out of her way to make as loathsome as possible, even "subhuman."[113] But then, joining other literary predecessors like Ivan Karamazov, the Misfit turns to consider the possibility of the Christian doctrine of salvation through faith in Jesus Christ.

This brings us to the final page of the story. The Misfit tells the grandmother that Jesus only makes matters worse. On the one hand, Jesus' death is just another example—indeed, the ultimate and most disturbing one—of unfair, undeserved suffering.[114] And if Jesus offers a way out of this cycle, he does so only by way of another example of supreme unfairness. According to the Misfit's final speeches, if Jesus appeared to each and every person and asked him or her to believe in him, that at least would be fair. Several times the Misfit indicates that if faced with such a decision, he would believe. But instead, Jesus appeared only to a handful of people in Palestine two thousand years ago, then disappeared, demanding that all the rest of humanity make the most momentous decision of their lives based on hearsay. Jesus has given us the chance to escape our undeserved suffering, but only by submitting to the constant, agonizing mental suffering of nagging, relentless doubt. Faced with such a maddening decision that only exacerbates and makes permanent a mental agony, the Misfit, much like Rufus, opts for destruction, violence, and loneliness to postpone the decision and distract himself as much as possible from it.

Let us consider the Misfit's position. First, as the examples alluded to above indicate, it is a position with a powerful history in world literature.[115] O'Connor has not said anything unique or new here, but it is her gift to do in just a few paragraphs of vernacular dialogue what takes Melville or Dostoyevsky literally hundreds of pages of dense prose and convoluted plot. And it is not quite fair to the Misfit's position to dismiss it as "a modern misreading."[116] I too disagree with it finally, but not because I'm any less modern, and definitely not because I haven't felt exactly like the Misfit does here. O'Connor parodies and dismisses Joy/Hulga's atheism, but not the Misfit's refusal to believe. It is a completely human need and longing to live according to observable facts. You could not navigate even the simplest of daily tasks if you could not assume a plethora of facts as given and stable, because you had observed them before. Then how farfetched or neurotic is it to expect the much more important relationship with God to be based on facts that you can see, rather than on unseen things you must take on faith? I am afraid that it's not at all farfetched or neurotic not to believe in God, or to choose not to have a relationship with God; on the contrary, it's perfectly reasonable. Atheists are not necessarily unintelligent nor mentally unbalanced; whatever it is that faith offers, it is not quite like a mathematical proof or a psychological cure, as much as some Christian apologists try to dress it up as either of those.

But, I think we must hasten to add, it's also perfectly reasonable to believe in God and to choose to have a relationship with him. As large a place as I grant to reason in our lives, all of us let enormous parts of our lives be ruled by nonrational decisions. These are often the most important and fulfilling parts of our lives—whom to marry, what music to listen to, where to go to school, where to live, what career to follow, which friendships to cultivate, which to let wither, whom to hold a grudge against, whom to forgive. So choosing God is as mysterious and frightening a prospect as choosing a friend or lover, but it offers the same high level of return, and not choosing offers the same level of safety and loneliness. Not enough atheists or Christians are as thorough and critical in their examination of their beliefs as the Misfit is. I think his final paragraphs powerfully call us all to introspection and honesty, as he shows how undeniable and central reason must be to our lives and faith, at the same time as he shows how it cannot be the only faculty on which we rely.

But this is no mere intellectual diversion or even obsession for the Misfit. As he describes the unfairness of Jesus' not appearing to him and therefore not letting him be a good man, this man who murders as nonchalantly as he straightens his glasses is almost overcome with tears. This theological problem does not keep him awake at nights because it's interesting, but because it hurts him inwardly, torturing his soul and twisting his emotions and will with its maddening uncertainty and with the fact that no amount of killing or any other distraction will ever make it go away. I think it would be an excellent measure of sound and perfect faith if someone could get as worked up over his or her belief as the Misfit has gotten over his disbelief. I would call truly blessed someone who could let a fascination and joy at the mystery of the incarnation grow into a constant bliss that sometimes flares up into ecstasy, the way the Misfit has let his obsession with God fester into a dull ache that occasionally flares up into overwhelming despair or murderous rage.

As the Misfit is intellectually and emotionally overwhelmed by his meditation on his life and on Jesus, something changes in the grandmother's reaction to him. Finally past her pleadings based on self-preservation and fear, the grandmother can give a reaction that is not flattery, manipulation, or panic, but a sincere and attentive reaction to what he is saying and feeling. Seeing him close to tears, she touches his shoulder and murmurs, "You're one of my own children!"[117] But the Misfit, unable to stand either the vulnerability he has displayed to her or the intimacy she has risked with him, springs back and shoots her three times in the chest. As she lies dead on the ground, the grandmother finally seems at peace; no longer frightened, selfish, or manipulative, she dies with serenity, even happiness. But why does she make this last gesture to the Misfit? What vision does she have in this last moment?

We have only her last words on which to base our interpretation, and O'Connor's choice here is one of the most brilliant in her stories, for she leaves it up to the reader to decide in what way the grandmother sees the Misfit as her child. Does she see his doubt and fear as like her own?[118] Or does she finally see her own sinfulness as like his?[119] Or does she finally see his real goodness and her own—not the fake goodness of politeness that she had mistakenly obsessed over before, but the goodness that is still struggling with and anguishing over all the evil and pain in life?[120] Or does she have compassion on his suffering, finally acting like a mother to him and feeling his pain?[121] I see nothing in the story that would preclude any of these interpretations, nor anything that would prevent one from suggesting and experiencing many more. Her loving gesture to the Misfit, regardless of its exact nuance and totally regardless of its immediate and fatal outcome, remains a perfect moment of love—powerful, free, and liberating. Compared to the other ways we have seen her interact with people in the story—bickering, flattering, or lying—there seems to be little question that this last moment is to be preferred to all the others, that it even redeems her false life. That such a moment comes at such a gory, staggering cost is only O'Connor's testimony to the power of evil in this life, not a diminishment of the goodness that glimpses heaven in this last moment.[122]

And what of the Misfit? Does the grandmother's gesture change him at all? O'Connor said that she liked to imagine that it did,[123] but she has left us only the barest of hints in the story itself. Right before he shoots the grandmother, the Misfit snarls that because of the uncertainty Jesus brought to the world, there was "no pleasure but meanness"[124] in life. But the last words of the story have him silencing his shallow and sadistic accomplice with the observation "It's no real pleasure in life."[125] The Misfit has at least learned not to enjoy cruelty.[126] He has not yet learned how to love, but he has learned that violence and brutality bring no relief to him, not even in the immediate circumstances, let alone ultimately. It seems optimistic but not naive to think that this newfound dissatisfaction with violence will one day lead him to abandon it, and perhaps one day to embrace its opposite. Because of the grandmother's beautiful and unexpected gesture, the Misfit has made at least one small step away from evil and toward good.

Besides the succinctness and crystalline concentration of this brief passage, these paragraphs are powerful and worth returning to over and over because of their indeterminacy. Studying them repeatedly is important, because it reveals more and more interpretations we had previously overlooked, but it can never fully explain or solve the meaning of the passage. Like real life, the end of the story admits of many interpretations, and no amount of interpretations can exhaust its beauty and mystery. But concentrated examination of such a profound passage can lead us to a different kind of understanding—not a figuring out, or an explanation, or a solution, but rather an experience of "standing in awe, and in humility, before an abyss of silent unknowing."[127] This kind of understanding is of infinitely more value than any mere explanation, for by it we discard all our masks, deceptions, and rationalizations to stand before the infinite, loving presence of God.

For Reflection: Only God Is Righteous—"The Artificial Nigger"

As shown (above) in my analysis of self-righteousness, O'Connor brings out in shocking vividness the ugliness and sinfulness of our attempts to fix other people by being mean to them "for their own good." This dynamic is so powerful in O'Connor's stories that I would like to underline it one more time and propose it as an object for continued reflection. The faultiness of such "tough love" is the driving force in the story "The Artificial Nigger," which O'Connor described as her best story.[128] The story takes us through one harrowing day with Mr. Head and his grandson Nelson as they journey by train from their isolated town to Atlanta and back. Mr. Head has determined to teach the boy a lesson by taking him to the city to humble him, for the boy has some childish pretensions of grandeur because he was born in the big city. Part of this humbling or, more accurately, humiliation, will be to show the boy that the city is full of "niggers," so that he will see there is nothing to be proud of in being from such a place. The project has the doubly disgusting goal of humiliating an innocent child by teaching him to humiliate and degrade others.[129]

Needless to say, such self-righteous schemes do not unfold as planned. Mr. Head's attempts to mock African Americans on the train more or less backfire on himself, making him look foolish, while the black people impress Nelson with their regal bearing and composure. As soon as they leave the train station in Atlanta, the two get increasingly lost and confused. Here too a black woman overwhelms Nelson with her unfamiliar beauty that is both erotic and maternal, more powers that Mr. Head cannot counter.[130] Yet their real degradation happens not in the black neighborhood, but among middle-class whites. Exhausted from so much walking, Nelson falls asleep sitting on the sidewalk. Mr. Head cruelly thinks to humble the boy, who has been mocking him for getting them lost, by hiding twenty feet away, so that when Nelson wakes up, he will see how alone and helpless he is. This plan also misfires, for when Nelson wakes up, he's so terrified that he darts down the street and crashes into a pedestrian, injuring her. An angry crowd gathers, and Mr. Head cowardly denies knowing Nelson. Rather than humbling the boy, Mr. Head has shamed himself before his grandson, who, he now imagines, will never forgive him for this despicable treachery.

The two continue to wander, and the suspense of the story increases as they enter a wealthy suburb that O'Connor describes more and more outrageously with images from Dante's *Inferno*. It is a world of cold emptiness, white houses that look like icebergs, ugly dogs, labyrinthine paths that lead nowhere, and sewer grates that lead down to the rivers of hell.[131] When I read the story the first time, I was by this time literally paralyzed with fear, assuming that it would end in typical O'Connor fashion with one or both of them getting run over by a trolley or suffering some other violent death. But instead, a man out walking his dogs solves their immediate problem of catching the train by easily directing them to the nearby suburban stop. And their more serious spiritual problem of how Mr. Head can be forgiven for his ultimate betrayal is mysteriously solved when they see a lawn decoration that is a small statue of an African American, which Mr. Head labels as an "Artificial Nigger." The statue is so aged and cracked that it no longer looks happy or silly, but only wretched and suffering. And Mr. Head and Nelson are both so miserable at this point that they stand mesmerized by this "monument to another's victory that brought them together in their common defeat. They could both feel it dissolving their differences like an action of mercy."[132] As with Jacob or Mrs. Turpin, God's grace comes to Mr. Head in terms he can understand: Mr. Head is perfectly ready and equipped to think of a black person as a weak, despicable object of scorn. But at the same time, God's grace overflows Mr. Head's narrow mind and sears away his self-righteousness. Mr. Head was never ready before to see himself as such a minuscule, crushed little object, but now he finally can, and the results are salvific: "By recognizing his identity with those he thinks contemptible, he can recognize himself for what he really is."[133] Realizing his own sinfulness, Mr. Head lets God's mercy overwhelm him and reconcile him to Nelson.

In reflecting on this story, I think it has helped me to focus on the ridiculousness and pervasiveness of my sin. Usually when we think of sin or evil, we go for the really big instances of them—murder, rape, cannibalism, torture—acts that almost all of us avoid our whole lives long. But Mr. Head reminds me so effectively that sins are also all those nasty little acts of cruelty and callousness that I perpetrate all the time. I don't have the willpower to be a Hitler or a Charles Manson, but I don't usually use my willpower enough to avoid being a Mr. Head, to avoid hurting the people I should be helping. I am nowhere near eradicating such absurdly petty and self-righteous behavior in my life, but I think reflection on this story would help anyone to begin to diagnose and treat this most minor but pervasive manifestation of sin.

On the other hand, the mysteriousness of grace so accurately depicted by O'Connor is also worthy of reflection. Just as with thinking only of big sins, I wonder how much we get distracted and misled when we think only of big moments of grace. Let's say that most people— even most avowed atheists, I would say—would acknowledge that the birth of a healthy child, or a miraculous recovery from some fatal illness, are moments graced by God. I think they are, too, but maybe that makes grace a little too easy to identify—it feels really good and you didn't do it on your own—and a little too infrequent to help me in my seeking for God's presence. But the moments of grace in O'Connor's stories are quite different from these examples. They usually involve violence, grotesquerie, and comedy; they don't look the least bit like childbirth or miraculous recovery, and they don't feel good at all to the characters who undergo them. By reflecting on this, O'Connor has helped me to become more aware of God's grace coming to me in less overt and less happy occurrences.[134] If even atheists can feel a little bit of God's grace at the birth of a child, then Christians should be striving to find grace in the seemingly less likely, less obvious places—in sicknesses that others dismiss as misfortunes, in events that others dismiss as coincidences, in secular art or music that others dismiss as meaningless or even as an ungodly temptation. Grace is there even in the most horrible or the most trivial of circumstances, exactly when we need it most. I think it is a very difficult but necessary spiritual exercise to sharpen our eyes and widen our hearts to notice and accept it. But with her usual wry humor, O'Connor has shown us Mr. Head accepting God's grace, even though he is one of the most stubborn and foolish of her many stubborn and foolish characters. If he can accept such grace without even trying, then all of us should make the effort.

For Prayer: Praising God—"A Temple of the Holy Ghost"

> God done this to me and I praise Him. . . .
>   This is the way He wanted me to be.[135]

I take our last prayer from "A Temple of the Holy Ghost," one of O'Connor's lesser known stories. O'Connor herself expressed surprise and regret that the story received less attention than her others and had not been anthologized,[136] and others have also singled it out as an epitome of her work. "This story contains all the elements which vitalize Miss O'Connor's work."[137] In the story, a twelve-year-old girl who is never named but always called "the child"—a reminder that we are all children, both in the negative sense of "childish," and in the positive sense of "children of God"[138]—observes the mysterious antics of her two second cousins. They are two years older than she, just at the beginning of experimenting with their sexuality—makeup, high heels, flirtations, pretended worldliness and sophistication, flippant mockery of the idea that they might be "A Temple of the Holy Ghost" and might want to refuse the sexual advances of young men. Meanwhile, the child indulges in her own arrogance and grandiosity, dreaming of her future as either a doctor, engineer, or Christian martyr—the latter being preferable not for its holiness, but for its greater fame and briefer duration. One night the two older girls go to a fair, and when they return home, they are obviously trying to keep a secret from the child. She tricks them into telling it. They describe how in one of the mysterious tents into which children are not allowed, they had seen a hermaphrodite—they don't know to call the person that, of course, though they remember that the person had a strange name that they now forget. The child doesn't exactly understand how a person can be both male and female, but what strikes her much more deeply is the hermaphrodite's speech that the girls recount, and it is from this that these two lines are taken. Throughout the speech and the retellings of it, the hermaphrodite expresses an earnest desire to accept the physical affliction given by God, and even to praise and thank God for this. When the child retells the speech to herself as she's falling asleep, she even embellishes it more to include the hermaphrodite and the audience vowing that they will be temples of the Holy Ghost, dwelling places for God, at the same time as they ecstatically praise God for his blessings.

I have chosen these simple sentences partly because I think the story encapsulates so many aspects of O'Connor's writing. This is true in its details—the observant but isolated child who contemplates religious questions far beyond her years, a character who alternates between thinking herself a terrible sinner and a great saint, the cruelty of older children, the focus on physical deformities, a single-parent home, the pain and unfairness of life. It is also true in its brief but intense experience of mysterious grace that we have seen in more extended form in other stories. The revelation of God's grace and presence to the child at the end of the story comes about because of her meditation on these lines, and their unexpected occurrence to her while praying. Like Mrs. Turpin's experience, the child's revelation comes about following an unsuccessful prayer in which she echoes the Pharisee of Luke 18:9–14, thanking and praising God for making her a Catholic and not a member of the Church of God—an ironically named denomination, because by her childish self-righteousness, she has excluded herself from the real church and presence of God. But this prayer is again the worst kind of gratitude, thanking God for supposedly making us better than other people, thanking God for our own false distinctions and pride that keep us from him: one might as well thank God for making us sinful. Real gratitude is thanking God for the way he made us, when the way he made us is not quite what we expected or desired, and which we usually find impossible to understand, accept, or appreciate, let alone to be grateful for it. It is thanking God for making us according to his plan, and not according to ours. It is delight in being itself, and it precludes all sinfulness, especially the judging of others. Perhaps more than any other O'Connor story that we have looked at, the passionate gratitude expressed here is part of a realization about God's own self and nature, more than about our own sinfulness and alienation from him.

But as we have seen repeatedly in our analysis, human sinfulness can always find a way to twist some good aspiration or feeling into something sinful, something oriented toward oneself and not toward God, something that drags us away from God rather than lifts us up toward him. In this case, it is our human tendency to take the idea "This is the way God wanted me to be," and apply it to the things we can and should change about ourselves. If I'm lustful, it's because God made me that way—perhaps even with good biological reasons, if one finds those convincing—and the same for angry, or greedy, or any other sinful attitude. And lest one think that sinfulness is always so easily recognized, consider more ambiguous attitudes such as ambition or pride: are these part of how God made me? Maybe, but it's no reason to accept or revel in them unreflectively and uncritically. In essence, I think O'Connor is advocating a startling, startled, loving affirmation of God's goodness in the face of human suffering, but it can be turned into a complacent, denying excuse for human sinfulness.

O'Connor knew perfectly well how human sinfulness and selfishness could take such an idea and turn it into something ugly. When Joy/Hulga utters almost the same words in "Good Country People," the effect is the opposite of the child's prayer: "If you want me, here I am—LIKE I AM."[139] But the difference in Joy/Hulga's statement is more significant than the similarity, for she does not say this to God, nor does she even acknowledge God's existence, let alone his role as Father and Creator. If anything, her bald assertion of ego is almost blasphemous, perversely echoing God's "I AM" of Exodus 3:14.[140] It is a statement of proud defiance, not loving acceptance. Yet we can somewhat ameliorate Joy/Hulga's egoism: asking others to accept us the way we are and not try to fix us is probably appropriate most of the time in our dealings with other sinful human beings. After all, other people really can't fix us, and it's often mean, selfish, and destructive of them to try, as we saw with Mr. Head, Mr. Fortune, and Sheppard. But with God it is the exactly wrong and self-destructive attitude, for God is the only one who can and will fix us.[141]

In "A Temple of the Holy Ghost," however, the child's final experience is completely God-centered, and therefore totally liberating and revelatory. She does not ask God to accept her the way she is; she accepts herself and thanks God for her self. She acknowledges that she is the way she is because her very being is a gift of God, for which she can finally show real gratitude. And this is exactly what could keep one from slipping into the specious rationalizations for sin outlined above. One cannot sin as long as one submits to God, for the essence of sin is rebellion against God, the attempt to bend other creatures and even God to one's own will. When the child finally knows and feels that she is a beloved creature of God, she is no longer accepting of her sinfulness, but repentant for it. She feels God's presence everywhere—in herself; in others, no matter how unwashed and uncouth they may be; in the Word of God; in the sacraments; in the natural world—a vision of all of creation not merely pointing to its Creator, but embodying him. "[O'Connor] believes that the material world embodies the spiritual world. One is almost tempted to say that for O'Connor the material world *is* the spiritual world."[142] This convergence of spirit and matter would become more explicit in her later stories, but never perhaps as beautiful as here in this very early story.[143] And the beauty and profundity of O'Connor's sacramental thought is that it not only redeems all matter, but just as importantly, all time: "Both grand and humble events alike can take on the sacramental quality of the mediation of grace through the eruption of the timeless into the temporal."[144] By centering ourselves on God, every part of space and time becomes precious and joyful to us, every part an embodiment and experience of God.

The last page of the story is one of the few in O'Connor where grace and revelation are not violent or fatal. It is an ecstatic vision worth striving for, or more accurately, worth opening ourselves up to, in humble and awestruck vulnerability, acceptance, gratitude, and love. Let us pray to the God who made us the way he wanted, who made us for him, with this kind of spirit.

For Further Reading

Giannone, R. *Flannery O'Connor and the Mystery of Love.* New York: Fordham University Press, 1999. Now available in paperback, its somewhat difficult academic prose offers sophisticated readings of O'Connor's stories and novels, showing the many connections and developments among them.

Kilcourse, G. A., Jr. *Flannery O'Connor's Religious Imagination: A World with Everything off Balance.* New York: Paulist Press, 2001. Offers accessible analyses of O'Connor's stories and novels, with a deep appreciation of her theology, usefully reinforced by references to her letters.

O'Connor, F. *The Complete Stories.* New York: Farrar, Straus & Giroux, 1971. All her stories in one volume, twelve of them never before published, arranged chronologically and with an engaging introduction.

———. *The Habit of Being.* Edited by S. Fitzgerald. New York: Farrar, Straus & Giroux, 1979. Presents her letters, some of the most entertaining and important of any twentieth-century writer.

Notes

1. On this experience of isolation, see S. Fitzgerald, "Rooms with a View," *Katallagete* 8 (1982): 4–11, esp. 6–10; also R. C. Wood, "Talent Increased and Returned to God: The Spiritual Legacy of Flannery O'Connor's Letters," *Anglican Theological Review* 62 (1980): 153–67, esp. 162–67.

2. On this experience, see R. Giannone, *Flannery O'Connor, Hermit Novelist* (Urbana, IL: University of Illinois Press, 2000), 15; and very movingly, R. Martin, "Flannery O'Connor—Twenty Years After," *Center Journal* 4 (1984): 29–37, esp. 29–33. Cf. R. Drake, "Flannery O'Connor: Some Afterthoughts," *Christianity and Literature* 46 (1996): 111–18, who rightly cautions against a distorting hagiography of O'Connor and her experience.

3. R. Drake, "The Harrowing Evangel of Flannery O'Connor," *Christian Century* 81 (1964): 1200–1202, esp. (quotation from) 1202.

4. Cf. H. Davies and M. H. Davies, "The God of Storm and Stillness: The Fiction of Flannery O'Connor and Frederick Buechner," *Religion and Life* 48 (1979): 188–96, esp. 191: "In her short stories as in her life the mother is the dominant figure."

5. The perceptive label of S. Fitzgerald, "The Invisible Father," *Christianity and Literature* 47 (1997): 5–18, esp. 10.

6. Cf. R. F. Morneau, "Spirituality: Five Twentieth–Century Witnesses of Discipleship," in *The Catholic Church in the Twentieth Century*, ed. J. Deedy (Collegeville: M. Glazier, 2000), 217–33, esp. 228: "Here Flannery O'Connor has a double vision. God, from one point of view, is unlimited, infinite, almighty. With the other eye she sees a God revealed specifically in the person of Jesus who became one of us, entered into the violence of our world, rose from the dead, and calls us home."

7. Drake, "Harrowing Evangel," 1201. See also Wood, "Talent Increased," 154–55.

8. P. Friesen, "The Missionary Calling of Flannery O'Connor," *Direction* 27, no. 2 (1998): 157–64, esp. 160.

9. G. A. Kilcourse, Jr., *Flannery O'Connor's Religious Imagination: A World with Everything off Balance* (New York: Paulist Press, 2001), 11.

10. E. Sewell, "Is Flannery O'Connor a Nonsense Writer?" *Soundings* 73 (1990): 273–302, esp. 298.

11. J. Zornado, "A Becoming Habit: Flannery O'Connor's Fiction of Unknowing," *Religion and Literature* 29 (1997): 27–59, esp. 34.

12. J. Zornado, "Negative Writings: Flannery O'Connor, Apophatic Thought, and Christian Criticism," *Christianity and Literature* 42 (1992): 117–40, esp. 117.

13. Quoted by J. Polter, "Obliged to See God," *Sojourners* 23 (1994–95): 16–22, esp. 21.

14. J. Andreas, "'If It's a Symbol, the Hell with It': The Medieval Gothic Style of Flannery O'Connor in *Everything That Rises Must Converge*," *Christianity and Literature* 38 (1989): 23–41, esp. 25.

15. Andreas, "Medieval Gothic Style," 27; see also Friesen, "Missionary Calling," 162–63; G. W. Shepherd, "The Example of Flannery O'Connor as a Christian Writer," *Center Journal* 4 (1984): 39–63, esp. 47–49 and 55–56.

16. M. C. McEntyre, "Mercy That Burns: Violence and Revelation in Flannery O'Connor's Fiction," *Theology Today* 53 (1996): 331–44, esp. 331.

17. J. Sykes, "Christian Apologetic Uses of the Grotesque in John Irving and Flannery O'Connor," *Literature and Theology* 10 (1996): 58–67, esp. 63.

18. See S. McFague, "The Parabolic in Faulkner, O'Connor, and Percy," *Notre Dame English Journal* 15 (1983): 49–66, esp. 54–60.

19. Cf. Drake, "Harrowing Evangel," 1201: "But whatever role the grotesque plays in her fiction, it is always dramatically functional, never extraneous to the central design"; also Drake, "Afterthoughts," 117: "But they *work* in the dramatic context, and they also *mean*. They're not there just to be lurid or titillating."

20. Wood, "Talent Increased," 156.

21. K. Martin, "Flannery O'Connor's Prophetic Imagination," *Religion and Literature* 26, no. 3 (1994): 33–58, esp. 50.

22. J. G. Parks, "Losing and Finding: Meditations of a Christian Reader," *Christianity and Literature* 38 (1989): 19–23, esp. 20.

23. Martin, "Twenty Years After," 35.

24. M. P. Gillespie, "Baroque Catholicism in Southern Fiction: Flannery O'Connor, Walker Percy, and John Kennedy Toole," in *Traditions, Voices, and Dreams: The American Novel since the 1960s*, ed. M. J. Friedman and B. Siegel (Newark, DE: University of Delaware Press, 1995), 25–47, esp. 30.

25. J. F. Desmond, "Flannery O'Connor and the Idolatrous Mind," *Christianity and Literature* 46 (1996): 25–35, esp. 26.

26. On O'Connor's study of the Old Testament prophets and of modern scholarship on them, see Martin, "Prophetic Imagination," esp. 33–50.

27. Wood, "Talent Increased," 156.

28. H. Ben-Bassat, "Flannery O'Connor's Double Vision," *Literature and Theology* 11 (1997) 185–99, esp. 188.

29. R. Giannone, "Stabbing the Heart: *Catanyxis* and *Penthos* in Flannery O'Connor's 'Greenleaf,'" *Christianity and Literature* 45 (1996): 331–44, esp. 332.

30. Martin, "Prophetic Imagination," 56.

31. D. Stokes, "Grit, Grace and Miss O'Connor," *Theology* 80 (1977): 107–10, esp. 108; see also Martin, "Prophetic Imagination," esp. 34; M. J. Weaver, "Thomas Merton and Flannery O'Connor: The Urgency of Vision," *Religion in Life* 48 (1979): 449–61, esp. 457–58.

32. Weaver, "Merton and O'Connor," 452.

33. Recently pointed out in a contemporary context, but with timeless applicability, by B. W. Tuchman, *The March of Folly: From Troy to Vietnam* (New York: Random House, 1984), as quoted by Maureen Dowd, "The Springs of Fate," *New York Times*, May 16, 2004, online: http://www.nytimes.com, accessed May 16, 2004: "Wooden-headedness, the source of self-deception, is a factor that plays a remarkably large role in government. It consists in assessing a situation in terms of preconceived fixed notions while ignoring or rejecting any contrary signs."

34. As described by S. Fitzgerald, "Happy Endings," *Image: A Journal of the Arts and Religion* 16 (Summer 1997): 73–80, esp. 79; also referred to by Sewell, "Nonsense Writer?" 281; and Wood, "Talent Increased," 160.

35. Drake, "Harrowing Evangel," 1201, emphasis in original.

36. A. DiRenzo, *American Gargoyles: Flannery O'Connor and the Medieval Grotesque* (Carbondale, IL: Southern Illinois University Press, 1993), 5. On the other hand, for the possibly negative aspects of the grotesque, see J. C. VanRys, "Reclaiming Marginalia: The Grotesque and the Christian Reader," *Christianity and Literature* 44 (1995): 345–57, esp. 349–50.

37. See Andreas, "Medieval Gothic Style," 24; Wood, "Talent Increased," 160.

38. Cf. Wood, "Talent Increased," 166: "She regarded her lupus not as an affliction to be stoically endured but a distraction to be wittily deprecated. Spiritually she was so liberated from it that she could still discern the humor implicit in her adversity."

39. Cf. J. R. Michaels, "Images of Grace in Flannery O'Connor's Strong Women," *Daughters of Sarah* 16 (1990): 27–30, esp. 29: "Sometimes the grace of God and the angel of death come simultaneously, and the reader looking for the traditional 'happy ending' comes away empty." See also Sewell, "Nonsense Writer?" 279–81, who compares the violence in O'Connor to that in "nonsense" writers, esp. Edward Lear and Lewis Carroll.

40. O'Connor, quoted in J. L. Gay, "The Literary Apologetic of Flannery O'Connor," *Crux* 19 (November 1983): 27–32, esp. 28.

41. H. T. Harmsel, "Getting Kilt: Death in the Stories of Flannery O'Connor," *The Reformed Journal* 37 (1987): 13–15, esp. 15.

42. Morneau, "Witnesses of Discipleship," 227.

43. K. Scullin, "Transforming Violence in O'Connor's *The Violent Bear It Away*," in *Wagering on Transcendence: The Search for Meaning in Literature*, ed. P. Carey (Kansas City: Sheed & Ward, 1997), 206–29, esp. 209.

44. Cf. Michaels, "Strong Women," 29: "Because human pride and self-sufficiency must be broken down before redemption can take place, redemption and judgment in many of O'Connor's stories look very much alike."

45. Ben-Bassat, "O'Connor's Double Vision," 192.

46. See R. Giannone, *Flannery O'Connor and the Mystery of Love* (Urbana, IL: University of Illinois Press, 1989) 97–101; Kilcourse, *O'Connor's Religious Imagination*, 176–79.

47. On the tentativeness of the General's epiphany, see F. Asals, *Flannery O'Connor: The Imagination of Extremity* (Athens, GA: University of Georgia Press, 1982), 207–08. Cf. the more optimistic evaluation of Kilcourse, *O'Connor's Religious Imagination*, 179.

48. Zornado, "Negative Writings," 117.

49. Cf. Michaels, "Strong Women," 29: "The world of O'Connor's short stories is to a considerable degree a woman's world. This does not make O'Connor a feminist in any ideological sense. It does mean that she saw women so clearly as human beings, and often as very strong and self-sufficient human beings, that she did not hesitate to ascribe to them the same *hubris*, the same overweening

pride, that we see in the great male tragic heroes." See also S. Maddux, "Flannery O'Connor and the Christian Pharisee," *Communio* 11 (1984): 335–49, esp. 338: "Another character type that occurs very frequently, in a number of different forms but usually with negative connotations, is the more or less aggressive, possessive, self-possessed, self-confident woman."

50. Ben-Bassat, "O'Connor's Double Vision," 196.

51. Giannone, *Mystery of Love*, 168–69.

52. Harmsel, "Getting Kilt," 14.

53. Cf. Giannone, "Stabbing the Heart," 334: "Not one to forget that the rich and famous also suffer, Mrs. Greenleaf clips accounts of divorcing movie stars."

54. Ibid., 334.

55. Giannone, *Mystery of Love*, 170.

56. See ibid., 167, on O'Connor's satisfaction and her critics' dissatisfaction with the story's ending.

57. F. O'Connor, *The Complete Stories* (New York: Farrar, Straus & Giroux, 1971), 334.

58. Consider the different interpretations of Friesen, "Missionary Calling," 163, who sees no redemption at the end of the story; Harmsel, "Getting Kilt," 14, and McEntyre, "Mercy That Burns," 338–39, who see the ending as ambiguous, but do not criticize it for that reason; D. P. Mehl, "Sex and Sacrament in Contemporary Literature: The Incarnation as Method," *Currents in Theology and Mission* 10 (1983): 351–64, esp. 357–58, who sees it as ambiguous and therefore flawed; and Giannone, "Stabbing the Heart," 340–43, who sees Mrs. May's redemption as complete.

59. Cf. Giannone, *Mystery of Love*, 172–73: "O'Connor discerns a connection between sexuality and death that is impressive for all its triteness. . . . The amatory embrace tells us that love is the way of ascent." See also E. Startzman, "Christ the Lover in the Works of Flannery O'Connor and C. S. Lewis," *Christianity and the Arts* 6 (1999): 32–36.

60. O'Connor, *Complete Stories*, 317.

61. Giannone, "Stabbing the Heart," 334.

62. See Giannone, *Mystery of Love*, 211; Kilcourse, *O'Connor's Religious Imagination*, 252–53.

63. Cf. Giannone, "Stabbing the Heart," 338, describing her as "a victim in search of assailants to justify her wrath."

64. Kilcourse, *O'Connor's Religious Imagination*, 285.

65. O'Connor, *Complete Stories*, 500. I have always wondered at the recurrence of this line in the movie *Raising Arizona*, but cannot confirm it as a direct allusion.

66. McEntyre, "Mercy That Burns," 336. See also Martin, "Prophetic Imagination," 52: "Turpin eventually becomes angry at God, whom she accepts as the originator of the message delivered by Mary Grace."

67. O'Connor, *Complete Stories*, 507.

68. Ibid., 508.

69. J. Goss, "O'Connor's Redeemed Man: Christus et/vel Porcus?" *The Drew Gateway* 44 (1974): 106–19, esp. 119.

70. It is probably another influence of Teilhard de Chardin, the French Jesuit and scientist, whose work O'Connor was reading at the time, and of which she approved enthusiastically for its integration of spirit and matter, science and spirituality: see E. Archer, "'Stalking Joy': Flannery O'Connor's Accurate Naming," *Religion and Literature* 18 (1986): 17–30, esp. 28–29; R. Bowen, "Christology in the Works of Flannery O'Connor," *Horizons* 14 (1987): 7–23, esp. 13–21; Kilcourse, *O'Connor's Religious Imagination*, 270–78.

71. See the analyses of J. C. Holbert, "Revelation according to Jacob and Mrs. Turpin: Early Reflections on Preaching and Contemporary Literature," *Journal for Preachers* 17 (1993): 11–21; and L. Munk, "Shouting at the Lord across a Hogpen: Flannery O'Connor's 'Revelation,'" *Theology* 97 (1994): 283–92.

72. See Kilcourse, *O'Connor's Religious Imagination*, 284; Maddux, "Christian Pharisee," 335–40.

73. Maddux, "Christian Pharisee," 345.

74. Thus Goss, "Redeemed Man," 118–19; Maddux, "Christian Pharisee," 340–49.

75. The astute connection made by Andreas, "Medieval Gothic Style," 36; Munk, "Shouting at the Lord," 290.

76. Morneau, "Witnesses of Discipleship," 228.

77. O'Connor, quoted in Wood, "Talent Increased," 156.

78. Giannone, *Mystery of Love*, 55.

79. Ibid.

80. O'Connor, *Complete Stories*, 153. Kilcourse, *O'Connor's Religious Imagination*, 141, misreads it as "seventy-five."

81. O'Connor herself seems a bit too harsh on Mr. Shiftlet, identifying him as the devil himself: see Giannone, *Mystery of Love*, 57; J. R. Lindroth, "A Consistency of Voice and Vision: O'Connor as Self-Critic," *Religion and Literature* 16, no. 2 (Summer 1984): 43–59, esp. 54–55. His possible redemption after the story seems almost as likely as that of the Misfit in "A Good Man Is Hard to Find."

82. Cf. Giannone, *Mystery of Love*, 57: "Grief over an imagined slight to his angelic mother gives the drifter the illusion of atoning for his desertion of the real angel in his life. At the base of Mr. Shiftlet's dejection is a trick that language itself plays on him: he misreads a lie, taking it literally.... Weepy conceit has Mr. Shiftlet around the heart so that he keeps up the charade of moralist even when he is alone."

83. Another good label from Kilcourse, *O'Connor's Religious Imagination*, 142.

84. O'Connor, *Complete Stories*, 156.

85. Cf. Kilcourse, *O'Connor's Religious Imagination*, 143: "Unlike Ruby Turpin in 'Revelation,' Mr. Shiftlet lacks the vision to recognize how he is

deprived of grace. But the story ends on an unmistakable note of original sin as this man with scars of violence and calluses of sin self-righteously condemns the world he has helped to corrupt."

86. The perceptive label of Kilcourse, *Flannery O'Connor's Religious Imagination*, 143.

87. Kilcourse, *O'Connor's Religious Imagination*, 186.

88. Giannone, *Mystery of Love*, 65.

89. See Kilcourse, *O'Connor's Religious Imagination*, 184.

90. Archer, "Accurate Naming," 25.

91. O'Connor, *Complete Stories*, 289.

92. Cf. Giannone, *Mystery of Love*, 64, who labels his sexuality "a weird combination of bravado and impotence."

93. O'Connor, *Complete Stories*, 290.

94. Giannone, *Mystery of Love*, 66, 68. See also Asals, *Imagination of Extremity*, 102–8.

95. The wonderfully concise description of Kilcourse, *O'Connor's Religious Imagination*, 187.

96. This time it is Giannone, *Mystery of Love*, 68, who offers the overly optimistic reading of the end of the story.

97. On the story as an inversion or complement to "Good Country People," see Asals, *Imagination of Extremity*, 99–102.

98. E. M. Budick, "'American Israelites': Literalism and Typology in the American Imagination," in *Biblical Patterns in Modern Literature*, ed. D. H. Hirsch and N. Aschkenasy (Chico, CA: Scholars Press, 1984) 187–208: 204.

99. Giannone, *Mystery of Love*, 176.

100. O'Connor, *Complete Stories*, 352; see the analysis of Asals, *Imagination of Extremity*, 101.

101. Suggested by Giannone, *Mystery of Love*, 179.

102. O'Connor herself offered a Christological interpretation of the woods: see Giannone, *Mystery of Love*, 180–81; see also Budick, "American Israelites," 204–5. This does not necessarily make the ending hopeful, for Mr. Fortune's willful blindness seems emphatic and unabated right through to the end of the story.

103. Giannone, *Mystery of Love*, 175.

104. Cf. the eloquent description of the names in Asals, *Imagination of Extremity*, 101: Fortune is "the assertion of the egoistic seeker of power, self-inflating and self-aggrandizing, devotee of the ancient bitch-goddess of this world," while Pitts is "powerlessness and suffering . . . pain, loss, and worldly defeat, from which opens an appalling glimpse of the bottomless pit and the inescapable awareness of that earthly pit to which we all go." I have wondered if "Pitts" could be even more hopeful: some fruit seeds are called "pits" and therefore the name could suggest fertility, life, and rebirth.

105. Giannone, *Mystery of Love*, 175.

106. Cf. Kilcourse, *O'Connor's Religious Imagination*, 259, who writes that Mr. Fortune has "gone to hell. . . . Love again miscarries through a legacy of stubborn selfishness and greed."

107. See the psychological analysis of J. M. Mellard, "Flannery O'Connor's Others: Freud, Lacan, and the Unconscious," *American Literature* 61 (1989): 625–43, esp. 642: "Killing the child who is pure PITTS now, the old man kills not his mirroring, narcissistic, Imaginary other, but his Other in the register of the Symbolic—a far graver crime, indeed, one that in psychoanalytic terms equals the murder of God in the Christian subject's denial of God's grace."

108. Andreas, "Medieval Gothic Style," 32.

109. Ibid., 31.

110. O'Connor, *Complete Stories*, 454; emphasis in the original.

111. On the identity between Rufus and the devil, see Kilcourse, *O'Connor's Religious Imagination*, 267–68; Lindroth, "Consistency of Voice," 55–57; D. Z. Phillips, "The Devil's Disguises: Philosophy of Religion, 'Objectivity' and 'Cultural Divergence,'" in *Objectivity and Cultural Divergence*, ed. S. C. Brown (Cambridge: Cambridge University Press, 1984), 61–77, esp. 65–66.

112. O'Connor, *Complete Stories*, 481.

113. Fitzgerald, "Happy Endings," 75.

114. Cf. Kilcourse, *O'Connor's Religious Imagination*, 132: "In effect, he argues that Jesus' undeserved suffering became the warrant for endless occasions of innocent suffering."

115. See my *In Praise of Wisdom: Literary and Theological Reflections on Faith and Reason* (New York: Continuum, 2004) for a discussion of some of these.

116. Giannone, *Mystery of Love*, 50.

117. O'Connor, *Complete Stories*, 132.

118. Thus Zornado, "Negative Writings," 132.

119. Thus Archer, "Accurate Naming," 26; Gay, "Literary Apologetic," 28.

120. Thus Kilcourse, *O'Connor's Religious Imagination*, 133–35; P. Mariani, "God and the Imagination," *Image: A Journal of the Arts and Religion* 18 (Winter 1997): 97–109, esp. 106.

121. Thus Asals, *Imagination of Extremity*, 147; Giannone, *Mystery of Love*, 50–53.

122. Cf. Giannone, *Mystery of Love*, 52–53: "Goodness has a gain of its own. The grandmother achieves the liberty to choose a response beyond the anger and revenge that violence induces in its victim. She chooses to love, and her tenderness crushes the gunslinger's might."

123. O'Connor, *Mystery and Manners*, ed. S. and R. Fitzgerald (New York: Farrar, Straus & Giroux, 1969), 113, quoted by Archer, "Accurate Naming," 26; Fitzgerald, "Happy Endings," 76; Giannone, *Mystery of Love*, 53.

124. O'Connor, *Complete Stories*, 132.

125. Ibid., 133.

126. Cf. the similar conclusions of Fitzgerald, "Happy Endings," 76; Kilcourse, *O'Connor's Religious Imagination*, 134.

127. Zornado, "Negative Writings," 133.

128. See G. N. Boyd, "Parables of Costly Grace: Flannery O'Connor and Ken Kesey," *Theology Today* 29 (1972): 161–71, esp. 168; Kilcourse, *O'Connor's Religious Imagination*, 151.

129. Cf. R. Giannone, "Flannery O'Connor Tells Her Desert Story," *Religion and Literature* 27 (1995): 47–68, esp. 57: "He finds in his grandfather's appeal to white male superiority a balm that moderates his aloneness. From now on, the lost backwoods child has a place in the larger social world that provides a black scapegoat to support his standing."

130. Cf. the analyses of the black woman in Asals, *Imagination of Extremity*, 86; Kilcourse, *O'Connor's Religious Imagination*, 155–56.

131. On the imagery, see Asals, *Imagination of Extremity*, 88–90; Giannone, *Mystery of Love*, 93.

132. O'Connor, *Complete Stories*, 269.

133. Boyd, "Parables of Costly Grace," 168–69.

134. This is part of the story's sacramental vision, of the spiritual and transcendent constantly and fully contained in the material: see Asals, *Imagination of Extremity*, 79; Bowen, "Christology in Flannery O'Connor," 79.

135. O'Connor, *Complete Stories*, "A Temple of the Holy Ghost," 246, 248.

136. See Kilcourse, *O'Connor's Religious Imagination*, 146–50, esp. 149. For another analysis, see Giannone, *Mystery of Love*, 76–81. On the Eucharist in the story, see R. H. Brinkmeyer, Jr., *The Art and Vision of Flannery O'Connor* (Baton Rouge, LA: Louisiana State University Press, 1989), 1–3. For an analysis that focuses on gender and sexuality in the story, see S. Gordon, *Flannery O'Connor: The Obedient Imagination* (Athens, GA: The University of Georgia Press, 2000), 152–64.

137. J. Jacobsen, "A Catholic Quartet," *The Christian Scholar* 47 (1964), 139–54, esp. 151.

138. O'Connor's fascination with children in her stories is again taken as evidence of her being a "nonsense" writer by Sewell, "Nonsense Writer?" 281–83.

139. O'Connor, *Complete Stories*, "Good Country People," 274.

140. Cf. Archer, "Accurate Naming," 24.

141. Cf. Giannone, *Mystery of Love*, 65: "She remains stiff-necked before the God Who knows her weakness, and wills to bow before her god of negation."

142. DiRenzo, *American Gargoyles*, 81, emphasis in original; his analysis of the story is on 81–91.

143. See Bowen, "Christology in Flannery O'Connor," 14.

144. P. W. Williams, "Perceptions of Time in American Catholicism," *Journal of Religious Studies* 11 (1983): 1–13, esp. 10.

5

CONCLUSION
The Truth Will Set You Free

It was only while actually writing this book that I was able to figure out why I was writing it, or why someone might want to read it or might benefit from such reading. I wondered why I was spending so much time and effort thinking and writing about evil and sin. And, indeed, why has the topic in different guises dominated most of my writing for the last ten years? Practically speaking, how could I expect readers to follow my lead into such dark and dismal realms of thought, especially when there's so much uplifting, inspirational writing out there? God is our light and our good shepherd, so why not brighten people's lives and make them feel safe, loved, and valued? Why not focus on other, more cheerful theological topics, like faith, hope, love, freedom, and salvation? I was having my own crisis about the validity of what I was doing; and unlike St. Paul or Luther or Pascal, it was not about feeling lost and sinful myself, but about my morbid fascination with such sinfulness. It was more like the kind of crisis that would be experienced by Stuart Smalley, Al Franken's neurotically self-deprecating character on *Saturday Night Live*. This was a crisis of feeling that I am inadequate to the task of explaining my work to others, of convincing them that sin is something important about which they should worry and contemplate. And even if I could explain it, why would I want to? Most people I know are nice enough, and some are downright virtuous, so why do I focus so much on the dark side of human nature and life? Isn't there enough ugliness in the world, so much that I have given up watching the local news for the last eight years, even long before September 11?

Indeed, there is, but in a strange way, that proves the relevance of this work. Before September 11, many Americans would barely have acknowledged the existence or the possibility of evil; at most, it would have occurred to them as some unpleasant memory of a distant, barbaric past. Hitler and the Holocaust are the distant past to many, and Rwanda and Bosnia are sufficiently obscure and geographically removed. In the supernatural realm, many more Americans believe in God and angels than in Satan and demons.[1] Guardian angels are especially popular as real and powerful beings who are eager to help you. Yet a "personal demon" is now just shorthand for any personal problem or neurosis, not for something with objective existence and power. It is something for which you need a twelve-step program or a pharmacological solution, not a priest or prayers. Even after September 11, most people think of evil as something "out there," something that only demented, unnatural people do. On the streets of the Bronx, where many of my students live, one may well meet an evil person, and this would be unpleasant, perhaps even fatal, but not really relevant to one's ideas about oneself or about human nature. We generally assume that evil people should be avoided and feared for the danger they pose, but need not be analyzed for any similarity they bear to "regular" people like you and me.

But ignoring or denying evil does not make it go away. Given the horrific track record of evil in the twentieth century, one would be quite justified in speculating that three centuries of secular humanism and declining religiosity in the West have let evil grow more virulent. Meanwhile, stunning advances in technology have rendered it infinitely more powerful and destructive. And making evil into something pathological that is irrelevant to most people renders it all the more insidious and pervasive in our own personal lives. As the John Huston character observes in the classic film noir *Chinatown*, every one of us is capable of every evil action imaginable, no matter how sick and depraved we deem it to be, and no matter how outraged we act when others commit it. But unlike him, we needn't use this as a cowardly excuse for our own evil, but rather as a more urgent call for its examination and eradication. Just because evil is all pervasive does not mean it's excusable. Like ignorance, sin is a disease that can only be cured once it is diagnosed. Left untreated it will really and inevitably become a sickness unto death (John 11:4 KJV).

But one needn't be so pessimistic and focus so much on sin as the actual commission of evil actions to appreciate what we have been studying in this book. The broader meaning of my work finally became clear to me as I was reading a perceptive rumination on Flannery O'Connor's writing:

> The beginning for the Christian reader is the awareness and experience of the decentered self, whose radical contingency and vulnerability put it at risk to new possibilities of understanding in dialogue with difference and otherness. For the Christian this awareness does not come from the exercise of our rationality, but rather, paradoxically, as a gift. . . . While this counsel may point, for some, to a source of human anguish, it is also a source of human greatness and joy.[2]

As I read this, I was taken back to my own conversion experience, which came about when I learned—from reading the Bible, Dante, Augustine, Pascal, and C. S. Lewis with the teachers to whom this book is dedicated—that the essence of Christianity is not in its teachings about the creation of the world or about the end of days, nor in its moralizing, nor in its dwelling on how wicked people are. Instead, the essence of Christianity that I have embraced is in its shocking but accurate evaluation of humans as weak, broken, and incomplete. I suddenly realized that original sin is not only about two people and a talking snake—which reduces it to a fairly quaint myth. Nor is it just about the sinful things I do—which, since I don't sin all that badly, reduces it to a fairly mundane and unimpressive list of minor infractions. These are hardly the sorts of things for which one would receive eternal damnation, or for which one would feel constantly racked with guilt. The most important part of original sin is this sense of a brokenness that I cannot fix by myself, an incompleteness that I cannot fill up on my own, no matter how many different things I try to grasp and hold on to as completion or fulfillment. This mundane and constant state of brokenness can be seen throughout our lives. It showed itself in the slow and painful deaths of my mother and of my friend Greg—endured by both, so far as I could tell, with Stoic patience, but experienced by those left behind

as nearly unbearable holes in our lives. It was human frailty and brokenness that then led my father to fill that void with hatred and rage against
the God whose existence he denied. Original sin besets me in the petty
grudges and maliciousness that I myself can so easily hold on to until I
find perverse enjoyment in them. These common experiences are the
things that prove to me daily the utter truthfulness of the Christian
claim that the world is not exactly the way God made it at first, that
there is something wrong with it that only God can fix.

This is the truth about ourselves that we must learn in order to be set
free. Belief in sin and redemption is therefore the essence of Christianity,
and it is worth emphasizing that this is the very concept that makes
Christianity different from every other world religion. According to
Christianity, it is not enough just to meditate until we get enlightenment, as in Buddhism. It is not enough just to strive for detachment
from our actions until we are released from the karmic cycle, as in
Hinduism. It is not enough just to flow with the Way, as in Taoism. It is
not enough just to perfect ourselves morally through our own efforts,
as in Confucianism. It is not enough just to follow the laws God has
given us so that we can be his chosen people, as in Judaism or Islam. As
Christians, we would do well to learn and practice all these spiritual dis-
ciplines of the other world religions. But we should also acknowledge
that Christianity depicts the present human situation as much worse
than any other world religion does, as much more in need of divine
intervention and not just human action.

We should take none of this to mean that Christianity is necessarily
more pessimistic than other religions. Though the severity of the disease—or dis-ease—is more dire in Christianity, the joyousness of the
cure is all the more extreme. And the final, blissful state is as beautiful
and ecstatic as that described in any other tradition. But the way to that
redemption is as paradoxical as it is true. Though I took the title of this
conclusion from John's Gospel (8:32 NIV), I think Luke's Gospel best
summarizes our examination of sin and redemption with the prayer of
the sinful tax collector that we looked at in chapter 1: "God, have mercy
on me, a sinner" (Luke 18:13 NIV). That's all that really needs to be
said to God from a Christian perspective, and the prayer has taken on
a huge importance in the Orthodox tradition for its succinct profundity. But as simple as the prayer is, its difficulty and paradox are then
explained by Jesus, who says that "all who humble themselves will be

exalted" (Luke 18:14). Learning to humble ourselves as God humbled himself is the unique challenge and paradox of Christianity. For twenty years, I have been humbled by the books we have examined here, as I have been by the kind and loving people mentioned in the acknowledgments. Together they have given me small glimpses of what exaltation will be like. And in that sense, thinking for so long about sin has not been depressing at all, but redemptive, joyous, and uplifting.

Notes

1. As shown in many recent polls, usefully collated and summarized online: http://www.religioustolerance.org/chr_poll3.htm#god (site visited on March 9, 2003).

2. J. G. Parks, "Losing and Finding: Meditations of a Christian Reader," *Christianity and Literature* 38 (1989): 19–23, esp. 23.

BIBLIOGRAPHY

Adam, K. *Saint Augustine: The Odyssey of His Soul*. Translated by D. J. McCann. New York: Macmillan, 1932.

Agaesse, P. "Saint Augustine." Pages 25–29 in *Jesus in Christian Devotion and Contemplation*. Edited by E. Malatesta. St. Meinrad, IN: Abbey, 1974.

Andreas, J. "'If It's a Symbol, the Hell with It': The Medieval Gothic Style of Flannery O'Connor in *Everything That Rises Must Converge*." *Christianity and Literature* 38 (1989): 23–41.

Archer, E. "'Stalking Joy': Flannery O'Connor's Accurate Naming." *Religion and Literature* 18 (1986): 17–30.

Arnold, M. "Wise Blood: Flannery O'Connor's Lonely Gospel of Hope." *The Drew Gateway* 46 (1975–76): 78–84.

Asals, F. *Flannery O'Connor: The Imagination of Extremity*. Athens: University of Georgia Press, 1982.

Auerbach, E. *Dante: Poet of the Secular World*. Translated by R. Manheim. Chicago: University of Chicago Press, 1961.

Augustine. *City of God*. Translated by H. Bettenson. New York: Penguin Books, 1972.

———. *Confessions*. Translated by M. Boulding. Edited by J. Rotelle. Hyde Park: New City, 1997.

———. *The Confessions of St. Augustine*. Translated by J. K. Ryan. New York et al: Image Books, 1960.

———. *Soliloquies*. Translated by K. Paffenroth. Edited by J. Rotelle. Hyde Park: New City, 2000.

Baasten, M. "Humility and Modern Ethics." *The Reformed Review* 38 (1985): 232–37.

Bacchi, L. F. "A Ministry Characterized by and Exercised in Humility: The Theology of Ordained Ministry in the Letters of Augustine of Hippo." Pages 405–15 in *Augustine: Presbyter factus sum*. Edited by J. T. Lienhard, E. C. Muller, and R. J. Teske. Collectanea Augustiniana. New York: P. Lang, 1993.

Balthasar, H. U. von, "Jesus and Forgiveness." *Communio* 11 (1984): 322–34.

Barker, M. "The Time Is Fulfilled: Jesus and Jubilee." *Scottish Journal of Theology* 53 (2000): 22–32.

Barolini, T. "Dante and Francesca da Rimini: Realpolitik, Romance, Gender." *Speculum* 75 (2000): 1–28.

Barrachina, I. M. *Spiritual Doctrine of St. Augustine*. Translated by E. J. Schuster. St. Louis: Herder, 1963.

Barton, S. C. "Parables on God's Love and Forgiveness (Luke 15:1–32)." Pages 199–216 in *The Challenge of Jesus' Parables*. Edited by R. N. Longenecker. Grand Rapids: Eerdmans, 2000.

Baumgaertner, J. P. "The Meaning Is in You." *Christian Century* 104 (1987): 1172–76.

Ben-Bassat, H. "Flannery O'Connor's Double Vision." *Literature and Theology* 11 (1997): 185–99.

Bernstein, J. A. "Ethics, Theology and the Original State of Man: An Historical Sketch." *Anglican Theological Review* 61 (1979): 162–81.

Bolin, T. M. "A Reassessment of the Textual Problem of Luke 23:34a." *Proceedings, Eastern Great Lakes and Midwest Biblical Societies* 12 (1992): 131–44.

Bolt, P. G. "'With a View to the Forgiveness of Sins': Jesus and Forgiveness in Mark's Gospel." *The Reformed Theological Review* 57 (1998): 53–69.

Bourke, V. J. *Augustine's Quest of Wisdom: Life and Wisdom of the Bishop of Hippo*. Milwaukee: Bruce, 1944.

Bowen, R. "Christology in the Works of Flannery O'Connor." *Horizons* 14 (1987): 7–23.

Boyd, G. N. "Parables of Costly Grace: Flannery O'Connor and Ken Kesey." *Theology Today* 29 (1972): 161–71.

Brandeis, I. *The Ladder of Vision: A Study of Dante's Comedy*. Garden City, NY: Doubleday, 1961.

Brinkmeyer, R. H., Jr. *The Art and Vision of Flannery O'Connor*. Baton Rouge: Louisiana State University Press, 1989.

Brown, P. *Augustine of Hippo: A Biography*. Berkeley: University of California Press, 1967.

Browning, P. M. "Flannery O'Connor and the Grotesque Recovery of the Holy." Pages 133–61 in *Adversity and Grace: Studies in Recent American Literature*. Edited by N. A. Scott. Chicago: University of Chicago Press, 1968.

Budick, E. M. "'American Israelites': Literalism and Typology in the American Imagination." Pages 187–208 in *Biblical Patterns in Modern Literature.* Edited by D. H. Hirsch and N. Aschkenasy. Chico, CA: Scholars Press, 1984.

Burghardt, W. J. "A Brother Whom I Have Pardoned." *The Living Pulpit* 3 (1994): 10–11.

Burnaby, J. *Amor Dei: A Study of the Religion of St. Augustine.* London: Hodder & Stoughton, 1938.

Burns, J. P. "Augustine on the Origin and Progress of Evil." *Journal of Religious Ethics* 16 (1988): 9–27.

Campbell, D. "Flannery O'Connor Is Not John Updike." *American Quarterly* 43 (1991): 333–40.

Cary, P. *Augustine's Invention of the Inner Self: The Legacy of a Christian Platonist.* Oxford: Oxford University Press, 2003.

———. "Book Seven: Inner Vision as the Goal of Augustine's Life." Pages 107–26 in *A Reader's Companion to Augustine's Confessions.* Edited by K. Paffenroth and R. Kennedy. Louisville: Westminster John Knox Press, 2003.

Cavadini, J. "Book Two: Augustine's Book of Shadows." Pages 25–34 in *A Reader's Companion to Augustine's Confessions.* Edited by K. Paffenroth and R. Kennedy. Louisville: Westminster John Knox Press, 2003.

Chadwick, H. *Augustine.* Oxford: Oxford University Press, 1986. Reissued as *Augustine: A Very Short Introduction.* Oxford: Oxford University Press, 2001.

Chilton, B. "Forgiving at and Swearing by the Temple." *Forum* 7 (1991): 45–50.

Clark, M. T. *Augustine: Philosopher of Freedom: A Study in Comparative Philosophy.* New York: Desclée, 1958.

Clements, R. J., ed. *American Critical Essays on The Divine Comedy.* New York: New York University Press, 1967.

Cogan, M. *The Design in the Wax: The Structure of the Divine Comedy and Its Meaning.* Notre Dame, IN: University of Notre Dame Press, 1999.

Coles, R. "Reflections." *Religion and Intellectual Life* 1 (1984): 11–13.

Collins, J. *Pilgrim in Love: An Introduction to Dante and His Spirituality.* Chicago: Loyola University Press, 1984.

Collum, D. D. "Nature and Grace." *Sojourners* 23, no. 10 (December 1994–95): 22–24.

Cooper, S. A. *Augustine for Armchair Theologians.* Louisville: Westminster John Knox Press, 2002.

Cross, R. "Atonement without Satisfaction." *Religious Studies* 37 (2001): 397–416.

Dante Alighieri. *The Divine Comedy.* Translated by G. L. Bickersteth. Oxford: Blackwell, 1981.

———. *Inferno.* Translated by J. Ciardi. New York: Penguin Books, 1954.

———. *Inferno.* Translated by M. Musa. New York: Penguin Books, 1984.

———. *Paradise.* Translated by M. Musa. New York: Penguin Books, 1986.

———. *Purgatorio.* Translated by J. Ciardi. New York: Penguin Books, 1957.

————. *Purgatory*. Translated by M. Musa. New York: Penguin Books, 1985.

Davies, H., and M. H. Davies. "The God of Storm and Stillness: The Fiction of Flannery O'Connor and Frederick Buechner." *Religion and Life* 48 (1979): 188–96.

Day, S. M. "Moral Vision and the Grotesque: Another Look at Flannery O'Connor's Novel *Wise Blood*." *The Grail* 13 (1997): 11–27.

DeGennaro, A. A. *Dante's Divine Comedy*. New York: Philosophical Library, 1986.

Demory, P. "Faithfulness vs. Faith: John Huston's Version of Flannery O'Connor's *Wise Blood*." *The Journal of Southern Religion* 2 (1999).

Deschene, J. M. "The Divine Comedy: Dante's Mystical and Sacramental World–View." *Studia Mystica* 4 (1981): 36–46.

Desmond, J. F. "Flannery O'Connor and the Idolatrous Mind." *Christianity and Literature* 46 (1996): 25–35.

DiLorenzo, R. D. "Augustine's Sapiential Discipline: Wisdom and the Happy Life." *Communio* 10 (1983): 351–59.

DiRenzo, A. *American Gargoyles: Flannery O'Connor and the Medieval Grotesque*. Carbondale: Southern Illinois University Press, 1993.

Drake, R. "Flannery O'Connor: Some Afterthoughts." *Christianity and Literature* 46 (1996): 111–18.

————. "The Harrowing Evangel of Flannery O'Connor." *Christian Century* 81 (1964): 1200–1202.

Dungan, D. L. "Jesus and Violence." Pages 135–62 in *Jesus, the Gospels, and the Church: Essays in Honor of William R. Farmer*. Edited by E. P. Sanders. Macon, GA: Mercer University Press, 1987.

Ehrman, B. *The New Testament: A Historical Introduction to the Early Christian Writings*. 2d ed. New York: Oxford University Press, 2000.

Evans, G. R. "*Alienatio* and Abstract Thinking in Augustine." *Downside Review* 98 (1980): 190–200.

Ferrari, L. "The Theme of the Prodigal Son in Augustine's *Confessions*." *Recherches Augustiniennes* 12 (1977): 105–18.

Ficken, C. "Theology in Flannery O'Connor's *The Habit of Being*." *Christianity and Literature* 30 (Winter 1981): 51–63.

Fiorini, P. "Beatrice, That is, 'On Fidelity.'" Translated by M. Hickin. *Communio* 24 (1997): 84–98.

Fitzgerald, S. "Assumption and Experience." *Cross Currents* 31 (1981–82): 423–32.

————. "Happy Endings." *Image: A Journal of the Arts and Religion* 16 (Summer 1997): 73–80.

————. "The Invisible Father." *Christianity and Literature* 47 (1997): 5–18.

————. "A Letter from Flannery O'Connor about *Wise Blood*." *Katallagete* 9 (Summer 1985): 5–13.

————. "Rooms with a View." *Katallagete* 8 (1982): 4–11.

Fitzmyer, J. A. *The Gospel according to Luke*. 2 vols. New York: Doubleday, 1981–83.

Forman, C. C. "The Search for Authenticity in Flannery O'Connor's *Wise Blood*." Pages 396–405 in *Festchrift in Honor of Charles Speel*. Edited by T. J. Sienkewicz and J. E. Betts. Monmouth, IL: Monmouth College Press, 1996.

Foster, K. "The Mind in Love: Dante's Philosophy." Pages 43–60 in *Dante: A Collection of Critical Essays*. Edited by J. Freccero. Englewood Cliffs, NJ: Prentice–Hall, 1965.

———. *The Two Dantes, and Other Studies*. Berkeley: University of California Press, 1977.

Fowlie, W. "Faith and Narrative in Dante." *Notre Dame English Journal* 15 (1983): 67–76.

Francis, B. J. "The Mysticism of St. Augustine." Pages 95–108 in *Prayer and Contemplation*. Edited by C. M. Vadakkekara. Bangalore: Asirvanam Benedictine Monastery, 1980.

Freccero, J., ed. *Dante: A Collection of Critical Essays*. Englewood Cliffs, NJ: Prentice–Hall, 1965.

———. *Dante: The Poetics of Conversion*. Edited by R. Jacoff. Cambridge, MA: Harvard University Press, 1986.

Friesen, P. "The Missionary Calling of Flannery O'Connor." *Direction* 27, no. 2 (1998): 157–64.

Garvey, M. O. "Communication and the Arts: Lost: The Mind of the Church." Pages 203–15 in *The Catholic Church in the Twentieth Century*. Edited by J. Deedy. Collegeville: Michael Glazier, 2000.

Gay, J. L. "The Literary Apologetic of Flannery O'Connor." *Crux* 19 (November 1983): 27–32.

Giannone, R. *Flannery O'Connor and the Mystery of Love*. Urbana: University of Illinois Press, 1989.

———. *Flannery O'Connor, Hermit Novelist*. Urbana: University of Illinois Press, 2000.

———. "Flannery O'Connor Tells Her Desert Story." *Religion and Literature* 27 (1995): 47–68.

———. "Stabbing the Heart: *Catanyxis* and *Penthos* in Flannery O'Connor's 'Greenleaf.'" *Christianity and Literature* 45 (1996): 331–44.

Gibble, K. "A Talent Increased." *Christianity Today* 26 (1982): 78.

Gill, D. "Socrates and Jesus on Non-Retaliation and Love of Enemies." *Horizons* 18 (1991): 246–62.

Gillespie, M. P. "Baroque Catholicism in Southern Fiction: Flannery O'Connor, Walker Percy, and John Kennedy Toole." Pages 25–47 in *Traditions, Voices, and Dreams: The American Novel since the 1960s*. Edited by M. J. Friedman and B. Siegel. Newark: University of Delaware Press, 1995.

Girard, R. *"To Double Business Bound": Essays on Literature, Mimesis, and Anthropology*. Baltimore: Johns Hopkins University Press, 1978.

Gordon, S. *Flannery O'Connor: The Obedient Imagination*. Athens: The University of Georgia Press, 2000.

Goss, J. "O'Connor's Redeemed Man: Christus et/vel Porcus?" *The Drew Gateway* 44 (1974): 106–19.

Green, W. M. *Initium omnis peccati superbia*. University of California Publications in Classical Philology 13. Berkeley: University of California Press, 1949.

Greisch, J. R. "Violent Shakings." *Christianity Today* 18 (1974): 19–20.

Grimes, R. L. "Anagogy and Ritualization: Baptism in Flannery O'Connor's *The Violent Bear It Away*." *Religion and Literature* 21 (1989): 9–26.

Harmsel, H. T. "Getting Kilt: Death in the Stories of Flannery O'Connor." *The Reformed Journal* 37 (1987): 13–15.

Hart, H. "No Condemnation." *The Other Side* 29 (1993): 20–23, 30.

Harvey, J. F. *Moral Theology of the Confessions of Saint Augustine*. The Catholic University of America Studies in Sacred Theology 55. Washington, DC: Catholic University of America Press, 1951.

Hatzfeld, H. "The Art of Dante's *Purgatorio*." Pages 64–88 in *American Critical Essays on The Divine Comedy*. Edited by R. J. Clements. New York: New York University Press, 1967.

Hawkins, P. S. "Dante: Poet-Theologian." *Princeton Seminary Bulletin* 16 (1995): 327–37.

————. "'What Is Truth?': The Question of Art in Theological Education." *Anglican Theological Review* 76 (1994): 364–74.

Hein, R. "Divine Imagination." *Christian History* 20, no. 2 (2001): 11–16.

Hertig, P. "The Jubilee Mission of Jesus in the Gospel of Luke: Reversals of Fortunes." *Missiology: An International Review* 26 (1998): 167–79.

Holbert, J. C. "Revelation according to Jacob and Mrs. Turpin: Early Reflections on Preaching and Contemporary Literature." *Journal for Preachers* 17 (1993): 11–21.

Hollander, R. "Tragedy in Dante's Comedy." *Sewanee Review* 91 (1983): 240–60.

Horsley, R. "Ethics and Exegesis: 'Love Your Enemies' and the Doctrine of Nonviolence." Pages 72–99 in *The Love of Enemy and Nonretaliation in the New Testament*. Edited by W. M. Swartley. Louisville: Westminster John Knox Press, 1992.

Jacobsen, J. "A Catholic Quartet." *The Christian Scholar* 47 (1964): 139–54.

Jones, A. *The Soul's Journey: Exploring the Three Passages of the Spiritual Life with Dante as a Guide*. New York: HarperCollins, 1995.

Kenney, J. P. "St. Augustine and the Invention of Mysticism." Pages 125–30 in *Augustine and His Opponents, Jerome, Other Latin Fathers after Nicaea, Orientalia*. Edited by E. A. Livingstone. Studia patristica 33. Leuven: Peeters, 1997.

————. "Saint Augustine and the Limits of Contemplation." Pages 199–218 in *St. Augustine and His Opponents, Other Latin Writers*. Edited by M. F. Miles, E. J. Yarnold, and P. M. Parvis. Studia patristica 38. Leuven: Peeters, 2001.

Kenney, T. "From Francesca to Francesco: Transcribing the Tale of Passion from the Inferno to the Paradiso, or Thomas Aquinas as Romancer." *Religion and Literature* 31 (1999): 61–73.

Kilcourse, G. A., Jr. *Flannery O'Connor's Religious Imagination: A World with Everything off Balance.* New York: Paulist Press, 2001.

Kilgallen, J. J. "Luke 7:41–42 and Forgiveness of Sins." *Expository Times* 111 (1999): 46–47.

———. "A Proposal for Interpreting Luke 7, 36–50." *Biblica* 72 (1991): 305–330.

Kingston, M. "Forgiveness, Openness, Love." *Expository Times* 109 (1998): 238–39.

Lindroth, J. R. "A Consistency of Voice and Vision: O'Connor as Self-Critic." *Religion and Literature* 16, no. 2 (Summer 1984): 43–59.

Lorentzen, M. E. "A Good Writer Is Hard to Find." Pages 417–35 in *Imagination and the Spirit: Essays in Literature and the Christian Faith.* Edited by C. A. Huttar. Grand Rapids: Eerdmans, 1971.

MacQueen, D. J. "Augustine on Superbia: The Historical Background and Sources of His Doctrine." *Mélanges de science religieuse* 34 (1977): 193–211.

Maddux, S. "Flannery O'Connor and the Christian Pharisee." *Communio* 11 (1984): 335–49.

Mallard, W. *Language and Love: Introducing Augustine's Religious Thought through the Confessions Story.* University Park, PA: Pennsylvania State University Press, 1994.

Mariani, P. "God and the Imagination." *Image: A Journal of the Arts and Religion* 18 (Winter 1997): 97–109.

Markus, R. A. "De ciuitate dei: Pride and the Common Good." Pages 245–59 in *Augustine—Second Founder of the Faith.* Edited by J. C. Schnaubelt and F. Van Fleteren. Collectanea Augustiniana. New York: P. Lang, 1990.

Martin, K. "Flannery O'Connor's Prophetic Imagination." *Religion and Literature* 26, no. 3 (1994): 33–58.

Martin, R. "Flannery O'Connor—Twenty Years After." *Center Journal* 4 (1984): 29–37.

Mayer, D. R. "The Blazing Sun and the Relentless Shutter: The Kindred Arts of Flannery O'Connor and Diane Arbus." *Christian Century* 92 (1975): 435–40.

———. "'Like Getting Ticks off a Dog': Flannery O'Connor's 'As If.'" *Christianity and Literature* 33 (1984): 17–34.

———. "Outer Marks, Inner Grace." *Asian Folklore Studies* 42 (1983): 117–27.

Mazzeo, J. A. "Dante's Conception of Love." Pages 140–57 in *American Critical Essays on The Divine Comedy.* Edited by R. J. Clements. New York: New York University Press, 1967.

McDonald, R. "Comedy and Flannery O'Connor." *South Atlantic Quarterly* 81 (1982): 188–220.

McEntyre, M. C. "Mercy That Burns: Violence and Revelation in Flannery O'Connor's Fiction." *Theology Today* 53 (1996): 331–44.

McFague, S. "The Parabolic in Faulkner, O'Connor, and Percy." *Notre Dame English Journal* 15 (1983): 49–66.

McMahon, R. *Augustine's Prayerful Ascent: An Essay on the Literary Form of the Confessions.* Athens: University of Georgia Press, 1989.

McVeigh, D. M. "The Western Canon: Bloom, Dante, and the Limits of Agon." *Christianity and Literature* 44 (1995): 181–94.

Mehl, D. P. "Sex and Sacrament in Contemporary Literature: The Incarnation as Method." *Currents in Theology and Mission* 10 (1983): 351–64.

Mellard, J. M. "Flannery O'Connor's Others: Freud, Lacan, and the Unconscious." *American Literature* 61 (1989): 625–43.

Meyer, W. E. "The American Religion of Vision." *Christian Century* 100 (1983): 1045–47.

Michaels, J. R. "Images of Grace in Flannery O'Connor's Strong Women." *Daughters of Sarah* 16 (1990): 27–30.

Morneau, R. F. "Spirituality: Five Twentieth-Century Witnesses of Discipleship." Pages 217–33 in *The Catholic Church in the Twentieth Century.* Edited by J. Deedy. Collegeville: Michael Glazier, 2000.

Munk, L. "Shouting at the Lord across a Hogpen: Flannery O'Connor's 'Revelation.'" *Theology* 97 (1994): 283–92.

———. "Understanding Understatement: Biblical Typology and 'The Displaced Person.'" *Journal of Literature and Theology* 2 (1988): 237–53.

Musa, M. *Advent at the Gates: Dante's Comedy.* Bloomington: Indiana University Press, 1974.

Neuleib, J. W. "Comic Grotesques: The Means of Revelation in *Wise Blood* and *That Hideous Strength.*" *Christianity and Literature* 30 (Summer 1981): 27–36.

Niemeyer, G. "Why Marion Montgomery Has to 'Ramble.'" *Center Journal* 4 (1985): 71–95.

Nietzsche, F. *Nietzsche Briefwechsel: Kritische Gesamtausgabe.* Berlin: W. de Gruyter, 1982.

Nisly, P. W. "Faith Is Not an Electric Blanket." *Christianity Today* 29 (1985): 21–24.

O'Connor, D. K. "The Ambitions of Aristotle's Audience and the Activist Ideal of Happiness." Pages 107–29 in *Action and Contemplation: Studies in the Moral and Political Thought of Aristotle.* Edited by R. C. Bartlett and S. D. Collins. Albany: State University of New York Press, 1999.

O'Connor, F. *The Complete Stories.* New York: Farrar, Straus & Giroux, 1971.

———. *The Habit of Being.* Edited by S. Fitzgerald. New York: Farrar, Straus & Giroux, 1979.

———. "Novelist and Believer." Pages 159–67 in *The Christian Imagination: The Practice of Faith in Literature and Writing.* Edited by L. Ryken. Rev. and expanded ed. Colorado Springs: Shaw Books, 2002.

O'Connor, M. P. "The Universality of Salvation: Christianity, Judaism, and Other Religions in Dante, *Nostra aetate*, and the New Catechism." *Journal of Ecumenical Studies* 33 (1996): 487–511.

O'Connor, T. S. J. "Climbing Mount Purgatory: Dante's Cure of Souls and Narrative Family Therapy." *Pastoral Psychology* 49 (1999): 445–57.

Owens, V. S. "Fiction and the Bible." *The Reformed Journal* 38 (July 1988): 12–15.

Paffenroth, K. "Bad Habits and Bad Company: Education and Evil in the *Confessions*." Pages 3–14 in *Augustine and Liberal Education*. Edited by K. Paffenroth and K. Hughes. Aldershot, UK: Ashgate Books, 2000.

———. "Friendship as Personal, Social, and Theological Virtue in Augustine." In *Augustine and Politics*. Edited by J. Doody, K. Hughes, and K. Paffenroth. Lanham, MD: Lexington Books, 2005.

———. *In Praise of Wisdom: Literary and Theological Reflections on Faith and Reason*. New York: Continuum, 2004.

Paffenroth, K., and Robert Kennedy, eds. *A Reader's Companion to Augustine's Confessions*. Louisville: Westminster John Knox Press, 2003.

Park, C. C. "Crippled Laughter." *American Scholar* 51 (1982): 249–57.

Parks, J. G. "Losing and Finding: Meditations of a Christian Reader." *Christianity and Literature* 38 (1989): 19–23.

Payton, R. J. *A Modern Reader's Guide to Dante's Inferno.* New York: P. Lang, 1992.

Perkins, P. *Reading the New Testament.* 2d ed. New York: Paulist Press, 1988.

Phillips, D. Z. "The Devil's Disguises: Philosophy of Religion, 'Objectivity' and 'Cultural Divergence.'" Pages 61–77 in *Objectivity and Cultural Divergence*. Edited by S. C. Brown. Cambridge, UK: Cambridge University Press, 1984.

Poggioli, R. "Paolo and Francesca." Pages 61–77 in *Dante: A Collection of Critical Essays*. Edited by J. Freccero. Englewood Cliffs, NJ: Prentice–Hall, 1965.

Polter, J. "Obliged to See God." *Sojourners* 23 (1994–95): 16–22.

Prior, M. *Jesus the Liberator: Nazareth Liberation Theology (Luke 4:16–30)*. Sheffield, UK: Sheffield Academic Press, 1995.

Pritchard, J. "Jesus and Jubilee." *Epworth Review* 26 (1999): 52–59.

Procopé, J. F. "Initium omnis peccati superbia." Pages 315–20 in *Cappadocian Fathers, Chrysostom and His Greek Contemporaries, Augustine, Donatism and Pelagianism*. Edited by E. A. Livingstone. Studia patristica 22. Leuven: Peeters, 1989.

Raiger, M. "Large and Startling Figures." Pages 242–70 in *Seeing into the Life of Things: Essays on Literature and Religious Experience*. Edited by J. L. Mahoney. New York: Fordham University Press, 1998.

Reynolds, B. "Dante, Poet of Joy: A Celebration." *Theology* 97 (1994): 265–75.

Rich, F. "It Was the Porn That Made Them Do It." *New York Times*, May 30, 2004. Online: http://www.nytimes.com. Accessed May 30, 2004.

Ringe, S. H. *Jesus, Liberation, and the Biblical Jubilee*. Philadelphia: Fortress Press, 1985.

Rolland, H. "Divine Imagination." *Christian History* 70 (2001): 11–17.

Ross, A. "Protagonist Corner." *Journal for Preachers* 5 (1982): 28–30.

Ryan, C. "The Theology of Dante." Pages 136–52 in *The Cambridge Companion to Dante*. Edited by R. Jacoff. Cambridge, UK: Cambridge University Press, 1993.

Ryan, J. K. *The Confessions of St. Augustine*. New York: Image Books, 1960.

Ryan, L. "Stornei, Gru, Colombe: The Bird Images in *Inferno* V." *Dante Studies* 94 (1976): 25–45.

Sandnes, K. O. "The Death of Jesus for Human Sins: The Historical Basis for a Theological Concept." *Theology and Life* 15/16 (1993): 45–52.

Schall, J. V. "Plotinus and Political Philosophy." *Gregorianum* 66 (1985): 687–707.

Schlabach, G. W. "Augustine's Hermeneutic of Humility: An Alternative to Moral Imperialism and Moral Relativism." *Journal of Religious Ethics* 22 (1994): 299–330.

Schroeder, S. "From the Church without Christ to the Absolute Absence of God: Thinking about the First Coming." *Philosophy and Theology* 2 (1988): 387–98.

Scullin, K. "Transforming Violence in O'Connor's *The Violent Bear It Away*." Pages 206–29 in *Wagering on Transcendence: The Search for Meaning in Literature*. Edited by P. Carey. Kansas City: Sheed & Ward, 1997.

Sewell, E. "Is Flannery O'Connor a Nonsense Writer?" *Soundings* 73 (1990): 273–302.

Shepherd, G. W. "The Example of Flannery O'Connor as a Christian Writer." *Center Journal* 4 (1984): 39–63.

Siegfried, R. "The Search for the True Self: Thomas Merton and Flannery O'Connor." *Studia mystica* 10 (1987): 5–18.

Skehan, P. W., and A. A. Di Lella. *The Wisdom of Ben Sira: A New Translation with Notes*. New York: Doubleday, 1987.

Smith, W. A. "The Christian as Resident Alien in Augustine: An Evaluation from the Standpoint of Pastoral Care." *Word and World* 3 (1983): 129–39.

Soares-Prabhu, G. "'As We Forgive': Interhuman Forgiveness in the Teaching of Jesus." Pages 57–66 in *Forgiveness*. Edited by C. Floristán and C. Duquoc. Edinburgh: T & T Clark, 1986.

Startzman, E. "Christ the Lover in the Works of Flannery O'Connor and C. S. Lewis." *Christianity and the Arts* 6 (1999): 32–36.

Stokes, D. "Grit, Grace and Miss O'Connor." *Theology* 80 (1977): 107–10.

Stormon, E. J. "The Spirituality of St. Augustine." Pages 129–44 in *Christian Spiritual Theology: An Ecumenical Reflection*. Edited by N. J. Ryan. Melbourne: Dove Communications, 1976.

Swing, T. K. *The Fragile Leaves of the Sibyl: Dante's Master Plan*. Westminster, MD: Newman, 1962.

Sykes, J. "Christian Aplogetic Uses of the Grotesque in John Irving and Flannery O'Connor." *Literature and Theology* 10 (1996): 58–67.

Teselle, S. M. "Experience of Coming to Belief." *Theology Today* 32 (1975): 159–65.

———. "The Parabolic in Faulkner, O'Connor, and Percy." *Notre Dame English Journal* 15 (1983): 49–66.

Tuchman, B. W. *The March of Folly: From Troy to Vietnam.* New York: Random House, 1984.

Van Bavel, T. J. "De la raison à la foi: La conversion d'Augustin." *Augustiniana* 86 (1986): 5–27.

Van den Brink, J. N. B. "Humility in Pascal and Augustine." *Journal of Ecclesiastical History* 19 (1968): 41–56.

VanRys, J. C. "Reclaiming Marginalia: The Grotesque and the Christian Reader." *Christianity and Literature* 44 (1995): 345–57.

Vijayakumar, J. "Non-Violence and Peaceful Co-Existence: A Biblical Persepctive." Pages 45–55 in *Bible Speaks Today: Essays in Honour of Gnana Robinson.* Edited by D. J. Muthunayagom. Delhi: Indian Society for Promoting Christian Knowledge, 2000.

Weaver, M. J. "Thomas Merton and Flannery O'Connor: The Urgency of Vision." *Religion in Life* 48 (1979): 449–61.

Weithman, P. J. "Toward an Augustinian Liberalism." *Faith and Philosophy* 8 (1991): 461–80.

Wessling, J. H. "The Newman Connection: Notional Assent and Real Assent in the Novels of Flannery O'Connor." Pages 233–57 in *The Literary and Educational Effects of the Thought of John Henry Newman.* Edited by M. Sundermeier and R. Churchill. Roman Catholic Studies 7. Lewiston: E. Mellen, 1995.

Williams, C. *The Figure of Beatrice: A Study in Dante.* New York: Boydell & Brewer, 1994.

———. *Outlines of Romantic Theology.* Edited by A. M. Hadfield. Grand Rapids: Eerdmans, 1990.

———. "The Theology of Romantic Love." In *Charles Williams: Essential Writings in Spirituality and Theology.* Edited by Charles C. Hefling, Jr. Cambridge, MA: Crowley Publications, 1993.

Williams, P. W. "Perceptions of Time in American Catholicism." *Journal of Religious Studies* 11 (1983): 1–13.

Wink, W. "Neither Passivity nor Violence: Jesus' Third Way (Matt. 5:38–42 par.)." Pages 102–25 in *The Love of Enemy and Nonretaliation in the New Testament.* Edited by W. M. Swartley. Louisville: Westminster John Knox Press, 1992.

Wood, R. C. "C. S. Lewis and the Ordering of Our Loves." *Christianity and Literature* 51 (2001): 109–17.

———. "Flannery O'Connor's Racial Morals." *Christian Century* 111 (1994): 1076–81.

———. "Recent Flannery O'Connor Criticism." *Religion and Literature* 26 (1994): 81–88.

————. "Talent Increased and Returned to God: The Spiritual Legacy of Flannery O'Connor's Letters." *Anglican Theological Review* 62 (1980): 153–67.

Yarian, S. O. "The Twentieth-Century Role of the Hell of St. Francis of Assisi and Dante." *Soundings* 66 (1983): 331–47.

Yearley, L. H. "Genre and the Attempt to Render Pride: Dante and Aquinas." *Journal of the American Academy of Religion* 72 (2004): 313–39.

————. "Selves, Virtues, Odd Genres, and Alien Guides: An Approach to Religious Ethics." *Journal of Religious Ethics* 25 (1998): 127–55.

Yoder, J. H. *The Politics of Jesus.* 2d ed. Grand Rapids: Eerdmans, 1994.

Zornado, J. "A Becoming Habit: Flannery O'Connor's Fiction of Unknowing." *Religion and Literature* 29 (1997): 27–59.

————. "Negative Writings: Flannery O'Connor, Apophatic Thought, and Christian Criticism." *Christianity and Literature* 42 (1992): 117–40.

INDEX